The Peril and Promise of Performance Pay

Making Education Compensation Work

Donald B. Gratz

ROWMAN & LITTLEFIELD EDUCATION
Lanham • New York • Toronto • Plymouth, UK

Published in the United States of America
by Rowman & Littlefield Education
A Division of Rowman & Littlefield Publishers, Inc.
A wholly owned subsidiary of The Rowman & Littlefield Publishing Group, Inc.
4501 Forbes Boulevard, Suite 200, Lanham, Maryland 20706
www.rowmaneducation.com

Estover Road
Plymouth PL6 7PY
United Kingdom

British Library Cataloguing in Publication Information Available

Library of Congress Cataloging-in-Publication Data

Gratz, Donald B.
  The peril and promise of performance pay : making education
        compensation work / Donald B. Gratz.
     p. cm.
  Includes bibliographical references.
  ISBN 978-1-60709-010-6 (hardcover : alk. paper) —
  ISBN 978-1-60709-011-3 (pbk. : alk. paper) —
  ISBN 978-1-60709-012-0 (electronic : alk. paper)
  1. Teachers—Salaries, etc.—United States. 2. Merit pay—United States. I. Title.
  LB2842.22.G73 2009
  331.2'81371100973—dc22   2009001034

♾™ The paper used in this publication meets the minimum requirements of
American National Standard for Information Sciences—Permanence of
Paper for Printed Library Materials, ANSI/NISO Z39.48-1992.
Manufactured in the United States of America.

Contents

Foreword

The national landscape is changing dramatically. In fields from health to utilities, a profound transition is under way, as institutions move from being resource-driven to becoming results-driven.

In education, the landscape is changing at three levels. First, at the level of the bully pulpit, the public's call for better results is providing a political and leadership opportunity for public officials. This opportunity has led to greater interest in forging a stronger link between the goals of school districts (to improve student achievement) and their budgets (where more than 80 percent of the operating budget is spent on compensation). Second, legislatively, both federal and state accountability initiatives are increasing local and national awareness of results. Third, demographic changes are having a marked yet underappreciated impact on public education.

Far fewer households now have children in the schools than during the baby boom generation. At the same time that these households have less immediate vested interest in the schools, there is correspondingly greater competition for public dollars. This competition will increase as boomers retire. The boomers are the wealthiest segment of the U.S. population and are largely white. The students going to school are less well off financially and far more diverse. What will lead the boomer generation to invest in today's students? Needs alone do not drive resources. Instead, getting the results the public is interested in—linking what students learn to what educators earn—will be increasingly pivotal in years ahead.

These conditions have already led to experiments with performance pay in many states and districts, but here is the key question: Will performance pay be done in ways that are helpful to students and teachers or will it continue to repeat the mistakes of the past, including the failed merit pay efforts of the early 1980s?

The lesson of performance pay is, at root, a lesson of institutional change. The Community Training & Assistance Center (CTAC) has assisted a range of districts and states, the U.S. Congress, and the U.S. Department of Education to develop new methods of compensation that support students, educators, and organizational goals, including the landmark compensation reform in Denver. Based on this experience, we have identified six cornerstones of compensation reform.

First, performance pay is a systemic reform. More than an ingredient of reform, it is a driver—not because money alone motivates teachers but because it catches and holds a district's attention.

Second, compensation reform must be done with teachers, not to teachers. Performance pay, if it is going to work, cannot be imposed from above in the form of management or policy fiat or achieved by copying models from elsewhere. It involves very intentionally building trust and collaboration so that program designs can be customized and mid-course corrections can be made as needed.

Third, performance pay must be organizationally sustainable. If the intent is to reward teachers' impact on student learning, the reform must address the full range of factors—from the boardroom to the classroom—that contribute to effective teaching. This is what distinguishes performance-based compensation from the more superficial test-based compensation.

Fourth, performance pay must be financially sustainable. It is essential to anticipate and plan on the front end of an initiative for the financing needed for long-term sustainability. Teachers and taxpayers alike have seen promises come and go regarding compensation schemes and are wary of any reform outlasting a budget crunch or a change in superintendent.

Fifth, a broad base of support is required within the district and community. Buy-in from the district is needed for effective implementation. Support from the community is vital for generating additional resources.

Sixth and most important, performance pay must go beyond politics and finances to benefit students. Both in planning and development, it has to focus on demonstrably affecting student learning. When done right, performance pay benefits students *and* teachers.

As both practitioner and researcher, Don Gratz has direct working familiarity with the challenges of designing and implementing performance pay initiatives and extensive knowledge of the historical results of this reform. His book—*The Peril and Promise of Performance Pay*— shows a deep understanding of these cornerstones and an appreciation that performance pay involves a fundamental shift in how we approach school reform, moving away from adopting models and programs and instead focusing on changing the conditions that most affect educational results.

In examining the current substance and historical roots of these issues, Gratz shows that the conventional wisdom of educational reform is often more conventional than wise. Demonstrating the perspective and courage to take on some of the most sacred cows in the field, he identifies and then addresses key questions that are increasingly central to the national educational discussion:

- What is the definition of performance?
- Whose performance should be the basis for pay?
- Is the focus on promoting student learning or measuring it?
- What are the effects of educational standards?
- Are schools in crisis truly driving an economy in crisis?
- Should the problem of unequal distribution of income be placed at the door of the schools?
- What do practitioners understand about performance pay that ideologues fail to grasp?
- What opportunities are generated by performance pay?

These questions cut to the heart of performance pay and school reform. The stakes for students, teachers, and communities are too high for the responses to these questions to be anything other than well informed. This book is a critical read.

William J. Slotnik
Founder and Executive Director
Community Training & Assistance Center (CTAC)

Founder and National Convener
Institute for Teacher Compensation and School Improvement
Boston, Massachusetts

Preface

The initial ideas for this book arose out of my work on Denver's Pay for Performance pilot. Most of the players in Denver were dedicated to conducting a thorough, thoughtful, and honest experiment with performance pay. The staff of the Community Training & Assistance Center (CTAC), of which I was a part, was similarly dedicated to its technical assistance and research roles. We discovered together how considerations of pay and performance permeate every aspect of schooling. Our discussions over the course of several years were stimulating, enlightening, frustrating, and intellectually challenging, as we explored the difficulties of providing a good education to an impossibly wide range of different children and families, in the politically charged environment that is public education today.

Denver's pilot was a complicated experiment which kept encountering new issues and obstacles and which demonstrated the complexity of an idea that most people think is simplicity itself—paying teachers based on their performance. But it is not simple at all, either in concept or in implementation. Our work in Denver led to two major reports that analyzed these complexities, plus a companion volume on understanding student achievement data. It also led to my article on the pilot in the April 2005 edition of *Phi Delta Kappan*.

I had not planned to pursue the topic further—though I certainly recognized how poorly understood it is in public policy circles—but an email and subsequent discussions with Tom Koerner, editor at Rowman & Littlefield Education, convinced me that there was much more to say. It's not possible to think intelligently about performance pay without defining teacher and student performance, and defining that performance requires considering what Americans want their schools to do. Unless you believe that test scores fully measure the performance of students, teachers, and schools, this is a complex discussion. Three years and many drafts later—well after the initial deadline—I am pleased to present *The Peril and Promise of Performance Pay: Making Education Compensation Work,* as interest in performance pay continues to increase faster than understanding.

In addition to colleagues at CTAC, I would like to thank Curry College, which has supported this project through resources and time. And I would particularly like to thank my family—my dedicated, supportive (and long-suffering) wife, Fran, and my wonderful daughters, Jenny and Julie, now grown and out of the house. They put up with many years of my disappearing into my attic office to work on this and other projects of little interest to them but were available to offer both support and the occasional reality check, keeping me grounded in the real world and reminding me of what's really important. Love to all of you.

Donald B. Gratz
Needham, Massachusetts
September 2008

I

THE CURRENT CONTEXT

Introduction to Part I

More than twenty states and an unknown number of districts are currently experimenting with some form of performance-related pay for their teachers. Various performance pay plans can now be found on the agendas of many governors, state and national legislators, business organizations, think tanks, and political candidates, where they are often seen as a new idea that can solve the problems of education. Performance pay for teachers is not an idea on the horizon. It is here now.

But what is performance pay? How does it work? What is it supposed to accomplish? The plans that fall under the heading of performance pay today are far too varied and wide-ranging to be easily described or understood. Some are based on standardized test scores, while others define student achievement more broadly. Some focus on teacher skill development, others on filling hard to fill positions, still others on schoolwide goals. These plans, while they all move away from the single salary schedule and are loosely grouped under a heading of performance pay, have little else in common. Yet politicians, the press, and other civic leaders tend to discuss performance pay as if it were a single, well-understood approach to compensation. It's not. The plans in place and on the table are vastly different—aimed at different results and based on very different views of education.

Even so, teachers, district leaders, and politicians are beginning to agree that modification of the single salary schedule may be in order and to establish some common ground as to what forms of teacher compensation might help improve education. In this context, it is important that everyone involved understand the critical differences between the different forms of performance pay. Until it is clear what problem a plan is supposed to solve, what assumptions regarding teacher performance and student goals it is

3

based on, what success it has had in the past, and what direction it implies for the education of the nation's children, no plan deserves either support or rejection.

PLAN OF THE BOOK

The purpose of this book is to investigate the goals, assumptions, and methods that undergird performance pay plans in light of recent and distant history, lessons learned about human motivation from both education and industry, current attitudes towards teacher compensation, the impact of public education on students and society, and the purposes citizens ascribe to their public schools. It is divided into two parts.

Part I (chapters 1–5) sets the stage. Chapter 1 provides the current educational context for performance pay, including a description of the different forms it takes. These start with teacher pay based on the scores of their students on standardized tests, but they include many other ideas and plans. Chapter 2 explores the economic case proponents most often make for attempting to improve schools through pay incentives for teachers—the reasons cited for using performance pay, the benefits such plans may bring, and some of the counterarguments. Chapter 3 provides a brief history of performance pay, dating back to Britain's national attempt in the late nineteenth century and moving through the present day. This is followed by a summary of business, labor, and public attitudes towards performance pay today, based in part on that history (chapter 4).

Between 1999 and 2005, the Denver Public Schools conducted a thorough pay-for-performance pilot, and the district's teachers and voters have since approved a related plan—a dramatic departure from traditional forms of teacher compensation. A distinguishing feature of Denver's approach was that it included a four-year pilot and comprehensive study of the processes, problems, and results of the experiment. These provided significant information on what works and what doesn't in a school system. Chapter 5 considers some of the lessons of that pilot. By combining lessons from Denver, from earlier plans in education, and from industry, the book explores the needs and goals, the methods and problems, and the implications of performance pay for school leaders and policy makers seeking to implement such plans.

Part II begins with critical issues and assumptions raised in the first half of the book, each of which is addressed in a subsequent chapter. Chapter 6 explores the presumption that American schools are failing or in crisis and provides a discussion of the main problems performance pay is supposed to rectify. In particular, it looks at the relationship between education and the economy—often cited as a major reason for improving schools. Is education the route to success for struggling families? Do better schools lead to greater productivity? Are economic slowdowns related to school success? Further, chapter 6 considers international comparisons and other measures of school and teacher performance.

Chapter 7 addresses the relationship between family background and student achievement given the frequently stated goal of eliminating the "achievement gap." Do family income and related social factors shape student progress, or are student results shaped by the education they receive? Both? To what extent can schools overcome differences in family background? Is demography destiny, or does it not matter at all? How do the answers to these questions affect the discussion of teacher compensation?

Because many performance pay plans are designed to be motivational, chapter 8 looks at the theory and history of human motivation—not just in education, but in all aspects of work. It considers how our understanding of human motivation informs our choices of organizational structure and compensation. Do incentives, financial and other, motivate workers? What has been learned from a century of study, mostly in business, about what does motivate workers?

Chapter 9 reviews the purposes of education, along with the definitions and assessments of performance that these purposes imply. Any attempt to develop a performance pay plan presumes a definition of performance, both for teachers and for students. What do we mean by performance? What are our goals for our children and our country?

Once goals have been established and performance defined, performance pay also presumes that they can be measured. This is the subject of chapter 10. To what extent and in what ways can we measure our educational goals? Should we limit our goals to what can be easily measured? As the country considers the need to improve and ways to bring about that improvement, it should also discuss what it means by improvement—what it expects its public schools to accomplish and how it will know. Given these goals, purposes, and plans, how should teacher compensation be designed?

Finally, chapter 11 sums up where these discussions lead. It reviews lessons learned and provides a brief framework that may lead to fruitful discussions at both the state and local level. What do we know about performance pay for teachers from historical examples, recent examples, and lessons from other industries? How can we define performance so that we achieve what we want for our children and our society? What are the practical implications of potential policies that might effectively be implemented? And where do we go from here?

Like many participants in and observers of the public school system (including politicians, business people, union leaders, and many citizens), I believe our current compensation system is in need of change. Agreeing on that point is easy; determining what comes next is harder. Our next steps depend on the problems we want to solve and the goals we want to pursue. Success in pursuing these goals also requires that the solutions we choose be closely linked to the problems and goals we identify.

Alfie Kohn quotes Jone L. Pearce as observing in 1987 that "it is the rare author who does not end the list of 'merit pay problems' with upbeat suggestions for the successful implementation of such a program."[1] I'm guilty of that in this book, but only to a point. Performance pay won't work where it's simply test-based, both because it is conceptually flawed and because it simply cannot be implemented in any meaningful way. It won't work in some districts because they won't have the patience and courage to review their practices and align purposes, goals, structures, practices, and methods of compensation.

It *can* work, however, where it means differentiated compensation based on mutually developed goals and strategies, and where teachers, administrators, and parents work together to develop a plan that addresses these goals and strategies with mutually agreed definitions of performance. It can work where the district understands that changes in teacher compensation are not a reform—they are not an end in themselves, but a means to an end. For changes in teacher compensation to have a positive effect, they have to serve a larger organizational end, and all affected parties have to agree on both the end and the means of achieving it.

Thus, while I don't propose a single solution to a set of goals and concerns that may differ from one community to the next, I do offer many lessons to be learned, and I propose some guidelines and principles—based on history, analysis, and my own experience—as to what might work and what probably will not. If we pay attention to these lessons and guidelines, it is my hope and belief that some schools and districts may find a means to improve compensation, performance, and the educational interests of children and families all at the same time.

NOTES

1. Alfie Kohn, *Punished by Rewards* (New York: Houghton Mifflin, 1993), 332.

1

Setting the Stage

Our Nation is at risk.... We report to the American people that while we can take justifiable pride in what our schools and colleges have historically accomplished and contributed to the United States and the well-being of its people, the educational foundations of our society are presently being eroded by a rising tide of mediocrity that threatens our very future as a Nation and a people....

Salaries for the teaching profession should be increased and should be professionally competitive, market-sensitive, and performance-based. Salary, promotion, tenure, and retention decisions should be tied to an effective evaluation system that includes peer review so that superior teachers can be rewarded, average ones encouraged, and poor ones either improved or terminated.[1]

In the first decade of the twenty-first century, we find ourselves in a period of uncertainty and change in education. Local communities have lost much control over their schools to federal and state authorities, and these authorities have mounted an assault on current practice with the stated purpose of improving student achievement, reducing the achievement gap, and preparing students for what is described as a more competitive world. Fueled by a drive for standards and test-based accountability, an ideology favoring private enterprise, and the widespread declaration that America's schools are failing, many conservatives and some liberals believe that state and federal mandates provide the best means to force improvement on an educational system they see as substantially broken.

The refrain that American schools are failing is hardly new. The roots of the current view may be traced back to Sputnik in 1957, or at least to 1983, when the National Commission on Excellence in Education (NCEE) proclaimed that "a rising tide of mediocrity" was threatening to engulf the country's schools, destroy its economy, and quite possibly bring down the nation.[2] Many of the two hundred reports that followed in the next fifteen to twenty years, often sponsored by business-backed organizations or business-oriented think tanks, also linked problems of the U.S. economy to poor public schools.[3]

Although President Reagan's "morning in America" was followed by an initial surge in prosperity during the early 1980s, the economy was performing poorly by the end of the decade. As Americans watched, a Japanese company bought Rockefeller Center, prompting fears that the United States was falling so far behind that it could never catch up. *A Nation at Risk* and other reports fueled this national fear with the accusation that low standards, lazy teachers, and poor-quality schools were to blame. They raised a cry for "world class standards" both to save the nation from economic collapse and to save children from the streets.

"While we still desire a strong work ethic, we must appreciate the implications for education of an economy that changes with striking and unprecedented rapidity," said one proponent of standards in the 1990s. "This rapidly changing economy requires workers who are flexible, adaptable, quick learners, critical thinkers, and above all else, problem-solvers. *And these are precisely the skills our schools are not teaching.*"[4]

During the presidency of George H. W. Bush (1988–1992), IBM chief Louis Gerstner and other business and political leaders initiated a coalition called The Teaching Commission. This group launched a move towards educational improvement called America 2000, which once again proclaimed that America's schools were failing and attempted to spur improvement with business-like approaches, educational standards, and broad goals. When Bill Clinton became president in 1992 this effort continued, ending up in legislation with a new name—Goals 2000: Educate America Act—but the same primary goals.

By the end of the 1990s, most states had introduced academic standards in the core subject areas, as well as tests to measure whether schools were meeting them. Because state standards varied widely, national standards were also proposed for a time during the 1990s, but many educational groups and local districts opposed them. This effort was abandoned in favor of state standards and tests, though some educators and policy makers still support national standards.

The Clinton years saw a major economic boom in the United States, even as the Japanese economy and some others collapsed. Some describe the 1990s as the greatest era of sustained growth in the history of the world, a time that put the country in surplus for the first time in decades.[5] This economic success did not, however, translate into a change of stance towards the public school system. Schools were still seen as failing; only the evidence of that failure and the goals for the standards and tests had changed.

Whereas the evidence of school failure in the 1980s was the country's inability to compete in the world economy, the evidence of that failure in the

1990s was the achievement gap between the poor and middle-class students, and between whites and most minorities, as shown on national tests. This shift of purposes has been critiqued by some as specious reasoning—that the standards and testing regime was a solution in search of a problem—but the condemnation of America's failing schools continues, as does the push for higher levels of achievement in more subject areas measured by "rigorous" tests.

In 2001, during his first year in office, President George W. Bush pushed changes to the Elementary and Secondary Education Act (ESEA), creating the first national bill to demand student proficiency in every school system across the country. Using his substantial Republican majority—and building a coalition that embraced people from all political stripes—Bush forged a bill that, while it does not establish national standards, substantially increases both federal and state involvement in public schools.

Under this law—the No Child Left Behind act of 2001 (NCLB)—all states have now developed standards and tests to measure student performance. By 2014, all schools must demonstrate that their students are "proficient" in reading and math according to the standards created in the various states. In the meantime, all schools must make Adequate Yearly Progress (AYP) towards this goal according to varying state formulae. While many teachers and parents oppose the tests and the proficiency goal, which they view as both unrealistic and unfair to urban and minority students, others believe that the status quo (particularly in urban schools) is unfair to those same students.

(RE-) ENTER PERFORMANCE PAY

NCLB is by far the largest national foray into education policy in U.S. history, which local communities have managed with state oversight since the U.S. Constitution awarded that power to the states in 1788. One of the goals of NCLB is accountability for results, which is addressed primarily at the district and school level. Despite more than a decade of educational standards and increasingly stringent accountability measures, however, it is not clear that achievement levels have significantly changed.

As each year of Adequate Yearly Progress passes, more schools and districts are being labeled inadequate. States are struggling to determine how to apply the sanctions they have threatened, given numerous schools to which these sanctions could apply, and to find and implement new means to improve schools. The National Assessment of Education Progress (NAEP), the federally mandated "nation's report card," shows modest progress in some areas. But it does not provide evidence that an increase in the number of standards, the number of tests, or the rigor of those standards and tests has resulted in a significant overall improvement in test scores, let alone any broader definition of student achievement.

Considerable opposition to the testing mandates exists among parents and the public, but until recently most educational and political leaders have stood behind NCLB and the need for students to achieve proficiency. As this book is being written, and as NCLB is being considered for reauthorization, concern over its more punitive provisions has delayed further action indefinitely. Even though the future of NCLB is uncertain, the drive for higher standards and tougher tests is still strong.

The attitudes, goals, and practices embodied in No Child Left Behind are far from universal, but they do influence policy makers. The growing number of schools failing to meet their Adequate Yearly Progress goals has led many of the nation's governors, and the boards and superintendents of some large communities, to seek a way to strengthen NCLB's accountability measures. These leaders hope to find both a solution and, in some views, a culprit. Bringing accountability down to the level of the individual teacher seems a logical next step. Given this national mood, initiatives to bring accountability into the classroom through a link between teacher compensation and student achievement (or some other measure of teacher performance) are on the rise.

This movement towards greater accountability grows, in part, from the belief that all children can learn. If all children *can* learn but many aren't (according to the tests), someone, or perhaps some institution, must be to blame. The link between teaching and learning is both well established and easy to grasp. Further, the fact that teachers are not paid according to their level of success, and (for some observers) the fact that teachers are members of unions, makes them appealing targets.

Thus, though the traditional "steps and lanes" approach to teacher pay remains the norm for the vast majority of districts across the country, a new wave of policy makers is attempting to build incentives of various types into their compensation systems, and a significant number of states have proposed or mandated some form of performance pay. Questions as to the effectiveness and impact of these measures remain, however, and substantial opposition has surfaced both to specific requirements of No Child Left Behind and to other aspects of this national drive towards accountability.

It's important to remember, however, that paying teachers based on their performance is not a new idea. It has many different forms, and has been tried regularly in this country and others for at least two hundred years. Rather than simply accept or reject proposals to differentiate teacher pay, many of which are only conceptual and only some of which have actually been implemented, now is the time to look carefully at the proposals—putting aside ideology as much as possible—and to consider what they are intended to accomplish, whether they are likely to be effective, and whether, if they are effective, the results will be those the country wants and expects.

TYPES AND CATEGORIES OF TEACHER COMPENSATION

Incentive compensation schemes come in many varieties. *Merit pay*, by definition, is based on some determination of merit. Teacher unions, among others, often view merit as a subjective judgment made by a principal or other supervisor. As such, even union leaders who have supported pay based on *performance* often adamantly oppose pay based on *merit*. They see merit pay as a thinly disguised example of an "old boy" network, in which a principal (or superintendent or school board) rewards favored teachers based on loyalty or whether they rock the boat—a subjective and unaccountable measure of a teacher's worth that puts teachers at the mercy of their supervisors and therefore of politics and favoritism.

Performance-based compensation, by contrast, is pay based on some objective measure of performance—at least in theory. This may be an output such as student achievement or demonstrated proficiency in class (according to various measures of effective teaching). In practice, it may also be based on an input—a surrogate for performance—such as professional development sessions taken or college credits earned.

In fact, though merit is often seen as subjective and performance as objective, the distinctions are fluid and many use the terms interchangeably. In either case, the specifics matter. The effectiveness of any program and the support it may garner from teachers, parents, or other citizens depends on how merit and performance are defined and measured. The simple announcement that a politician or district is interested in pursuing merit or performance pay tells the listener little. The program's goals and mechanisms determine its nature, and these vary considerably.

Below are the primary categories of teacher compensation, starting with the nearly universal steps and lanes approach. The default term used in this book for the various forms of performance-based compensation is *performance pay*, which broadly encompasses all the different forms in a general notion of differentiated teacher pay, but the distinctions between terms such as merit and performance are critically important. Indeed, the unraveling of some of these differences and their implications is one of the book's primary purposes. Most districts and states attempting performance pay use some combination of the approaches below, and the basic definitions are drawn primarily from several studies of these experiments.[6]

Steps and Lanes

The traditional structure of teacher salaries is a "steps and lanes" approach, also known as the "single salary schedule." Steps are based on longevity (years of service) while lanes reward merit as indicated by degrees or coursework. Most districts provide a set of step increases for all teachers for the first eight to fifteen years of service and allow teachers to move from one lane to the next as they add degrees or graduate credits. Increases generally fall in the 2 to 5 percent range for both step and lane changes, with starting salaries in the low $30,000s to $45,000. A teacher who starts at $40,000 with a 2.5 percent step increase will earn $41,250 the next year. If she moves to the next lane through graduate coursework and earns an additional 3 percent, her percentage increase becomes 5.5 percent.

Further, the entire scale moves up each time a cost of living adjustment (COLA) is awarded, which is most years, so this teacher might earn an additional 2.5 percent on top of the other adjustments, depending on how calculations are made. This would boost the teacher's increase in this example to 8 percent—a considerable percentage raise. While some observers criticize these kinds of percentages as overly generous, unfair to taxpayers, and out of step with corporate reality, it is also true that teachers tend to start lower than many professions requiring a similar level of education, and that they max out on increments fairly early in their careers.

By the time she has taught ten years, our fictional teacher may have reached the maximum on her step raises and may have earned all the coursework or lane increments short of a doctorate. If that is the case, she will only receive COLA raises for the rest of her career (a standard range of 1 to 5 percent). Though results will vary considerably by district, this would cap her salary perhaps between $50,000 and $60,000 (as high as $80,000–90,000 in a few districts) using 2008 dollars. This is higher than many nonprofit arts and social service organizations but generally below the salary opportunities of professions in the private sector with comparable education requirements.

Certification and Degrees

The typical teacher compensation system is not based solely on longevity, as described above, though critics often make this charge. The "lanes" portion assesses teacher effectiveness through certification and degrees, a general approach common to many professions (doctors, lawyers, accountants). Teachers are initially licensed and earn additional levels of licensure, or additional special licenses, through coursework and field experience. Once licensed, teachers are presumed competent. Unlike professionals in other fields, teachers are awarded tenure after a few years. They are evaluated regularly prior to receiving tenure, and periodically after that, but pay increments are based either on longevity (steps) or on coursework (lanes) rather than these evaluations. Teachers are also paid for extra duties such as coaching.

Increasingly, states have required additional levels of licensure and recertification, but these have not substantially altered the basic structure of the profession. These additional requirements, along with additional pay, are based on external certification through approved training, degrees, or other forms of professional development for teachers. Though the use of degrees and external licensing bodies is common in the professions, tenure and the single salary schedule are not. Nor do most professions base increases on external input rather than worker output. At the same time, it is also true that the majority of lawyers, doctors, and accountants don't work for the government and that opportunities for remuneration based on effort and perceived effectiveness are much greater in these professions than in education.

Teacher Skill and Knowledge

While certification and degree requirements may indicate skill and knowledge, a range of new assessment materials has been developed both by individual states and by national organizations. ETS's Praxis series is designed to assess teacher proficiency at the earlier stages and is used for licensure in many states. A few states (such as Massachusetts) have developed their own tests, often at great expense.

At the other end of the profession, the National Board for Professional Teaching Standards (NBPTS) offers a complex assessment for national certification of experienced teachers which relies in part on a demonstration of teacher performance in the classroom. Standards such as those developed by INTASC of the Chief State School Officers attempt to include more complex measures of teacher skill and knowledge. One well-known model of this approach comes from the Consortium for Policy Research in Education (CPRE), which has provided the basis for several district experiments.

While some assessments of skill and knowledge are primarily based on earning credits or completing courses, others require a "demonstration" of the new skills. This may take the form of observation, a portfolio, a videotaped lesson, or a live demonstration. Assessment may include planning and preparation, the classroom environment, instruction, and professional responsibilities, as well as the Praxis exams.[7]

Group and Individual Incentives

Some programs emphasize group rather than individual goals, in which all teachers in a school or other group receive the same reward if the school as a whole achieves a goal. Sometimes the school receives the reward rather than the teachers. Schools may identify both academic goals such as improving test scores and behavioral goals like reducing absenteeism or dropout rates.

Supporters of the group approach believe that individual bonuses are divisive, discouraging teachers from working together, while group bonuses promote cooperation. As CPRE explained in 1995, "Student outcomes are the joint product of many teachers working together at a school," and individually based models breed competitive rather than collegial environments.[8]

While some policymakers and many districts favor a group incentive, most of the proposals advanced by states and districts do not. Proponents of individual incentives seek to reward specific teachers as a measure of individual accountability, embodying their belief that both the problem and the potential solution of increased motivation lie with individual teachers.

This category overlaps with the previous one, in that performance may also be judged through a demonstration of teacher knowledge or proficiency, such as a portfolio, or through an outside agent such as NBPTS rather than directly through an assessment of student results. While several existing programs provide funding directly to teachers, only a few have so far attempted to systematically assess the performance of individual teachers based on student achievement, though that number is growing. Most of these rely primarily on standardized test scores. Many recent proposals have emphasized individual teacher accountability, a method that produces many complex problems that will be discussed later in this book.

Though both group and individual incentives are considered objective to the extent that they judge performance based on an assessment of student work, there is a substantial difference between those plans that attempt to measure the performance of individual teachers and those that measure the performance of schools. Many who support group incentives do not support using test scores or other student assessments to judge the success of individual teachers because they believe it will be either divisive or unfair, but do support the use of student assessments at the school level. Because teacher and school performance can be assessed in so many different ways, no uniform practice has emerged.

Job and Market Incentives

A significant variation on these models compensates teachers who choose to work in low-performing schools in urban areas, for example, or in hard-to-fill subject areas. Some plans also consider a teacher's other contributions to the school, such as serving on committees, mentoring other teachers, or additional contact with parents. These variations have been called job-based and market-based,[9] terms which begin to illustrate the complexity of the variations even though they do not cover all of the models in use.

Career-Ladder Approaches

Career ladder plans feature supervisor assessments, progress on professional growth plans, additional training, or the achievement of particular agreed-upon goals, and are based on creating a career path with differentiated duties. Some state plans, such as Minnesota's Q-Comp, encourage this approach. They include opportunities for experienced and well-qualified teachers to become mentors or master teachers and offer additional pay for these roles. These compensation proposals recognize the lack of opportunity for teachers to advance professionally, except for the few who move to administration, and attempt to provide a career path as a means to keep good teachers and improve student results.[10]

Individual Objectives

A performance-by-objective approach was popular in some districts in the 1980s[11]—the product of an era in which Management by Objectives (MBO) and similar organizational approaches were in vogue in business. While few if any of these 1980s experiments continue, individual teacher-set objectives were a critical factor in Denver. However, the objectives used in Denver's pilot and final plan differ from these earlier versions in two significant respects. First, earlier versions of MBO did not tie compensation to the objectives. Denver does. Second, Denver's teacher-set objectives focus directly on student achievement, whereas the 1980s experiments could also include teachers' personal and professional goals.

Following the business model, MBO is more a management approach than a compensation system. As Hatry notes, "The motivational effectiveness of performance-targeting plans does not depend on monetary awards. Instead, such plans are based on the psychological theory of goal-setting, which postulates that human actions are triggered by conscious intentions that are expressed as specific goals."[12]

Though Denver's new compensation plan includes bonuses tied to the achievement of teacher objectives, it is important to note that responses from teachers indicate that they agree with Hatry's analysis: objective-setting in Denver's pilot was highly beneficial, but that benefit was largely unrelated to the financial incentive.[13]

Bonuses and Base Pay Increments

So far, experiments with direct pay to teachers are based largely on a bonus system, a one-time payment for increased performance. Denver adds compensation to a teacher's base salary, in certain circumstances, which makes the pay increase permanent. Base pay increments are significantly more valuable to recipients than a bonus, as they will be repeated each year and will increase any subsequent percentage-based increment. Salary increments also count towards retirement benefits, while bonuses do not. Because additions to a teacher's base pay also increase the cost to the district substantially, administrators are often reluctant to grant a permanent increase based on a year's results.

RECENT PROPOSALS AND PLANS

Several waves of experiments have occurred in the two hundred- to three hundred-year history of performance pay, including attempts in this country through the 1970s and 1980s (see chapter 3). While few of these have lasted, the dawning of the twenty-first century has seen another flurry of new proposals. Currently, more than twenty states and a range of districts are implementing or discussing some form of performance plan for teachers, including Florida, California, Minnesota, and Texas (district and state plans), plus cities such as Denver and New York, to name just a few.

For example, Florida's first statewide plan in 2003 mandated that districts set aside 5 percent of their salary pool for performance pay. While Florida's state achievement tests were to be the basis for bonuses, districts were given leeway in determining how to distribute the funds. In 2005, state leaders decided to "crack down" on districts they believed were violating the spirit of the law and to tighten requirements, causing considerable resistance. In 2006, two new variations on the existing law were passed by the legislature, each with different requirements. In 2007, however, with the election of a new governor, yet another plan—dramatically revised—was put into place. In response to the complaints and controversy, the new plan was designed to focus less on test scores, to be subject to collective bargaining, to provide more local control, and to be more flexible. Each of the changes was actively debated in the press. Each was actively championed by some political and educational leaders and vigorously opposed by others. Each responded to various changes in both public attitudes and election results. Even with the less restrictive plan, there is still resistance and confusion, and results are unclear.

Florida's story is not unusual. Many states and districts have put forth plans with similarly stormy histories, and few have shown clearly positive results. Most of these have been imposed plans, rather than negotiated or jointly developed, and few have taken the time to address the critical issues and assumptions of performance pay set forth in this book. Houston, Dallas, and Austin, Texas, have each implemented or have been developing their own plans in the past decade, as has the state. The oldest of these—Houston's—has been modified several times and subject to massive controversy and resistance among both teachers and parents.

The current and past governors of California (one Democrat, one Republican) have each proposed some form of performance pay plan, neither of which has been implemented. So have the current and past governors of Massachusetts (one Republican, one Democrat). Minnesota's Q-Comp program (Quality Compensation for Teachers) is a much discussed model for performance pay in that it invites applications from districts rather than attempting to establish specific guidelines for performance or specific rewards or incentives for teachers.

At the national level, the federal government's $100 million Teacher Incentive Fund, an outgrowth of No Child Left Behind, has now distributed two rounds of awards to states, districts, and charter schools seeking to develop incentive pay plans for teachers and/or principals in high-need districts. The specific goals of the fund, according to the request for proposals, include: "Improving student achievement by increasing teacher and principal effectiveness; reforming teacher and principal compensation systems so that teachers and principals are rewarded for increases in student achievement; increasing the number of effective teachers teaching poor, minority and disadvantaged students in hard-to-staff subjects; and creating sustainable performance-based compensation systems."

Many districts across the country have attempted some form of performance pay plan, from Cincinnati to Charlotte to Denver. The method of development used in Denver—the inclusion of a wide range of affected parties, and the willingness of those parties to address critical issues and questions described in this book—is one of the reasons Denver's plan was implemented with wide support and is seen as a national model for educational change across the country.

CRITICAL ISSUES AND QUESTIONS IN PERFORMANCE PAY

There are significant differences among the various plans proposed and implemented by different states and districts, along the lines discussed above. These differences result from the diverse goals, purposes, and assumptions of the proposals, and from different views regarding school purposes and measures of progress. They also reflect a lack of knowledge of past experiments with performance pay and a misunderstanding of what motivates humans in a work setting—both in the corporate world and in education. Before adopting any such far-reaching plan, proponents would be well advised to consider the following major issues and questions, each of which is addressed later in the book.

Program Purposes

In too many proposals, the solution is the focus of discussion rather than the problem to be solved. A solution is selected—high standards and tough tests or individual teacher accountability based on test scores—followed by a list of problems it will address. Performance pay has been proposed to improve teaching, motivate good teachers, weed out poor teachers, attract the best college graduates into teaching, eliminate the achievement gap, improve the economy, prepare students for working in today's economy, heighten international competitiveness, and so forth. While each of these goals may be legitimate, it is highly unlikely that any one strategy could address them all.

Instead, districts or states should consider whether they want to recruit more teachers into the profession, improve school accountability, or eliminate the achievement gap, and then should focus on each of those goals individually. As specifically as possible, the root causes of particular problems should be uncovered. Strategies can then be developed to address those root causes. Focusing on solutions without clearly establishing a link to the problems they are meant to solve is a common route to program failure. It is the kind of thinking that allowed standards and tests to be the solution to two very different problems—the economy in the 1980s and the achievement gap in the 1990s—with little consideration for how well the strategy actually addressed the root causes of either (more on this later.) Politicians often gravitate to appealing solutions, which they then attach to a range of problems. This is, perhaps, why so many of these solutions fail to produce the desired result.

It should be clear that a strategy to recruit top college graduates into teaching may differ from one aimed at closing the achievement gap. In each instance, the starting place is identifying the problem and its causes. A range of specific, targeted strategies can then be identified to address specific causes.

Defining and Assessing Performance

In order to implement any plan effectively, planners must define their terms and goals, and these should relate directly to the purpose of the program. What does performance or merit mean? Does performance mean teacher performance, and if so, how will that performance be defined and measured? Will student performance be used as a gauge of teacher performance? If so, how will student performance be measured, and how will planners isolate the effects of one teacher from the cumulative effects of many teachers, the impact of parents, local conditions, and individual interests and circumstances?

Will student performance be measured in a narrow range of academic skills and knowledge reflected by standardized tests, or does the definition of student achievement encompass other areas of academic skill? Will it include students' social, emotional, and physical growth? What are the implications of each strategy? Clearly, if pay is to be awarded based on teacher performance, teacher performance must be defined. If teacher performance is defined relative to student performance, that must also be defined.

The need for definition is demonstrated by the Teacher Incentive Fund, which, similar to many such proposals, provides vague goals like "improving teacher effectiveness" and rewarding teachers for "increases in student achievement." These terms may mean standardized test scores, which are presumed to be objective (see chapter 9), but if test scores provide the definition of performance, a host of questions and problems follow.

If student achievement is to be measured objectively, it must be quantifiable with sufficient rigor to determine whether an outcome is the result of some contribution of the teacher, or whether it might be demographics, outside influences, the work of earlier teachers, or chance—the luck of the draw of a particular set of students on a particular test. If student achievement is to be measured more subjectively, or if the definition of achievement is to expand beyond a few limited academic skills, the parameters must also be spelled out. Either way, definitions must be clear and agreed to or results will be neither meaningful nor motivational.

Even in the case of objective measures of a limited number of skills, measurement problems are significant. Linn and Haug[14] have shown that year-to-year test comparisons for the same grade in individual schools are highly unreliable, and that schools recognized as excellent or outstanding through state and national awards rarely continue at that high level. Conversely, schools identified as needing improvement are most likely to gain the next year, simply because their classes are moving towards the average result based on other school factors. This suggests that test results may have limited reliability (and therefore limited validity for such uses) and that chance—different classes, different students, different years—is a significant factor.

Tying Teacher Pay to Student Outcomes

The concept of performance—whether teacher or student or both—implies a linkage to outcomes. Typically, scores on standardized tests serve as outcome indicators, replacing all of the outcomes parents, employers, and citizens want for students. The debate as to whether standardized tests are acceptable as the sole indicator of student success continues to rage throughout the country with regard to No Child Left Behind, the use of grade level and high school exit exams, and efforts to close the gap between the social classes and racial/ethnic groups.

But consider: whatever position one takes in this debate, adding teacher compensation to the equation substantially increases the stakes. If testing primarily reading and math does narrow the curriculum, that curriculum will become considerably narrower if these tests become the basis of teacher compensation. If student creativity and interest are stifled now, increasing the stakes will pull teachers further away from activities that engage students. If teaching to the test or cheating on the test are problems, these problems will be heightened as the incentives for teaching to the test or cheating increase.

Conversely, if current testing practices are improving results for students in a way that satisfies the purposes of schools, these results will also be enhanced. These arguments will intensify, the pressure will increase, and the burden of proof will be higher in direct relationship to the extent to which compensation is linked to results. The continuing controversies in states such as Florida and Texas clearly demonstrate this effect.

When asked, however, most parents and citizens want more for their students than test scores, and many also want fewer tests. They want students to learn good nutrition, critical thinking skills, good citizenship, and to come home motivated to learn. If we value these, how do we measure them? If they are hard to define and harder to measure, how do they figure into the compensation plan? At the beginning of this chapter, a frequent critic of the public schools was quoted as claiming that the schools are not providing students with the skills and attributes they need to succeed: to be critical thinkers, flexible, adaptable, quick learners, and problem solvers. If these are the goals, will tying teacher compensation to standardized test scores help achieve them? How will we be able to tell?

Denver's new compensation system (Professional Compensation, or Pro-Comp) uses a range of measures: student test scores and other evidence of achievement based on teacher-set objectives, a career ladder, incentives to teach in hard to fill positions or hard to serve schools, and a traditional evaluation. According to its designers, ProComp "should not be confused with 'merit pay' and 'performance pay'—which have been used to describe earlier experiments in teacher compensation plans that were not successful. These earlier attempts were unpopular due to the perceived subjectivity of the process and the often narrow focus used to evaluate an employee." Instead, they say, "ProComp is actually *results-based pay*, using multiple criteria to assess teachers' performance [emphasis in the original]."[15] This may be the best term yet, but it still begs the main question: what results do we want, and how will we know whether we have achieved them?

Incentives and Motivation

The next question concerns human motivation. Two clear premises provide the foundation for most performance pay schemes that tie compensation to results (test scores) rather than to actions (taking on new duties). These are that higher pay leads to greater motivation and that greater motivation leads to better results. If we believe that additional pay will improve teaching—without additional training or resources —we must believe that the key is motivation.

Further, if we believe that extrinsic motivation is the key to improving teaching without the need for additional training and other supports, we must also believe that teachers already have the skills and tools to do the job—that the primary issue is simply that they aren't trying as hard as they could. How true is this? What can we learn from industry about incentive pay plans that have been tried—whether they work, when they work, and what circumstances make them workable? In what ways might these lessons carry over into education?

Many teachers make a related distinction between financial incentives aimed at motivating them to try harder, which they disdain, and rewards for good performance, which they find acceptable. The terms *incentive* and *reward* often get used interchangeably and tend to overlap. The distinction is in the purpose, and it is important to teachers. This point must also be considered by those who would implement a performance pay plan. An "incentive" that is considered demeaning is unlikely to be motivational.

History and Experience

What do history and past experiments teach us about the effectiveness of performance pay? Under different names and with different attributes, performance pay has been tried repeatedly for more than two hundred years, in large districts and small and in countries such as Great Britain, Canada, and the United States.

Two chapters of this book address the question of experience. One takes the historical view, reaching back into eighteenth-century England and looking at British and American attempts through modern times. The second considers Denver's experiment, which is far more comprehensive than most. Past performance may not guarantee future results, but the lessons of history add much to our current understanding of the promise and pitfalls of performance pay in education. The history of attempts at performance pay both in education and in business should, if nothing else, convince us to proceed with caution.

Implementation

Finally, once goals and purposes are established, the practical issues of implementation remain. In describing a massive federal employment project mounted by the Economic Development Administration in Oakland, California, in the 1960s, Pressman and Wildavsky make the following comment:

> When we say that programs have failed, this suggests we are surprised. If we thought from the beginning that they were unlikely to be successful, their failure to achieve stated goals or to work at all would not cry out for any special explanation. If we believed that intense conflicts of interest were involved, if people who had to cooperate were expected to be at loggerheads, if necessary resources were far beyond those available, we might wonder rather more why the programs were attempted instead of expressing amazement at their shortcomings. The problem would dissolve, so to speak, in the statement of it. No explanatory ingenuity would be required.[16]

Implementing any complex new program in a large system is difficult. A controversial program that involves compensation will be doubly so, and all the lessons of change and systems management apply. Denver's four-year Pay for Performance pilot and its eventual ProComp plan provide many lessons in implementation that will be widely applicable. While many of the most significant issues in performance pay are conceptual, even a well-conceived program will fail if it is too hard or expensive to implement, or if it is implemented too quickly or without careful planning.

This is not to say that improvements in teacher compensation cannot be implemented, or that components of a new system that address either results or motivation are predestined for failure. It is to suggest, however, that even if a district determines its goals and defines its results, it still needs to look at the practical implications of any policy change to determine what it will cost in time, effort, and money to implement completely, and whether it is prepared to pay that price.

U.S. President James A. Garfield once described the ideal education as philosopher and educator Mark Hopkins sitting on one end of a log with the student on the other.[17] This notion, however quaint it sounds, suggests what many might consider the ideal teaching arrangement: one teacher and one student interacting. Assuming that a one-to-one teacher–student relationship is the ideal, it is easy to see that there is no practical way it could be implemented for the simple reason that no state or district could afford to pay for enough teachers to individually educate every child. Therefore, we create a compromise between what we want (as best we can define it) and what resources we are willing to devote to achieving that end. So it is with teacher compensation. If we want to accomplish a change, what must we do to implement it? And if we can't afford to do everything, what might we reasonably expect to do within the constraints of our willingness as a society to pay?

CONCLUSION

The impetus for this book is the need to unpack the different types of teacher compensation mentioned above, in order to understand the assumptions they are built on, the success they have had in the past, and, most important, their implications for students and the schools. Performance pay requires a greater level of agreement than currently exists as to what we as citizens mean by performance for schools, teachers, and students. Test scores may be one indicator of student learning, but they do not encompass either the goals most parents have for their students or the vision most citizens have for their country.

Until we can establish a broader consensus concerning what goals we want schools to accomplish and how we might assess their success—either district by district or in the form of a national dialogue—performance pay is unlikely to bring about positive change. With greater agreement, however, and in the wake of extended controversy over No Child Left Behind, the current moment presents an ideal opportunity to chart a more constructive way forward.

NOTES

1. National Commission on Excellence in Education, "A Nation at Risk: The Imperative for Educational Reform," April 1983, *A Nation at Risk*, U.S. Department of Education. Accessed 12 December 2004 at www.ed.gov.

2. National Commission on Excellence in Education, "A Nation at Risk," Paragraph 1.

3. Dale Ballou and Michael Podgursky, *Teacher Pay and Teacher Quality* (Kalamazoo, MI: W. E. Upjohn Institute, 1997), 2.

4. Theodore Hershberg, "The Case for New Standards in Education," *Education Week*, 10 December 1997. Accessed 27 December 2004 at http://www.edweek.org/ew/articles/1997/12/10/16hersh.h17.html?qs=Hershberg.

5. Richard W. Stevenson, "The Wisdom to Let the Good Times Roll; The Clinton Legacy," *New York Times*, 25 December 2000: A.1, Late Edition (East Coast). Accessed 26 November 2007 at http://query.nytimes.com/gst/fullpage.html?res=9D0CEEDB1238F936A15751C1A9669C8B63&scp=1&sq=&st=nyt.

6. Sharon Conley, Donna E. Muncey, and Jewell C. Gould, "Negotiating Teacher Compensation: Three Views of Comprehensive Reform," *Educational Policy* 16, no. 5 (November 2002): 675–706; Charlotte Danielson, *Enhancing Professional Practice* (Alexandria, VA: ASCD, 1996); Harry P. Hatry, John M. Greiner, and Brenda G. Ashford, *Issues and Case Studies in Teacher Incentive Plans* (Washington, DC: Urban Institute Press, 1994); Allan Odden, "New and Better Forms of Teacher Compensation Are Possible," *Phi Delta Kappan* 81, no. 5 (January 2000): 361–365.

7. Odden, "New and Better Forms of Teacher Compensation Are Possible," 363–364.

8. Carolyn Kelley and Allan Odden, "Reinventing Teacher Compensation," in *CPRE Financial Briefs* (Consortium for Policy Research in Education, 1995). Accessed 8 May 2000 at http://www.cpre.org/images/stories/cpre_pdfs/fb06.pdf.

9. Conley, Muncey, and Gould, "Negotiating Teacher Compensation."

10. Allan Odden and Carolyn Kelley, *Paying Teachers for What They Know and Do* (Thousand Oaks, CA: Corwin Press, 1997); Danielson, *Enhancing Professional Practice*.

11. Hatry, Greiner, and Ashford, *Issues and Case Studies in Teacher Incentive Plans*.

12. Hatry, Greiner, and Ashford, *Issues and Case Studies in Teacher Incentive Plans*, 83.

13. Donald B. Gratz, William J. Slotnik, and Barbara J. Helms, *Pathway to Results: Pay for Performance in Denver* (Boston: Community Training & Assistance Center, 2001).

14. Robert L. Linn and Carolyn Haug, "Stability of School-Building Accountability Scores and Gains," *Educational Evaluation and Policy Analysis* 24, no. 1 (Spring 2002): 29–36.

15. Denver Public Schools, *ProComp: A Collaborative Project of Denver Public Schools and Denver Classroom Teachers Association* (Denver, CO: Denver Public Schools, 2005).

16. Jeffrey L. Pressman and Aaron Wildavsky, *Implementation*, 3rd ed. (Berkeley, CA: University of California Press, 1984), 87.

17. Fred Rudolph, "Mark Hopkins (1802–1887)," (Williamstown, MA, Williams College Archives).

2

Education and the Economy: Exploring the Case for Performance Pay

In particular, despite economic theory to the contrary and any problems that may exist in the schools, the productivity of the individual worker has increased dramatically in the past decade without conveying additional economic benefits to the worker or his family.

Instead, it appears that productivity has increased without a substantial increase in worker education level or compensation, and with the benefits reaped almost entirely by those already at the uppermost economic level. Thus, the assumptions that schools are not producing productive workers, and that the productivity of individual workers drives economic success for the workers themselves as well as their employers, have both been proven false over the last decade.

Removed from their organizational contexts, many performance pay plans are composed of the same carrot-and-stick elements and pursue similar goals. Despite the variations described in the previous chapter, the elements and goals of most such plans have not changed for hundreds of years. At root, they are built on a concept of human motivation centered on incentives. Align incentives with organizational goals, the argument goes, and watch as those goals come closer to being met. Economically speaking, this is a "rational man" or "rational actor" argument. The rational man naturally desires higher compensation with which to improve his life, and he will work harder to get it. Incentives are intended to increase effort, improve performance, attract and retain the best workers, and sometimes to identify poor performers. The belief that financial rewards drive human motivation provides the foundation for these plans.

But ideas cannot be removed from their contexts. In the world of education, which has centuries of history with performance pay, the context includes differing perceptions of the purposes of education (to create workers for business or help individuals develop skills and talents), a widespread perception that these purposes are not being met, competing beliefs about the impact of incentives on human motivation, and a confusing array of details that arise from the complex nature of schools. In short, since the goals of education are not universally agreed upon and not easily measurable, and since the behaviors needed to reach the goals are not always known (and differ depending on the goals), performance pay becomes much more complex.

This chapter considers the primary underlying assumptions upon which the case for performance pay is built.

THE CASE IN BRIEF

The brief case for performance pay goes like this: There is a crisis in education, indicated by the continued failure of American students to surpass students from other countries on international tests, the continued failure of schools to improve test scores and bring students to proficiency across the country—particularly in urban and poor communities—and the persistent achievement gap.

This failure is leading to two results. First, many students lack the skills to compete in our increasingly knowledge-based society, leaving them unprepared for the world of work, and unable to be productive citizens. Second, businesses are unable to fill the skilled positions they have created with graduates of American schools, leaving them increasingly unable to compete in the global marketplace. These businesses are forced either to hire foreign workers or to do without the skilled workers they need, leading the country towards economic catastrophe and a substantial reduction in the American standard of living.

Thus, the failures of the education system are driving a downward economic spiral that will ultimately affect every citizen in the country. The need for higher standards and better teaching is urgent and immediate. The current "one-size-fits-all" compensation system provides a disincentive for better teaching, and for attracting and retaining better teachers. Create that incentive, and teaching will improve. As teaching improves, student results will also improve. As in industry, incentive pay (often coupled with other forms of accountability) provides a direct and meaningful way to build a stronger teaching force, more effective schools, and better-prepared future workers.

Underlying Assumptions

Dramatic words like "failure" and "crisis" have long been associated with the public schools. They have served to shape public perception and to drive the public policy agenda, including many of the school reform initiatives of the last several decades. The perception that schools are failing is often linked with the belief that education levels drive the economy—that the failure of schools to sufficiently educate students will lead (and has lead in the past) to economic crises.

Proponents of performance pay who believe schools are in crisis often support direct links between student results (test scores) and teacher compensation. As more than twenty states are currently involved in or have proposed or legislated performance pay plans—plans often based on these concerns about education and the economy—the discussion below begins with the assumptions behind these initiatives:

- Schools are in crisis, as shown by declining test scores and inferior performance relative to other countries on international tests.
- A close causal connection exists between public school effectiveness and the U.S. economy. The country's economic success and confidence are in jeopardy because of the crisis in the schools.
- A close causal connection also exists between students' success in school and their economic well-being following school. Student economic success is in jeopardy because of the crisis in the schools.
- Economic success for individual students and for the country is a primary purpose of education.
- Test scores represent student achievement and teacher performance with sufficient accuracy to serve as the basis for public policy decisions.
- The need for more teachers and more qualified teachers is increasing because of retirements, the number of teachers who leave in the first few years, the increasing demands of the job, and the low qualifications of some who choose to enter the profession.
- Teachers will do a better job if sufficiently motivated.

While these assumptions are not always stated, they provide the logic base not only for performance pay but also for many other initiatives directed at the public schools. There are significant flaws with these assumptions, as will become clear later in the book, but each represents a substantial body of both public opinion and political argument. Counterarguments and additional issues are discussed in chapters 6–10.

CRISIS IN THE CLASSROOM

The perception of schools in crisis is driving current educational reform efforts, as it has for generations. In fact, public schools were born in crisis, and the language of crisis has appeared in discussions of public education since the early 1800s. Immigration and the dramatic growth of the cities fueled fears that immigrants from alien cultures, with their strange languages and customs, would change the nature of society. This tension led both to riots between "nativists" and immigrants on one extreme and to the creation of an array of public institutions to help train new citizens and control the extent of change. Public schools were overburdened from their earliest days, and crises of access, facilities, funding, professionalism, and control were often the subject of active public debate.[1]

The current perception of crisis has its roots in the 1957 launching of Sputnik and took shape with the release of *A Nation at Risk* in 1983. In dramatic language, this report proclaims a national crisis in which the entire nation is falling behind. While its authors worry about learning in all subject areas, they focus on the educational challenges of the dawning technological age, seamlessly weaving a connection between the education of our students and the American way of life. Having proclaimed that the nation is at risk, they describe that risk this way:

> The risk is not only that the Japanese make automobiles more efficiently than Americans and have government subsidies for development and export. It is not just that the South Koreans recently built the world's most efficient steel mill, or that American machine tools, once the pride of the world, are being displaced by German products. It is also that these developments signify a redistribution of trained capability throughout the globe. Knowledge, learning, information, and skilled intelligence are the new raw materials of international commerce and are today spreading throughout the world as vigorously as miracle drugs, synthetic fertilizers, and blue jeans did earlier. If only to keep and improve on the slim competitive edge we still retain in world markets, we must dedicate ourselves to the reform of our educational system for the benefit of all—old and young alike, affluent and poor, majority and minority. Learning is the indispensable investment required for success in the "information age" we are entering.[2]
>
> Our concern, however, goes well beyond matters such as industry and commerce. It also includes the intellectual, moral, and spiritual strengths of our people which knit together the very fabric of our society. The people of the United States need to know that individuals in our society who do not possess the levels of skill, literacy, and training essential to this new era will be effectively disenfranchised, not simply from the material rewards that accompany competent performance, but also from the chance to participate fully in our national life.[3]

In just a few paragraphs, *A Nation a Risk* makes schools responsible for the U.S. economy, the economic future of students, the success of the country as a democracy, the common culture, morality, and individual freedom. Though it states that schools are "only one of the many causes and dimensions of the problem," it declines to name or address the others. Further, it concludes that the public schools are failing on all fronts.

A Nation at Risk sets forth the basic argument around school crisis that is still commonly heard today, but it was hardly the last word on the topic.

Many reports followed, most reinforcing or expanding on the conclusion that America's public schools were failing.

The National Commission on Excellence in Education, which published *A Nation at Risk*, was a largely business-oriented entity, with only one representative from education—at the university level. The members of the commission itself and the dramatic flair of its language captured the attention of the press and the public, as they were intended to. President Reagan chose to interpret the results as supporting vouchers and God in the classroom initially,[4] and later experimented with merit pay (see chapter 3). Both presidents Bush (senior) and Clinton participated in a series of national discussions through the late 1980s and early 1990s that led to the America 2000 agenda, later called Goals 2000. These discussions resulted in a series of lofty goals to improve learning for all students and end the crisis in education—for example: all children will enter school ready to learn—but offered few means to reach them.

In concert with these concerns and in pursuit of similar goals, most states began to develop standards for student learning, tests to see whether the standards were being met, and a series of sanctions to be applied where schools, teachers, or students were falling short. While some educators and politicians urged that national standards would be preferable to the wide range of standards developed by the various states, most thought that national standards would be politically impossible in the United States, given its long history of local control. By the end of the 1990s, most states had established their own standards.

A few years later, in 2001, President George W. Bush persuaded Congress to pass the No Child Left Behind act. This update of the longstanding Elementary and Secondary Education Act (ESEA) was a major departure from previous federal education legislation in the scope of its mandates, and while it listed flexibility, accountability, and choice as its stated goals, most of the emphasis has been on accountability. In support of the act, President Bush proclaimed that "too many of our neediest children are being left behind."[5]

International Comparisons

The evidence of crisis in the schools exists primarily in scores on standardized tests, which are used to demonstrate student achievement. Some of these tests are international, while some are national or local. All are subject to interpretation, as discussed in chapter 10, but low or declining test scores provide the *prima facie* evidence of crisis. This comment from 1997 is a typical reaction in America to the results of an international test: "Ample evidence from the National Academy of Sciences' Third International Mathematics and Science Study [TIMSS] . . . makes clear that nowhere in

America—even in our best school districts—are the majority of students performing at world class levels."[6]

While TIMSS results have been disputed both as to their comparability across countries and as to what can be inferred about the schools, the results from these kinds of tests have repeatedly been used to show U.S. students at a disadvantage (again depending on the interpretation). In fact, the failure of U.S. students to be anything short of first causes alarm in this country. After initial test results in the early 1990s that were seen as mediocre, a UN study in the mid-1990s proclaimed that U.S. students were not only failing to achieve, but getting worse. This analysis determined that, as the headline put it, "Surprise! Analyses Link Curriculum, TIMSS Test Scores."[7] By 1998, U.S. seniors were reported "near the bottom" on TIMSS.[8]

These results gave rise to the National Commission on Mathematics and Science Teaching for the twenty-first century, chaired by former senator John Glenn and known as the Glenn Commission. Its report, released in 2001, was titled "Before It's Too Late." Among its stated purposes was to "instill urgency among the public" regarding science and math teaching.[9]

In 2002, a UNICEF study determined that while Korea and Japan were at the top of the "best schooling list," the United States was near the bottom. This conclusion was based "not on the conventional yardstick of how many students reach what level of education, but on testing what pupils actually know and what they are able to do," according to a UNICEF official.[10]

The perception of crisis persists today. According to an Education Trust statement in April 2006, "The 2005 National Assessment of Education Progress (NAEP) science results released today show strong improvement in fourth-grade achievement, but offer very distressing news about the state of science literacy among secondary school students."[11] These kinds of results—not just in science and math, but often in reading and other areas—are frequently the subject of headlines. Indeed, as a 2005 *Education Week* article observed, despite the Bush administration's contention that No Child Left Behind was working, the 2005 NAEP results showed reading results as "relatively flat" and indicated that "progress in math has slowed during the past two years."[12] While these tests may be interpreted in many ways, it is worth noting that the news coverage tends to emphasize negative results over positive.

From the perspective of national and international test scores, many believe that math and science scores represent a failure of American students and their schools. According to the College Board, fewer than a third of fourth and eighth graders are proficient in math, while twelfth graders perform below average on international comparison tests in both math and science.[13] This, in the view of many organizations, represents a crisis. A closer look at test results and other international comparisons suggests a different interpretation of these results, as discussed in chapter 6. Still, the headlines and resulting public belief is that American students are losing ground to their international peers.

CRISIS IN THE ECONOMY

If the problem were simply confined to test scores, the continual talk of crisis might seem excessive. But to the extent that these results indicate a failure that connects to the American economy and lifestyle, many observers see the problem as both large and serious. The cyclical nature of the economy is paralleled by the cyclical nature of the crisis within the schools, at least since the 1950s, in a way that emphasizes the central role Americans believe public schools play in civic and economic life. When the economy is doing poorly, is changing, or is stressed, for example, the actions of the schools and attainment of students are directly associated with those problems. Unfortunately, the reverse is not true. When the economy is soaring, as it did in the 1990s, the connection between that success and education is not often recognized.

In the first decade of the 2000s, flux in the world economy has produced uncertainty in the United States. Changing economic conditions and fear that America might lose its economic dominance have led to a search for causes and solutions. The needs and failings of the schools once again occupy a central place in the discussion.

It is likely that some segment of society will always view the U.S. economy through a lens of impending doom. The economy is dynamic by nature, and where it benefits one party it is likely to disadvantage another. It is also true politically that crisis and the language of crisis have their uses. Still, widely acknowledged changes are taking place in both the American and world economies that could certainly spell difficulty, if not peril, for America. To the extent that these changes are connected to education, as many believe, education-based solutions could make sense. This case is built along the following lines.

Income Disparity—The Widening Income Gap

It is no longer news that the gap between rich and poor has been growing in the United States for some time. In 1999, for example, economic columnist Robert Kuttner reported that income for the bottom fifth of the population had declined from 5.4 percent of the national economy in 1979 to 4.2 percent in 1997, putting the purchasing power of this segment of the population below its 1979 level. At the same time, he noted, the benefits available to the lowest rung on the economic ladder "also keep being slashed in the name of economic incentive and budget discipline."[14] A month after Kuttner's column, *USA Today* published a cover story on suburban poverty, claiming that far from being just a city problem, the poverty rate was growing faster in the suburbs than anywhere else.[15]

A few years later, in 2004, a *Wall Street Journal* analysis based on Labor Department figures showed that the income divide was still growing sharply. The weekly wage of a worker at the tenth percentile rose only 0.6 percent after inflation, from $284 to $303, while the weekly wage of the worker at the ninetieth percentile rose 4.5 percent, from $1299 to $1440 during the same period.[16] By 2005, the *New York Times* was reporting a 12.7 percent increase in poverty, "the fourth consecutive annual increase" based on Census Department figures.[17] There are many similar analyses.

This growing income gap is partly due to a shift in capital distribution, according to the Brookings Institute, but Murnane and Levy see it as substantially the result of a growing division of labor—"a divide between those who can and those who cannot do valued work in an economy filled with computers." Murnane notes "an extraordinary widening" of the income in this country and concludes that "a key piece of it is this growth in the college-high school earnings differential. I see this as a real threat to democracy."[18]

This "middle-class dispersion"—a trend in which those with college degrees are rising into higher income brackets and those with a high school diploma or less are sinking—is creating an "hourglass-shaped society," according to Murnane and Levy. Workers with high-level skills will succeed to a greater extent than before, while those without the skills/education will fall further behind. They associate the income gap directly with the education gap and conclude that students must gain the skills of high school and college to succeed. They also believe that the economy will have good jobs for any students who increase their education.[19]

While there is much dispute about causes, effects, and the implications of change, few doubt that the economy of the country is changing. There is also a strong public perception that higher skills are needed in the workplace. Hershberg warns, "Sending a child into the economy of the future with the skills currently being taught in our schools is the equivalent of sending a child into a snowstorm dressed in a T-shirt and a pair of shorts."[20]

Most observers agree that the economy is changing, but many take a different view as to the role of schools. For example, the Brookings Institute considers the income disparity in its 2006 series introduction to *Opportunity in America: The Role of Education*, explaining that it takes five generations for the effects of family background to be overcome, on average, and that the "rags to riches" and "riches to rags" changes that are a staple of American mythology rarely happen in the United States. The report also states that the distribution of *earned* income in America is not substantially different from Europe, but that European societies "do a lot more to redistribute income— primarily through social welfare programs that are more generous than those in the United States."[21]

Further, despite the American belief in rags to riches stories through the schools, the Brookings report concludes that America "does not provide a lot of opportunity" and its schools do little to change economic status. "At virtually every level, education in America tends to perpetuate rather than compensate for existing inequalities." Oddly, the report rejects the idea of a more progressive tax and benefit system on the basis that it might lessen people's willingness to work and save, and because it's not "the American way." Thus, even though schools tend to perpetuate class distinctions rather than address them, the solution to economic inequality is to "strengthen the education system so that it compensates for differences in family background"—not to address those differences directly.[22]

Changing Job Patterns—Skills for the Twenty-first Century

In this technological age, many people believe that the best jobs will be related to technology. This belief, and the fear that American students underperform, drives much of the focus on math and science education. In concert with changes in income disparity, wage stagnation for workers, and enormous compensation packages for executives, the nature of jobs is indeed changing. Manufacturing jobs are being lost, while new jobs are being created either in industries requiring advanced skills (high technology and biotechnology) or in industries which require low skill and offer low pay (the service industry). Fast growing third world countries such as China, South Korea, and India threaten American industry. More highly skilled jobs are being outsourced to other countries, and some companies complain that the United States does not produce enough skilled workers in fields such as engineering.

Researchers at the Campaign for Educational Equity predict a shortfall of seven million college-educated workers by 2012, which suggests that the economy could accommodate these workers if they were available.[23] Though estimates as to the availability of high-skilled jobs vary, many citizens believe that lower corporate productivity due to poorly skilled workers is exacerbated by the need for more highly skilled workers than in the past.

Whereas the country has historically had a vibrant manufacturing industry in which many unskilled or semiskilled workers could earn a good living, too many manufacturing jobs have now migrated to other countries. Conversely, our growing technological sector, which includes development and some manufacturing, requires a higher level of skill than in the past—more mathematics and science skills, and more engineers. Indeed, these researchers argue, the engineering shortage is acute. The country is forced to import engineers from other countries.

The College Board, by contrast, estimates that the greatest job growth in the next decade will be in low-wage jobs (6.6 million) and that only 1.7 million new jobs will be created requiring a bachelor's degree or higher. It notes that Ford and General Motors have "suffered the indignity" of having their bonds rated at junk status (this was even before gas hit $4.00 and the recent economic collapse), and that of the 120 chemical plants being built around the world, only one is in the United States, while 50 are in China. In addition, college students in South Korea, China, Singapore, India, and even France are studying natural science and engineering at two or three times the frequency of U.S. students.

Where the Campaign for Educational Equity sees a shortage of college-educated workers in the near future, the College Board sees a different problem. It notes that a majority of the higher-level jobs are either not being created in this country or are moving abroad. So, while 22,000 software design jobs will be created annually in the next decade, there will be "five times as many jobs for janitors and cleaners, waiters and waitresses, and fast food servers."[24]

While taking pains to state that "the peril is not solely, or even principally, the failure of American schools and students to meet world class standards," the College Board nonetheless sees a crisis in teaching brought on by low pay and a huge need for new teachers due to impending retirements. It also believes that hiring more qualified new teachers and upgrading the profession will significantly reduce the coming economic crisis.

It's hard to know how to interpret these statistics, since the goal is not to train students to take low-wage jobs, but the College Board argues that a trade problem which threatens to turn America into a "sharecropper society" and which produced a trade deficit in high-tech products of $96 billion in 2005 is related, in part, to the educational system. The authors conclude that it is through education, specifically good teachers and good teaching, that we will prepare ourselves to handle the massive challenges of the coming decade: "A fiercely competitive global information economy, powered as never before by innovation and intellect, demands that America's young people be well educated. It is not only their individual potential that hangs in the balance; it is the nation's economic future."[25]

So what skills do workers need in the twenty-first century? Carnevale and Desrochers, in a study for Achieve's American Diploma Project (ADP), find that 84 percent of workers in well-paid professional jobs have taken Algebra II or higher, and an even higher percentage have taken at least four years of English. The American Diploma Project has identified the content within these courses, and developed a set of criteria, based on these content areas, which they claim students must attain to be successful. The twenty-two states that are members of the ADP Network have agreed, among other steps, "to make the college-preparatory curriculum the default curriculum for students, including the levels of math and English identified" by Carnevale and Desrochers.[26]

Significantly, however, the study also concludes that the students do not actually *use* the skills of Algebra II. It is simply that students who have *taken the course* are more successful, not that they needed or used the algebra skills.

This suggests that algebra skills are less the issue than opportunity to go to school in a community that regularly offers Algebra II. If this is true, it has significant implications for both student assessment and teacher compensation. What factors are associated with the opportunity to take Algebra II? Prior math training could be one factor, but are family income and neighborhood even more closely associated, as they are with standardized test scores?

A 2006 Conference Board report appears to support this view of academic skills. The Conference Board, along with three other business and employment-oriented organizations, set out to identify the skills needed in the twenty-first century by surveying more than four hundred employers across the nation. The critical skills most often identified by business in this report are *applied* skills in a range of areas rather than the basic skills measured by tests. Thus, while basic reading, math, and science are necessary, the real gap in workers coming out of schools now is in skills like teamwork and critical thinking.[27] This conclusion should also be considered in determining what kinds of incentives might be offered to teachers in support of what kinds of results.

Productivity and Competitiveness

Perhaps the greatest fear of politicians and businesspeople is that poorly skilled workers or a lack of workers will lead to a drop in productivity. This, they believe, will dampen the American economy such that we will be unable to compete. With higher labor costs and lower productivity, American firms will fall behind and the U.S. economy will no longer be able to keep up with its competitors—particularly the emerging economies such as China and Korea. This was the premise in 1983, when *A Nation at Risk* decried the "rising tide of mediocrity," and it remains the premise today. "Americans have long thought of education as the engine of economic growth and the purveyor of activity," notes *Education Week,* so it makes sense that a problem in education would extend itself to become a problem in the economy.[28]

Evidence of the drag of undereducated workers on the national economy is presented by the Campaign for Educational Equity at Teachers College, which has calculated what might happen if all of those currently without a high school degree had one. According to this analysis, only about half the nation's high school dropouts hold down regular jobs, compared with 69 percent of high school graduates and 74 percent of college graduates.

Beyond the difficulties these statistics indicate for the workers and their families, the costs to the economy incurred by those who are not working are substantial according to this report. Nearly 80 percent of dropouts depend on government health programs and pension plans, for example, costing the government hundreds of millions of dollars. High school dropouts have "higher rates of cardiovascular illnesses, diabetes and other ailments," and require $20,000 per year more in medical services than graduates. Similar figures are presented for the cost of crime and incarceration: a one percent increase in high school completion for men ages twenty to sixty "could save the U.S. up to $1.4 billion per year in reduced costs from crime."[29] Families on public assistance, a condition closely aligned with the education level of the mothers, cost the nation $1.5 billion a year.

On the earnings side, high school dropouts earn about $260,000 less in their lifetimes than graduates and pay $60,000 less in taxes, leading to annual losses of about $50 billion in state and federal taxes. Thus, study authors conclude, the United States could save "nearly $200 billion a year in economic losses," which—if it happened—would surely improve the lives of all Americans.[30]

While we have evidence of an increasing income gap relative to degrees earned, the evidence for this kind of connection between education and the economy is speculative at best. In particular, despite economic theory to the contrary and any problems that may exist in the schools, the productivity of the individual worker has increased dramatically in the past decade without conveying additional economic benefits to the worker or his family.

Instead, it appears that productivity has increased without a substantial increase in worker education level or compensation, and with the benefits reaped almost entirely by those already at the uppermost economic level. Thus, the assumptions that schools are not producing productive workers, and that the productivity of individual workers drives economic success for the workers themselves as well as their employers, have both been proven false over the last decade.

In fact, a series of 2006 reports shows that the recent increases in poverty and loss of wages are not directly connected with worker productivity at all. The Economic Policy Institute reports that the economy's productivity increased by "a remarkable 33.5%" from 1995 to 2005, while real wages declined. The median real income for working families was down 5.4 percent in that period, even though the economy had grown every year. All of the gains went to "upper-bracket people and corporate profits."[31]

There is little dispute that the number of people in poverty is growing, that the real income of working families is diminishing, or that the income gap between the rich and poor is increasing. However, the recent productivity findings call into question the presumed connection between education level and productivity, and between productivity and economic success for the worker. To the extent that a perception of crisis or need is founded on these connections, it appears to be an argument founded on myth rather than fact.

The case for increased earnings linked to educational attainment also assumes that there would be appropriate jobs available for all people without a high school or college degree if only they completed their education, an assumption that is open to question. Given the lure of highly skilled workers in other countries who command much lower salaries, it strains credulity to believe that if all students were to graduate from high school or college they would all earn what high school and college graduates earn now. Some would, but high school dropouts and graduates earn less than college graduates on average because they have different jobs. The range of available jobs would not necessarily change. Plus, an over-supply of educated workers could lead to salary reductions at the higher end.

If lower-educated workers were not available to perform service jobs, either college graduates who could not find high-skilled jobs would be performing them, or immigrants from other countries would. The economy is driven by considerably more than the availability of American labor and, as shown above, estimates of future job availability vary considerably. If higher-skilled jobs are actually unfilled in some instances because qualified workers cannot be found, some American students may be missing opportunities. But skilled jobs are exported to emerging countries not because there are no Americans to perform them but because foreign workers will do them for less. Producing more highly educated Americans will not change this dynamic.

The New Economy—Leaving Our Children (and Us) Behind

If schools help determine the financial success both of students and of society at large, crises in either or both of these areas may certainly be cause for concern. As the College Board concludes in *Teachers and the Uncertain American Future,*

> For more than two centuries, public schools have helped make America what it is today. They helped to form our understanding of what it means to be an American. They produced the workforce that long made the American economy the envy of the world. In knitting together strands from many different nations and peoples, they have made the United States immeasurably more powerful and secure than it would otherwise have been.[32]

Without a focus on teaching and teachers, the report's authors fear, and in the face of massive dislocation in the world and local economy, the changes that are coming could be cataclysmic.

> The United States and its people are likely to be swamped by a tidal wave of public and private debt; a sea of red ink in federal, state, and local budgets; catastrophic trade imbalances; and the continued flight of jobs abroad in the transnational search for cheap, skilled labor willing to manufacture products for American consumption."[33]

High school graduation, in particular, is increasingly seen as critical for success in life. In a 2006 special report titled "Diplomas Count," *Education*

Week declares, "The economic and social prospects for young people who don't finish high school are increasingly bleak." According to this report, high school graduates earn 34 percent more than dropouts, and college graduates earn "a whopping 132 percent more."[34] If we believe that all students could earn that whopping 132 percent increase by going to college, we have a strong argument for helping all students to achieve that goal.

But many dispute these points, as noted above and discussed in chapter 6. The income gap is widening, and there is a correlation between higher education and higher earnings. However, our regressive tax policies may be responsible for much of the income gap, as the Brookings Institute believes, and it's not clear that a shortage of skilled workers looms—it appears equally likely that more high-skilled jobs will move elsewhere. Also, while it may be that 40 percent of workers currently work in the field of high technology, for example, it does not follow that all of these workers need the skills of engineers. Most of the people in this industry, as in others, work in sales, marketing, manufacturing, security, management, and support jobs.

Whether these perceptions of crisis are truly driven by economic reality is a matter of some dispute, but crisis, as I've noted elsewhere, is politically convenient.[35] It provides a repository for political fears and is a useful target for policy change that costs proponents little. Crisis drives action, and action wins votes. It's also true that the language of crisis and the link forged between education and the economy have been so persistent for so many years that the public perception of crisis is common. If we believe that the problems are linked—schools are failing, students are in danger, the country is declining—the sources of and solutions to economic problems can then be found within the schoolhouse. The much harder tasks of reforming the tax code, or of solving the housing and health problems associated with poverty, can be taken off the table.

All of the foregoing is important to the extent that both national economic success and individual economic success are determined by educational attainment (test scores)—that the two are related, and that the relationship is causal. That is, these arguments assume that educational attainment doesn't just *predict* success, it *causes* individual and societal success.

But educational attainment is closely linked to other factors, including poverty, poor health, greater risk of crime, and so forth. It could be that both educational attainment and future economic success are driven to a significant extent by a child's economic and class status. If this is the case, lifting families out of poverty will create greater lasting success than changes to the educational system (see chapter 7).

Still, the public tends to believe in a causal relationship between education and the economy, based on reports such as those above. Many of the public policy arguments for performance pay also stem from such a belief. Thus, the need for performance pay is built on predicted economic consequences for students and for the U.S. economy. These consequences are driven by a perceived crisis in the schools, which is indicated by low scores on standardized tests. If this is true—if linking teacher compensation to test scores will increase those test scores—performance pay is a logical conclusion to this line of thinking. The economy–education link and the perceptions of crisis are discussed further in chapter 6.

APPROACHES TO IMPROVING SCHOOLS

Within this broader context of educational crisis, a range of specific school problems have been identified and various proposals have been developed to address them. The proposals to solve these problems break into three overlapping areas: organizational change, curricular and instructional change, and individual change—supports, incentives, and sanctions for individual teachers, students, and schools.

Organizational changes have been proposed at the school, district, and state levels and include everything from site-based management to charter schools. Curricular and instructional changes have led to state standards, tests, and the alignment of curriculum at every level from kindergarten to what colleges teach aspiring teachers. No Child Left Behind, with its requirement of 100 percent proficiency based on standards, tests, and sanctions, is a major driver of both of these reform areas.

With regard to individual change, the connection between the quality of teaching and school success is widely accepted. No one disputes the need for good teachers, but people debate how to define and measure good teaching. As the economy changes and schools continue to underperform on test scores, however, proponents of performance pay see prospects for both the country and individual students as getting worse. This, in turn, drives the need to improve teaching.

Most current school improvement proposals include supports and incentives. For students, these take the form of tutoring, state and federal tests (seen as a form of incentive), and minimum score requirements for graduation. For teachers, supports include mentoring and induction programs, which some states now mandate, and ongoing (often required) professional development. Proponents believe standards and tests motivate students, and they see pay incentives as similarly motivating.

On the disincentive side, states have generally been more willing to deny diplomas to students who can't pass tests than to fire teachers who don't meet student performance or other standards for their classes. Most proponents of performance pay do not suggest dismissing or otherwise penalizing teachers for poor performance. But states are willing to take over "failing" districts and schools on occasion, which can result in the dismissal of teachers and principals. Indeed, states are ultimately required to take over districts considered to be failing by No Child Left Behind. How many districts the states are willing to take over—and how much they are willing to spend—are unanswered questions.

TEACHERS AND TEACHING

The rationale for most proposed changes to the structure of teaching, including performance pay, comes from the perceived need to dramatically improve student achievement in the schools, described above. The core assumption is that better teaching will drive better learning; a corollary assumption is that incentives will spur teachers to better teaching. Several causes of poor teaching have been identified, and proponents believe that each of these problems can be addressed through a performance pay plan. The case for performance pay as a driver for school improvement may thus be broken into the following problem areas.

Recruitment and Retention

This problem has two components. First, given stark projections about the number of teachers who will be retiring in the next several years, the need to recruit new teachers could become acute. "In a nation employing approximately 2.9 million teachers," says the College Board, "school districts nationally will have to hire 2 million new teachers in the next decade to account for enrollment increases, and for teacher retirement, turnover and change."[36] In addition, it is widely believed that the best college students choose careers other than teaching (see below). If this is true, and if pay is a significant reason, increasing pay for high-achieving college graduates is appealing.

An additional factor, along with the general need for more teachers and the desire for more selectivity about who will be allowed to teach, is the need for teachers in particular subjects. The subjects most often identified are science and math, but the need in areas such as special education and English language learners is or will soon become acute in many communities. Teachers of foreign languages are also in short supply. This need is the basis for innovative recruitment techniques as well as differentiated pay for some positions.

The second significant component of the problem is the low retention rate for new teachers. According to the National Education Association, "Half of U.S. teachers are likely to quit within the first five years because of poor working conditions and low salaries."[37] Although many other professions also have significant initial turnover, this is still a poor retention rate. It demonstrates the need to find ways to retain the better teachers among those who leave the profession early. This need drives the widely popular mentoring programs that are increasingly in place in many districts and are mandated by some states, as well as the idea of performance pay and/or career ladders for teachers. There is little disagreement across the political spectrum or among the different interest groups that recruitment and retention are serious concerns.

Teacher Quality

The concern about teacher quality is linked to issues of recruitment and re-tention; it also gets to the heart of the concern about results. If good teaching leads to improved learning, better teachers should provide better learning. However, many observers describe the quality of college graduates who choose to enter the teaching force as fairly low and dropping. "Far too many of those entering the profession do not have the skills and knowledge base to succeed," according to the Teaching Commission. College graduates whose test scores are in the bottom quartile are "twice as likely as those in the top quartile to have majored in education." Further, students with the top grades and test scores are "the least likely among their peers" to enroll in teacher training programs, and only 14 percent of education majors in the study had scores in the top quartile, compared to 26 percent of social science majors and 37 percent of math and science majors.[38]

Several reasons are generally cited. Some critics describe teacher training programs as "cash cows" for colleges, and accuse them of accepting low standards in admissions and turning out licensed teachers unqualified for the role. This view has led to the creation of state tests which prospective teachers must pass for the different licenses they seek, and to create tighter standards for teacher training programs. The assumption of a low-quality teaching force also leads many to support the idea of differentiated teacher pay. The theory is that if the issue is teacher quality, and if a way can be found to reward the teachers of the highest quality, a performance pay plan can address recruitment, retention, and quality all at the same time.

Teacher Motivation

One of the most popular arguments for performance pay is that teachers currently have no financial incentive to try harder, since they will get paid regardless of how well they do or how hard they try. Sanctions now planned for underperforming schools and districts, some of which will reach the individual teacher, may provide a form of motivation for teach-ers who fear losing their jobs, but this is not most teachers (at least, not yet). Many policy makers believe that equal pay regardless of the quality of a teacher's output (student test scores) provides a disincentive for do-ing a good job. Pay related to output, they believe, will provide the incen-tive for all teachers to do their best, improving learning across the board. This fundamental motivator is at the core of many incentive plans, espe-cially those based on student results: spur teachers to do a better job by paying those who do a better job more.

For financial incentives based on test scores to spur harder work and better results, however, we must assume (1) that some teachers are not working as hard as they could and (2) that they have the knowledge, skill, resources, and institutional support to do a better job if they would only try. Most teachers scoff at the notion that motivation is an issue or that it can be improved by pay. Instead, they say, they are working as hard as they can and could not work harder for higher pay. Many teachers and administrators advocate instead for more and better training so that teachers can improve their skills with the newest techniques, and for better organizational support.

This view was demonstrated in Denver, where teachers supported the Pay for Performance pilot and later the Professional Compensation system but discounted the motivational aspects of the pilot. Instead, they emphasized the increased district and school focus on student achievement, the individual goals they set, and the training they received in setting and measuring goals as most critical to the pilot's success. The Teaching Commission's surveys of teachers produced similar responses. What might improve results, teachers agree, are better organization and focus, greater support of the schools, more time for planning, and professional development in needed areas.

Because motivation is a central component of the concept of performance pay, chapter 8 is devoted to it. If incentives do not effectively motivate better teaching, or if the need for motivation is not the issue, directing public policy and public resources into such incentives is counterproductive.

Higher Pay for All Teachers

Not surprisingly, the national unions emphasize the need for higher pay across the board. It does not seem to be as well known, however, that many of the major reports of the last several decades—including *A Nation at Risk* (1983) and the Teaching Commission's *Progress and Potholes* (2005)—have recommended increases in the base pay of teachers to make the salaries "more competitive with other professions."[39] It is also true that whereas unions have traditionally rejected most modifications to the current steps and lanes approach, the past decade has seen considerable shifting in this point of view (see chapter 4). As shown in Denver and in other local and national settings, many teachers are open both to accountability—if they believe the district will treat them fairly—and to changes in the current pay structure.[40]

PERFORMANCE PAY RATIONALE

Each of the problem areas above can be addressed by altering teacher compensation, according to proponents. If humans are "rational" actors, they will naturally pursue higher pay as in their best interests. Thus, the premise is that higher pay will attract more highly qualified new teachers, help retain current teachers, and provide incentives to work harder.

To summarize, proponents believe differentiated compensation improves teacher quality in several ways. First, to entice and retain the best teachers, we should pay the best teachers more. This is an argument to pay bonuses to starting teachers with better degrees or higher grade point averages, to students who come from "better" colleges, and to those who are otherwise exemplary. It is also an argument for providing teachers with opportunities for advancement, and for paying teachers more according to some measure of quality. If schools offer higher pay, proponents believe, more young people will decide to become teachers.

Second, to improve the quality of current teachers, schools should motivate improvement by increasing the pay for those with the best results. Increasing the motivation for each teacher to try hard and do his/her best through incentives is probably the most often cited and most compelling rationale for the majority of supporters of test-based performance pay. It is based on various economic and motivational theories, as well as the popular perception of money as a motivator. This approach requires a workable definition of teacher performance.

Two additional points have salience to some supporters and are sometimes heard. First, there is competition. Beyond the specific problem of the single salary schedule, some performance pay supporters see the entire education industry as anticompetitive and therefore ineffective. If this is the problem—if lack of incentive and competition have led to stasis and laziness in the schools—privatizing the entire system might be the solution. This philosophy leads some to support charter schools and vouchers to reward the best schools in the same way that the economy rewards the best businesses. Performance pay is another instance, possibly a powerful one, through which free market advocates see a fundamental change in the structure of education leading to improved results.

Similarly, some argue that many schools are organized around union rules and perquisites rather than student needs. Thus, according to Hess and West,

> Across the nation, contracts include clauses that prohibit principals from factoring student achievement into teacher evaluation, that allow senior teachers to claim the most desirable school and classroom assignments, and that engage in a dazzling array of minutiae. . . . As a result, schools are organized and managed more like mid-20th century factories than professional 21st century centers of learning. None of this serves students, valuable teachers, or communities.[41]

Unions have caused problems in some districts and been leaders in others (including Denver), but it is worth noting that the problems in states with "right to work" laws and weak unions are similar to those in states that allow strong unions.

CONCLUSION

We like success and achievement and we are going to reward achievement [through per-formance pay]. . . . The United States is in a "ranking war" with such countries as India and China and must reward classroom performance or else our kids are going to be behind.
State Rep. Dennis Baxley, Florida[42]

As Rep. Baxley neatly summarizes, the case for test-based performance pay is derived from the crisis in the schools, the perceived need to dramatically improve teaching and learning, and the belief that incentives within the teaching profession will accomplish this purpose. Many of these are assumptions—often unstated and unexamined, but outlined above and in subsequent chapters of this book. In public statements, proponents tend to link the components of the argument together, as Rep. Baxley demonstrates, and most arguments come back to the same core elements.

Though broad-scale state- and district-based initiatives tend to focus on test-based solutions to the school "crisis" described above, it is also true that educators and researchers across the country are working on skill and knowledge approaches and career ladders to enhance teaching and learning. The motivation for these initiatives is derived in part from the arguments presented above, but without a belief in the motivational power of financial incentives. Instead, these proposals proceed from the premise that improving the conditions of teaching and learning, and the skills of teachers, will attract and retain teachers and lead to the greatest improvement in student results.

In the end, the case for test-based performance pay rests on a series of assumptions with a degree of general acceptance. If the assumptions are correct, the case of performance pay is strong. To the extent they are flawed, however, the case for performance pay—particularly for paying teachers based on test scores—is weaker. The increasing willingness of various parties to work together indicates a gradual agreement on some of the fundamental assumptions of education, but that agreement is far from complete. Before engaging further in changes to teacher compensation, individual districts, and ultimately the citizenry at large, need to strengthen their understanding of how schools link to the economy, how economic conditions affect students, how teacher and other workers are motivated, and how they can jointly define and measure student and teacher performance.

NOTES

1. David B. Tyack, *The One Best System* (Cambridge, MA: Harvard University Press, 1974); Stanley K. Schultz, *The Culture Factory: Boston Public Schools, 1789-1860* (New York: Oxford University Press, 1973); Michael B. Katz, *The Irony of Early School Reform: Educational Innovation in Mid-Nineteenth Century Massachusetts* (Cambridge, MA: Beacon Press, 1968); David Nasaw,

Schooled to Order: A Social History of Public Schooling in the United States (New York: Oxford University Press, 1979).

2. National Commission on Excellence in Education, "A Nation at Risk: The Imperative for Educational Reform," April 1983, *A Nation at Risk,* U.S. Department of Education. Accessed 12 December 2004 at www.ed.gov.

3. National Commission on Excellence in Education, "A Nation at Risk," Paragraph 8.

4. Gerald Holton, "An Insider's View of 'A Nation at Risk' and Why It Still Matters," *Chronicle of Higher Education,* 25 April 2003: B13–15.

5. U. S. Department of Education, *No Child Left Behind Executive Summary,* 2001. Accessed 16 March 2005 at www.ed.gov/nclb/overview/intro/execsumm.html.

6. Theodore Hershberg, "The Case for New Standards in Education," *Education Week,* 10 December 1997. Accessed 27 December 2004 at http://www.edweek.org/ew/articles/1997/12/10/16hersh.h17.html?qs=Hershberg.

7. Debra Viadero, "Surprise! Analyses Link Curriculum, TIMSS Tests Scores," *Education Week,* 2 April 1997. Accessed 5 September 2008 at http://www.edweek.org/ew/articles/1997/04/02/27timss.h16.html?qs=Surprise.

8. Debra Viadero, "U.S. Seniors Near Bottom in World Test," *Education Week,* 4 March 1998. Accessed 26 February 1999 at http://www.edweek.org/ew/articles/1998/03/04/25timss.h17.html?qs=Near+Bottom.

9. Arthur Eisenkraft, "Rating Science and Math," *Education Week* 20, no. 22 (14 February 2001): 68.

10. Alexander G. Higgins, "UN: Korea, Japan at Top of Best Schooling List; U.S., Germany Toward Bottom," UN Report on International Comparisons, 28 November 2002, AP Wire Report. Accessed 26 November 2002 at www.sfgate.com.

11. Claire Campbell and Chris Granger, *Ed Trust Statement on NAEP Science Results,* 24 May 2006. Accessed 7 July 2006 at www.edtrust.org.

12. Lynn Olson, "NAEP Gains Are Elusive in Key Areas," *Education Week* 25, no. 09 (26 October 2005): 1.

13. Center for Innovative Thought, *Teachers and the Uncertain American Future* (New York: The College Board, July 2006), 8.

14. Robert Kuttner, "The Boom in Poverty," *Boston Globe* (Boston), 21 March 1999, E7.

15. Haya El Nassar, "Soaring Housing Costs Are Culprit in Suburban Poverty," *USA Today* (Arlington, VA), 28 April 1999, 1, 2.

16. Greg Ip, "The Gap in Wages is Growing Again for U.S. Workers," *Wall Street Journal,* 23 January 2004, A1.

17. "U.S. Poverty Rate Rises To 12.7 Percent," *New York Times,* 30 August 2005. Accessed 30 August 2005 at www.nytimes.com/aponline.

18. Lynn Olson, "Economic Trends Fuel Push to Retool Schools," *Education Week* 25, no. 28 (3 March 2006): 1.

19. Olson, "Economic Trends," 1.

20. Hershberg, "The Case for New Standards in Education."

21. Isabel Sawhill, *Opportunity in America: The Role of Education* (Princeton, NJ: Brookings Institute, Fall 2006), 2.

22. Sawhill, *Opportunity in America,* 2–3, 6.

23. Alan Richard, "Researchers Tally Costs of Education Failings," *Education Week* 25, no. 10 (2 November 2005): 1.

24. Center for Innovative Thought, *Teachers and the Uncertain American Future,* 8.

25. Center for Innovative Thought, *Teachers and the Uncertain American Future,* 26.

26. Olson, "Economic Trends," 1.

27. *Are They Really Ready to Work?* (The Conference Board, Partnership for the 21st Century, Corporate Voices for Working Families, Society for Human Resource Management, 2006), 9.

28. Lynn Olson, "The Down Staircase," *Education Week: Special Report.* 25, no. 41S (Diplomas Count 2006): 5.

29. Richard, "Researchers Tally Costs of Education Failings," 1.

30. Richard, "Researchers Tally Costs of Education Failings," 1.

31. Robert Kuttner, "Another Year, Another Wage Loss," *Boston Globe,* Op Ed 2 September 2006. Accessed 2 September 2006 at www.boston.com.

32. Center for Innovative Thought, *Teachers and the Uncertain American Future*, 29.

33. Center for Innovative Thought, *Teachers and the Uncertain American Future*, 7.

34. Olson, "The Down Staircase," 5.

35. Donald B. Gratz, "High Standards for Whom?" *Phi Delta Kappan* 81, no. 9 (May 2000a): 681–687.

36. Center for Innovative Thought, *Teachers and the Uncertain American Future*, 9.

37. Lisa Lambert, "Half of Teachers Quit in 5 Years," *Washington Post,* 9 May 2006: A07. Accessed 9 May 2006 at www.washingtonpost.com; Louis Gerstner et al., *Teaching at Risk: Progress & Potholes* (New York: The Teaching Commission, 2006), 16.

38. Gerstner et al., *Teaching at Risk*, 17.

39. Gerstner et al., *Teaching at Risk*, 18.

40. William J. Slotnik et al., *Catalyst for Change: Pay for Performance in Denver, Final Report* (Community Training & Assistance Center, January 2004).

41. Frederick M. Hess and Martin R. West, "Taking on the Teachers Unions," *Boston Globe,* 29 March 2006: Op Ed. Accessed 11 April 2006 at www.boston.com.

42. Bill Kaczor, "Florida Lawmakers Trying to Revamp Merit Pay Plan for Teachers," *Orlando Sentinel,* 1 April 2006. Accessed 11 April 2006 at www.orlandosentinel.com/news/education/sfl-0401lawmakers,0,6468689.story.

3

Merit and Performance Pay in Education—A Brief History

It is no doubt right that the teacher should take steps to test the industry of his pupils; but the information which the child has always to keep at the call of his memory, in order that he may give it back on demand in the form which he has received it, is the equivalent of food which its recipient has not been allowed to digest.

Chief Inspector Edmund Holmes of Britain, 1907[1]

During the early Greek and Roman civilizations and through the Middle Ages, the trade of teaching was an individual enterprise, practiced by independent scholars or tutors who were able to attract a following. These scholars, sometimes organized in early forms of the university, were paid directly by the students or their families—an early and direct form of performance pay. Schools were most often privately run and funded, sometimes through the church, with teachers serving at the whim of the master or religious leader. Wealthier Europeans hired (and dismissed) tutors for their children.

In publicly funded schools, performance pay for teachers dates back at least as far as England in the early 1700s, when teachers' salaries in parts of the country were based on examinations of student proficiency in reading, writing, and arithmetic, though neither the schools nor this practice were systematic. As British schools evolved into a national system, the practice of examination in British education grew until, in the middle of the nineteenth century, it was incorporated into the Revised Education Code, where it lasted for more than thirty years.[2] The British experience of the late nineteenth century serves as a useful starting point both because it bears similarities to the current discussion and because is it the largest effort at systemized performance pay yet implemented in education.

47

BRITAIN'S BIG TEST

Many factors came together to create the climate that produced Britain's Revised Education Code in 1862. The country was struggling with mechanization, urbanization, and a surge in population and was pondering the dire warnings of Rev. T. R. Malthus and others that the population was increasing faster than it could be sustained. The country was also debating the extent to which schools should be secular or religious—religious schools were the most common—and this debate was complicated and enlivened by a series of advances in science, notably the publication of Charles Darwin's *Origin of Species* in 1859.

Several committees of prominent individuals were advocating for increases in funding for education, some for reasons of efficiency or religious conviction, others to promote goals such as protecting children from long hours in the factories. Although new restrictions on child labor were not enacted until later, it had become clear to some child welfare advocates that "the best factory act would be an education act."[3]

The 1850s and 1860s were also a period of economic stress for the country, and four different Royal Commissions offered different perspectives on funding education and supporting the underprivileged.[4] The most influential of these, the Newcastle Commission, proclaimed a crisis in British education in 1861, having determined that "the children do not, in fact, receive the kind of education they require." As a remedy, it recommended a strict regimen of inspection to assure that children were being taught as required, and to tie grants to schools to the examination results. "There is only one way of securing these results, which is to institute a searching examination by a competent authority of every child in every school to which grants are paid . . . and to make the prospects and position of the teacher dependent, to a considerable extent, on the results of the examination."[5]

Some upper-class politicians supported the inspection regimen because they saw inspections as a way both to curtail spending and "to restrict the learning of the common classes by restricting teaching in the publicly supported elementary schools to basic skills."[6] Education Minister Robert Lowe, a champion of payment by results who had previously been vice president of the Board of Trade, told Parliament in 1861 that the plan might not increase learning, but that it would at least reduce costs: "I cannot promise the House that this system will be an economical one and I cannot promise that it will be an efficient one, but I can promise that it shall be one or the other. If it is not cheap, it shall be efficient; if it is not efficient, it will be cheap."[7] The minister, a businessman, saw the application of free trade methods as a mechanism to get spending under control—to produce better value for less money.

Cost savings were not the only motivation, however. Proponents of examinations also included many who were concerned for the welfare of children, particularly poor children. For example, some supporters believed that examinations would provide an incentive for teachers to concentrate on the weaker students—those who needed the most help.

The examination system was launched in 1862 by codifying the already common practice of holding annual examinations based on national standards in reading, writing, and mathematics, and by developing science exams. History, geography, and grammar were added in 1867. Schools were funded based on the level of attainment of each student on these examinations, and while schools were not required to pay teachers based on the success of their students, most financially strapped schools did so.

Schools received a set rate for each child who was judged satisfactory in the examination and were penalized for poor attendance rates and unsatisfactory scores. For "satisfactory" performance, each child in the infant school earned 6s. 6d. (six shilling and sixpence) for the school, and each older child earned 12 shillings. Penalties were exacted for unsatisfactory attendance (4s. for older children, 2s. 6d. for the evening school) and for unsatisfactory performance in reading, writing, or arithmetic (2s. 8d. per subject and 5s. in the evening school).[8]

Entry into the teaching profession was largely unregulated in Britain at that time, as in the United States, and many teachers came with few qualifications for the job. The 1862 Education Act did not replace unqualified teachers or provide training. Instead, it pressured them for better results. Not surprisingly, teachers transferred this pressure to children to perform well on the examinations. Teachers were forced to focus much more of their attention on drilling students in the skills necessary for passing the annual examination, and their journals from the time reflect the "intense preparation for the dreaded examination day."[9]

This period of British history has been graphically described by such authors as Charles Dickens. The classes of society were sharply separated, and conditions for many were grim. Children were often kept in school for long hours, and some spent half the day in school and the other half working in the factories. In the poorer areas, many were undernourished and hungry. But the pressure was present in schools of all social classes. Brighter students were held back while less able ones were pushed to reach higher levels.[10]

As time passed, additional requirements were added. The Code became more specific as to both subject and expected result so that, as one inspector wrote, it "did all the thinking for the teacher; it told him in precise detail what he was to do each year."[11] In response, attempts "to teach outside of the three R's," were largely abandoned, and "these basics were taught in the most mechanical, least flexible manner possible."[12] Many teachers decided that "drill and rote repetition produced the 'best' results," so most schools dropped subjects like drawing, science, and singing and devoted their efforts to passing inspection.[13]

Increasingly, "teachers felt 'overpressured' by the system and its enforcers, and they 'overpressured' students to cram to meet the standards."[14] As one teacher observed, "I do not deny that many teachers do overwork the youngsters in a terrible way, but the poor souls really act under the pressure of the law of self-preservation. They must either meet the requirements of their superiors or become professionally extinct."[15]

In addition, overpressured teachers and students often resorted to tricks to survive—"a game of mechanical contrivance," according to poet Matthew Arnold, the most famous of the inspectors, "in which the teachers will and must more and more learn how to beat us."[16] Some teachers falsified records, while others "poured energy into fooling inspectors." One inspector described children "reading flawlessly"—while holding their books upside down.[17] As Arnold wrote later, "It is found possible, by ingenious preparation, to get children through the Revised Code examination in reading, writing, and ciphering without their really knowing how to read, write, and cipher."[18]

Students were placed in one of three levels, depending on their ability, and were tested accordingly. Given the strong negative incentive of the tests, it is hardly surprising that most children were judged to be in the lowest level, so that expectations for performance would also be low. In one year, 84 percent of students of all ages in the country were identified as being in the lowest level, and were therefore given the easiest test.

The system became more complex as it went forward, with "merit grants" for greater efficiency and some expansion of the subjects tested. In addition, the education bureaucracy grew dramatically as the ministry decided it needed to hire examiners to review the inspection reports and oversee the inspectors. This new layer of bureaucracy added substantially to the cost.[19]

Among its unanticipated results, the system of national examinations led to the creation of the nation's first teachers union, the National Union of Teachers. The union was born in 1870 out of earlier defeat, according to a union history, "for in 1861, crashing down on the evolving prestige of the certificated teachers, had come the reactionary, economical, disastrous promulgation of the Revised Code and the system of 'payment by results.'" During this period, the union grew in close parallel with growing national disenchantment among teachers and citizens over the consequences of that payment system.

In 1889, when the system of payment was "on its deathbed," the union summarized its objections this way: "It had failed to provide the children with a good education; it had set up a false gauge of efficiency; it had necessitated a 'system of cram which encourages mechanical rather than intellectual methods of teaching,' it had hurt both the bright and the slow; it had created suspicion between inspectors, managers and teachers; it condemned poor schools to continued inefficiency; and it had forced the same curriculum on all schools irrespectively."[20]

Even as testing grew, the public appetite for this system of test-based accountability, which had started high, diminished. As conditions changed—as suffrage was extended, as the push for compulsory schooling was under way, as communities were given a measure of local control (later taken away), and as the public saw and heard results they did not support—it became less enamored of the testing system. As early as 1870 a union retrospective identified the climate as improving, and by the end of the 1880s, performance pay was largely out of fashion. But it wasn't until 1892, nearly thirty years after it began—when the "overwhelming judgment" in the country was that the practice was "unsound policy"—that it was dropped.[21]

By 1904, reflecting the strong adverse reaction to the tests and their negative impact, the new guidelines for the country embodied a substantially different approach to the education of children. The job of teaching was described as "assisting" children to learn. The ministry handbook in 1905 called for "unlimited autonomy" for teachers.

> The only uniformity of practice that the Board of Education desires to see in the teaching of Public Elementary schools is that each teacher shall think for himself and work out for himself such methods of teaching as may use his powers to the best advantage and be best suited to the particular needs and conditions of the school.[22]

Looking back in 1907, the chief inspector for Great Britain, Edmond Holmes, described the prior system in this way:

> In nine schools out of 10, on nine days out of 10, in nine lessons out of 10, the teacher is engaged in laying thin films of information on the surface of the child's mind, and then, after a brief interval, in skimming these off in order to satisfy himself that they have been duly laid. He cannot afford to do otherwise. If the child . . . is to be "saved" by passive obedience, his teacher must keep his every action and operation under close and constant supervision. Were the information which is supplied to him allowed to descend into the subconscious strata of his being, there to be dealt with by the secret, subtle, assimilative processes of his nature, it would escape from the teacher's supervision and therefore from his control.
>
> It is no doubt right that the teacher should take steps to test the industry of his pupils; but the information which the child has always to keep at the call of his memory, in order that he may give it back on demand in the form which he has received it, is the equivalent of food which its recipient has not been allowed to digest.[23]

Thus, Britain's thirty-year experiment with performance pay ended in the 1890s, after causing a dramatic narrowing of the curriculum, many unintended negative results in the schools, and a public outcry. It was replaced by a system of "unlimited autonomy" for teachers, and a different approach to education in Britain that was to last for many years.

A tightly controlled teaching system similar to Britain's was also tried in Canada in the late nineteenth century, with similar results. It produced a substantial increase in test scores (in large part by focusing on the students most likely to succeed) along with a substantial narrowing of the curriculum. Once again, the experiment was dropped after a public outcry.[24]

THE AMERICAN EXPERIENCE

The first teachers in the United States were paid based on merit or performance as judged by the communities they served. In this respect, merit pay was the starting point for teacher compensation, based on the country's frontier history and the growth of education as a local rather than a national issue. This approach did not last, however, as individual community-supported schools gave way to systems of schools, starting in Boston and eventually spreading across the country.

Though there have been many different experiments, compensation for teachers has changed only slowly in the United States, and has seen only three primary stages: boarding in the homes of townspeople, grade-based pay (where teachers at higher levels were paid more), and the single salary schedule.[25] This transition took more than a century, as the one-room schoolhouse gave way to consolidated school systems, and as the task of teaching evolved into a profession.

Rural Schooling—Boarding Around

In the initial phase of American schooling, rural communities hired teachers who "boarded around" at the homes of different townspeople. This provided a living to frequently young and itinerant teachers, was extremely cheap for the community, and allowed the community tight control not only over what was taught but over every other aspect of the teacher's life. A part of this control had to do with the expectation that teachers would serve as role models, and indeed, much of the schooling expected at that time—beyond basic reading, writing, and arithmetic—had to do with discipline and moral instruction.

Though their lives were on display as they moved from house to house in small rural communities (often staying only a week in each one), teachers were usually on their own in the schoolhouse, acting as their own principals and supervisors. They were expected to keep order and to put on a community show occasionally, most often in the spring, but were otherwise largely left to determine what and how to teach. Given the lack of supervision, the goal of moral instruction and the need to move frequently, they were judged more on the way they conducted themselves than on results in the classroom.

Teachers received no formal training, and most had only an elementary education themselves, so qualifications had more to do with the basics, comportment, and with the ability to control the class. As such, teaching was both a low-pay and low-status occupation, and one estimate puts the average stay in the job at eighteen months. For young women, teaching was often a transition from their parents' home to their husbands', whereas for men it often served to supplement their summer income. In neither case was it considered a profession.[26]

America remained largely rural through the end of the 1800s. In 1880, for example, 77 percent of Americans still lived in agricultural communities.[27] Nonetheless, dramatic economic changes brought about through industrialization and massive growth in the cities also led to change in rural communities. Many lost population to the growing cities, as young adults and families migrated to the cities in search of better lives. New equipment changed the nature of farming. Improved transportation brought farming communities closer in travel time and made them more interdependent economically. Many citizens of these communities saw these changes as a breakdown of the self-sufficient village life they had known.

For schools, demand increased while the boarding around system became less and less attractive—particularly as other options became available to people who might otherwise have taught. At the same time, teachers were expected to teach their students more as the century went on. Qualified teachers were harder to find and keep, and the poor quality of rural teachers became known as "the rural school problem."[28]

Urban Growth and the Common School

Although most Americans still lived and went to school in rural areas into the late 1800s, industrialization, immigration, and dramatic growth in the cities drove substantial changes in the nature of American life—including changes in the schools. Unprecedented growth and industrialization went hand in hand.

The rapid growth of the cities was closely linked to the country's change from a farming society to one more heavily based in manufacturing. As industrialization grew, commerce with other countries in the world also expanded and interdependence increased. Jobs moved to the cities and factories, forcing families to leave rural communities to find work in the cities. More factories were built and both internal migration and foreign immigration increased: nineteenth-century cities grew at rates not seen before or since, as the following description of Boston indicates:

> The four decades after 1820 witnessed the fastest rate of growth the country had known or would ever see. . . . Newcomers jammed into the historic heart of town. Every public facility was overwhelmed. The population quickly outstripped the

available housing, and new construction lagged; water supplies and sewers were hopelessly inadequate; streets could no longer handle the traffic. . . . Americans felt the shock of the nation's first 'urban explosion.'"[29]

Between 1820 and 1840, the number of people in "urban settlements" increased tenfold, from 693,253 to 6,216,518. In Boston, for example, population growth was driven substantially by immigration—first Irish, then Italian and other European countries. In a single year, 1847, Boston added 37,000 Irish immigrants to its population of 117,000, an astonishing rate of growth. Other cities experienced similar population explosions.[30] Not only was this increase in the number of people staggering, the change to the social and cultural fabric of society was potentially threatening.

Transportation systems were still primitive, so most people lived near where they worked. Cities became more dense and crowded, creating the need for—and then overwhelming—systems for sanitation, cleanliness, public order, and crime prevention. As the poor from the farms or other countries arrived to work in the factories, slums and tenements grew uncontrollably dense. Cities exploded in population and complexity as well as in noise, stench, crime, and decay. Some parts of the cities were bad-smelling, dark, and dangerous.

Most immigrants in East Coast cities like Boston and New York were poor, uneducated, and Catholic—a very different cultural background from the "native" Americans of that period. Midwestern cities experienced dramatic growth of German, Polish, and other populations. As large numbers of outsiders poured into the cities, many citizens feared the breakdown of civilization. In New York, the pressures led to riots and monumental clashes between "nativists" and immigrants, but even in cities where riots did not take place, concern for public morality and public order was paramount.

A substantial purpose of the growing public school network was to be a bulwark of that public order. Civic leaders believed that consolidating individual schools by bringing them under the control of established educators would help solve these problems. They also believed that providing a common school experience for all children from all walks of life would increase the understanding across the social classes, thereby promoting tolerance and lessening friction.

Among the purposes of the Common School, therefore, were to provide a common school experience for all students, promote cultural understanding, and teach the American values and ideals—including the need for civic order—to all children. As different states moved to create common schools funded by taxes, schools were reorganized into age-graded classes and new curricula were developed.

The growth of the student population, the expectation that more would be taught to students in different grades, and the growing chaos in the cities all led civic leaders to push for consolidated school management under professional leadership. The purpose of consolidation, according to civic leaders such as Horace Mann, was to improve efficiency, student results, and school conditions by creating a system of schools controlled by a central board of civic leaders rather than a collection of autonomous entities. In addition, the fear of societal breakdown in the cities led leaders to see schools as a means of control. By socializing children of the poor and foreign born, schools could bring them to understand American society and their place in it. For the children of poor immigrants, their place would likely be working in the factory, obedient to the rule of law, and accepting of their place in society.

The following examples show the range and prevalence of this view:

- Nebraska (where half of the teachers were foreign born early in the 1800s): "How can we have a national spirit in a Commonwealth where there is an infusion of the language and blood of many nations unless there is a very strong effort made to socialize the different elements and weld them into a unified whole. . . . It therefore becomes evident how important it is that the teacher be an American in sympathy, ideals, training and loyalty."[31]
- Boston: In the 1820s, before the mass of Irish immigration, Irish immigrants were described as "clannish," "licentious," "deceitful," "lazy," "riotous," and "hard drinking." By the 1840s and 1850s, their children were often roaming the streets, pilfering from the stores and lounging on the docks. These children were considered examples of the "vicious" poor. In 1889, the School Committee stated, in justifying the use of corporal punishment, that ". . . many of these children come from homes of vice and crime. In their blood are generations of iniquity. . . . They hate restraint or obedience to law. They know nothing of the feelings which are inherited by those who were born on our shores."[32]
- The Connecticut Board of Education, in 1872: "It is largely through immigration that the number of ignorant, vagrant and criminal youth has recently multiplied to an extent truly alarming in some of our cities. Their depravity is sometimes defiant and their resistance to moral suasion is obstinate."[33]

Schools—like jails, hospitals, asylums, workhouses for the poor, fire and police departments, and other institutions developed during this period—were also supposed to counteract societal breakdown.

Professionalizing Education

From the earliest days, school teaching was a temporary, low paying, low status position. To that extent, it was not a surprise (nor perhaps a concern) that the quality of teaching tended to be low. In the mid-1800s school boards often complained that their applicants were those who could not, or did not want, to do the hard work of any other job . . . so they became teachers. Mann observed that the reasons for inadequate teaching were not hard to find: "we pay best,—1st, those who destroy us,—generals; 2nd, those who cheat us,—politicians and quacks; 3rd, those who amuse us,—singers and dancers; and last of all those who instruct us,—teachers."[34]

As management became more professional, the first result was a centrally devised curriculum and methodology for instruction. Superintendents prescribed, sometimes in exacting detail, what was to be taught, when, and to whom. Teachers were viewed as uneducated (which they often were) and incapable of deciding what or how to teach. Like factory workers, their job was to execute the plan that was given to them. Many teachers were the products of the locally controlled schools which, even though they had been consolidated into a citywide system, were often parochial in their interests, and were sometimes corrupt. Teachers in some communities had to "buy" their jobs (bribe hiring authorities) and were sometimes hired because of local loyalties as much as competence.

The nature of teaching also came under increased scrutiny in the second half of the century. While the initial push of consolidation led to systems of schools, the introduction of age-graded schools in the mid-1800s and the subsequent interest in professionalism gave rise to the hiring of professional managers. Although many teachers were considered incompetent, this concept of management had more to do with the control of teachers and the curriculum they taught than with upgrading the teaching profession (in parallel with Britain's effort, but without the institution of performance pay). In fact, although increasing attention was paid to teaching at the end of the 1800s, teachers were still more often seen as laborers than professionals. The need for professional management meant a professional superintendent and (sometimes, but not always) professional administrators at individual schools.

At the same time, society was starting to expect more from its schools, both in rural and urban communities. As expectations for teaching increased, the consideration of teachers as professionals also grew. Where once good teachers were seen as fit by temperament to be role models and moral exemplars (an outgrowth of the innate qualities they were born with), they came to be seen as created through training and experience, not as born to the job.

Teacher training in the mid-1800s took place first in teacher institutes, before the Civil War, and then primarily in normal schools, if it took place at all. This training was mostly for young women, and had as much to do with morals and upright behavior as with academic subjects. As Spring observes, "After graduation from elementary schools but before being sent back to elementary schools as teachers, normal school students received a one- or two-year course that included a review of material that had been learned and was to be taught in the elementary school grades and instruction in classroom management and methods of teaching. Overriding this formal curriculum was the concern with moral character." Teacher training became better as the 1800s gave way to a new century, but "the second-class citizenship of women and the low salaries in teaching contributed to the generally low status of teaching as a profession."[35]

Even so, by the end of the 1800s, teachers were not supposed to simply teach spelling and math but were now expected to integrate these with grammar, literature, geography, history, and so forth. Several committees and commissions—including one on rural schools, another on high schools, and a third on elementary schools—were formed in the 1890s to report on curricular needs and expected outcomes. Rural schools were seen as partly responsible for poor farming and the drift to town.[36] High schools, which had barely existed at the beginning of the century, were expected to work with colleges to create a common, college-preparatory curriculum. Elementary schools needed to better prepare students for high school, and so forth.

The elementary curriculum was much in debate between humanists, developmentalists, progressives, and others. Though John Dewey recognized the centrality of teaching and the need to involve teachers in curricular change, the more common view was that teachers should present whatever curriculum they were given.[37] A "scientifically designed" curriculum should not require teacher input; indeed, it should not allow such input.

Despite the growing expectations, therefore, teaching was still considered as much a matter of training and the ability to follow directions as of creativity or curriculum development. Good teaching came to be seen as something that was possible—even simple—so that someone who was not successful at teaching must be either lazy, incompetent, or otherwise at fault. As Protsik observes, "Professional educators came to believe that there were scientific principles underlying teaching, and the proper training could 'cure' bad teachers as though it were medicine." These professional educators believed that they could train teachers appropriately, and that they could erase the stigma of low status attached to teaching and turn it into a true profession.[38]

The Single Salary Schedule

The consolidation of schools led to standardized teacher salaries, and by the end of the nineteenth century, most school districts were using a tiered salary schedule that recognized the level at which a teacher taught, number of years of service, training, and the supervisor's assessment of merit. This approach to compensation provided teachers with a roughly equivalent pay scale for the level at which they taught—at least within a school or district—recognizing that teachers at the higher levels usually had both more training and greater opportunities to work in other professions. Many districts offered a guaranteed minimum salary.

While the tiered system offered consistency and more money to most teachers, this level of fairness came with one enormous caveat: women and blacks at all levels were paid substantially less. The system also tended to place men in the upper-level positions (high school), keeping costs down by paying large numbers of women substantially less to teach at the lower levels. In Boston in 1876, for example, male grammar school teachers were paid $1,700 to $3,200, and female teachers $600 to $1,200. For high school, men earned $1,700 to $4,000; women, $1,000 to $2,000.[39]

The movement away from the tiered system and toward a single salary schedule was closely tied to the civil and equal rights movements of the time, particularly the demand for voting rights and equal pay for women. The suffrage movement focused primarily on the vote, but also addressed other forms of perceived discrimination. "An increasingly assertive female work force collectively demanded higher salaries under the principle 'equal pay for equal work,'" according to Protsik. Since teaching was one of the main occupations available to women, the campaign for voting rights and equal pay was deeply intertwined with a specific effort to change the pay formula in the public schools. Most cities had women's organizations, and many of these organizations were either explicitly organized around equal pay in teaching, or aligned closely with others that were.

Some men's organizations formed to fight this effort, though this countermovement was weak. Of these, some claimed that women did not need the same standard of living, that they were "inferior intellectually" or were "avoiding marriage," but at least some were simply fearful that equal pay would cause their own pay to be reduced rather than women's pay increased.

In 1920, the Nineteenth Amendment to the U.S. Constitution granted women the right to vote. The first single salary schedules were introduced in Denver and Des Moines in 1921. By 1925, almost 80 percent of women in the nation's largest cities had won equal pay for work equal to their male colleagues.[40]

The evolution of teacher pay schedules as they are commonly seen today is therefore steeped in the history of labor and the growth of factories, civil rights for women and blacks, and the move from rural communities to industrialized urban centers. The single salary schedule evolved for several cogent reasons—the substantial differences in pay between men and women teachers, between white and black teachers, and between teachers at the secondary and elementary levels, as well as the concomitant difficulty in budgeting experienced by school systems. In 1918, 48 percent of schools sampled in one survey described their compensation systems as "merit-based," but this number dropped to about 18 percent in 1928. A 1944 National Education Association report concluded that measures of merit used to construct compensation plans were unreliable, and by the early 1950s the number of districts reporting use of merit pay had dropped to 4 percent.[41]

Although the single salary schedule is the almost universal method of compensation for teachers in public schools in the United States, it must be noted that it is a single *schedule* rather than a single *salary*, so that teachers are paid based on longevity (number of years in the district) and on professional development or education, most often indicated by degrees and credits towards degrees. A common schedule will have eight to fifteen annual step increases for years in the district, plus a series of different columns or lanes representing additional credits and degrees. These generally start at the bachelor's degree and move through masters, masters plus 15 credits, 30 credits and so forth, up to a doctorate.

To the extent that experience and further education increase a teacher's skill and effectiveness, this system differentiates pay according to these two indicators. Despite some studies questioning the value of long experience (twenty-plus years), most professions recognize that skills improve in the first part of one's career, particularly with good mentoring and supervision. It is also the case, as described below, that hundreds of attempts to reintroduce performance pay in one or another guise have been made in various school districts across the country. Few but the most recent—if any—remain in force today.

Workplace Motivation and Performance Pay in Industry

The current structure of the public schools was driven in part by changes related to the industrial revolution—by the huge numbers of immigrants pouring into the country, the cultural differences between the immigrants and current residents of America's cities, and by changes in the economy that brought more people off the farms and into the cities and factories.

These same forces of the industrial revolution also led to new ideas about management and the nature of work. The late 1700s saw a series of inventions like the spinning jenny, the steam engine, and the power loom, all of which contributed to the mechanization and urbanization of the 1800s. As early as 1776 Adam Smith had proposed the idea of breaking work into smaller units to improve efficiency. By the 1800s, this idea began to catch on. Prior to the Civil War, Eli Whitney introduced the concept of interchangeable parts to speed the production of muskets. Each step towards mechanization also led to changes in the structure of labor.[42]

By the arrival of the 1900s, more attention was being paid to managing workers in the factory. Whereas previous arrangements had separated management from labor and left laborers to do their work in the best way that they could, efforts to introduce new and more efficient ways of production were increasingly on the minds of entrepreneurs. Beginning in the 1880s and lasting well into the 1900s, Frederick Taylor began to conduct studies of "method" and of time, and to develop theories of "scientific management."

At the same time, Sears and Roebuck of America introduced its famous catalogue, possibly using the first assembly line in the country, and the internal combustion engine advanced sufficiently to allow the creation of the automobile. In 1913, having watched a moving conveyer of carcasses at a Chicago slaughterhouse, Henry Ford developed a similar method of speeding up the assembly of his cars. Before the assembly line, a worker could assemble a complete car chassis in about twelve and a half hours; "eight months later with standardization and division of labor the total labor time had been reduced to just ninety-three minutes per car."[43]

During the 1920s and into the 1930s, scientific management became increasingly common. Henry Gantt developed a method to visualize complex scheduling tasks (the Gantt chart), and Frank and Lillian Gilbreth developed specific methods for studying time and motion to improve efficiency. The Gilbreths extended their theories to their own home, publishing a book on their large family, and were immortalized by the book and the 1950 movie, *Cheaper by the Dozen*.

Even as school systems were moving to the single salary schedule to reduce confusion and unfairness, new ideas about management were evolving in the broader society. Businesses began experimenting with the most effective and efficient organization of labor. These experiments were initially based on the principles of *scientific management* championed by Taylor, and later on *human relations* management, introduced by Elton Mayo of Harvard in the 1930s. Mayo emphasized the importance of group interactions and the structure of work among groups. He predicted that "factory managers are going to someday realize that workers are not governed primarily by economic motives."[44]

The era of scientific management was also the era during which *scientific testing* was introduced. The U.S. Army commissioned a test to gauge the intellectual fitness of recruits, which led to the Army Alpha, the first widely used test of intelligence. This later grew into the Stanford Binet scale or Intelligence Quotient test (IQ), and spawned a range of attempts to measure both intelligence and academic achievement. The Iowa Test of Basic Skills was developed along these same lines in the 1950s.

Despite all of the interest in scientific management and a formula for differentiated compensation developed by Taylor, there is little evidence that experiments with performance pay in business increased productivity. The famous experiments at Western Electric's Hawthorne plant in Cicero, Illinois, led to further theories of motivation, and seemed to affirm that treating workers better produced greater productivity than did increased compensation. This became known as the "Hawthorne Effect" in research, in which the special treatment of individuals was recognized as causing productivity improvements separate from, and possibly instead of, the specific intervention under study.[45]

The earliest studies of performance pay in industry did not appear until the 1960s and 1970s, and initially focused on timed studies of volunteers performing artificial tasks, such as assembling items as they might in a factory—hardly an appropriate test of methods for teaching. The examples of performance pay that exist today (as opposed to *merit* pay) tend to be in areas of piecework, such as sales commissions. It is not clear that their results are transferable to education.[46] A further discussion of human motivation is contained in chapter 8.

Twentieth-Century Experiments with Performance Pay in Education

As these developments around labor management and testing progressed during the twentieth century, many schemes were developed to rate teacher proficiency and productivity (student results). The problem was, as Cohen and Murnane note:

> . . . none of them could establish a stable connection between teachers' merits and students' performance. Teachers who had high quality ratings did not consistently produce students' [sic] with high achievement. This was problematic, for the great rationale for merit pay was to stimulate productivity. If better teachers didn't produce better students, why pay better teachers more?[47]

By 1950, 97 percent of all U.S. schools had adopted the single salary schedule. This compensation plan does have its advantages: it provides certainty and predictability, is consistent with the unions' obligations to represent all teachers fairly, and is easy and cheap to administer and maintain.[48] Designed to promote "equity and objectivity," it associates teacher pay with experience and with professional development in the form of degrees and college training, a move which has encouraged many more teachers to earn college degrees. It also protects teachers from the arbitrary or capricious actions of administrators and school boards, which could be driven by political considerations, and provides a measure of academic freedom by reducing administrative control over a teacher's work.

Naturally, each of these benefits has an associated deficit, some of which have been widely noted. Reducing administrator interference may be beneficial, but reducing administrator ability to intervene when a teacher is performing poorly harms children. Failing to reward or encourage excellent results or extra effort may discourage teachers who put in that effort or achieve those results, while treating all teachers the same when they all know that some work harder than others and are more effective may reduce morale.

For these reasons and others, despite the predominance of the single salary schedule in the United States since the early part of the twentieth century, forms of merit and performance pay have been tried repeatedly across the country. Some waves of these experiments have been driven by events, while others have simply arisen through the efforts of superintendents, school boards, and/or unions in various states.

Although the first recorded attempt to formally institute merit pay in the modern era took place in Newton, Massachusetts, in 1908,[49] the trend at the time was strongly in favor of the single salary schedule and away from salary differentiation. This trend continued through the depression and world wars, a period of less public scrutiny of the public schools.

In the late 1950s, Sputnik rekindled interest in and fear about the country's education system. In a 1963 report called *The Miseducation of American Teachers*, the Council on Basic Education noted that the poorest students were choosing to become teachers, blaming the problem on education schools: "A weak faculty operates a weak program that attracts weak students."[50]

During the 1960s, about 10 percent of districts developed variations on the merit pay model, but once again this number fell to 5.5 percent in 1972 and 4 percent in 1979. "In search of an explanation," according to Cohen and Murnane, "one study reported that the chief local reasons for abandoning merit pay included teachers' discontent with merit ratings and the difficulties of devising a scientifically defensible measure of teacherly merit."[51]

President Richard Nixon initiated an experiment in Texarkana, Arkansas, led by the Department of Health, Education and Welfare, based on "concern over the lack of educational achievement among the growing population of the urban poor." According to Nixon, ". . . [T]he avoidance of accountability is the single most serious threat to a continued, and even more pluralistic educational system." This experiment, which focused on "performance contracting," started with great improvements in test scores demonstrated by various educational contractors in Texarkana, and quickly spread to eighteen other cities. However, "scandal and the lack of results ultimately doomed performance contracting," and the experiment was abandoned as a failure.[52]

In 1977–1978, a study by the Educational Research Service looked at 183 districts that had tried some form of performance or merit pay and had discontinued it. The average length of the experiment was approximately six years. Reasons given for discontinuing the experiment were administrative problems (40 percent), personnel problems (38 percent), collective bargaining (18 percent), and other (6 percent).[53] To the extent that teacher opposition is seen as the major impediment to successful implementation of performance pay, this study suggests otherwise.

Hatry and his colleagues (1985, updated in 1994) present a discussion of eighteen to twenty communities that engaged in incentive pay plans. Most of these were begun in the 1970s or 1980s, although a few dated back to the post-Sputnik era. Most provided a combination of supervisor assessment and professional growth plans, but some also included student test scores. Of the eighteen districts included in the study, only five remained active at the time of the update.[54]

In the mid-1980s, the now famous *A Nation at Risk* recommended that teacher salaries be "professionally-competitive, market-sensitive and performance-based."[55] This report was followed by as many as two hundred others, the majority of which sounded similar themes of educational crisis and many of which recommended a variable pay scale. President Ronald Reagan endorsed the idea of merit pay, creating what some describe as the first *national* call for differentiated compensation. Once again, experiments with pay for performance flourished for a short time. These most often rewarded teachers based on supervisor reviews, and led to resentment among teachers for their subjectivity.[56]

Frase (1992) collected analyses and case studies or commentaries on attempts at performance pay in the 1980s, at least some of which were spurred by *A Nation at Risk* and the Reagan initiatives, including plans in Tempe, Arizona (career development); Lake Forest, Illinois (comprehensive evaluation); Rochester, New York (peer assistance and review); and Fairfax County, Virginia (professionalism: evaluation, and support).[57]

Few such experiments remain. As Odden observed in 2000, "It would be difficult to find many examples of changes in teacher pay enacted before the 1990s that survive today." Emphasizing the distinction between merit and performance, Odden notes that "nearly all past proposals offered some version of merit pay. . . . They have foundered in part because teachers are uncomfortable with differentiation of pay based on the subjective judgments of administrators and in part because of a lack of continued funding."[58]

Despite the failure of merit and performance pay schemes to succeed over the long term, however, these ideas once again found their way into public discussion by the end of the 1990s. "After decades of resistance, the barriers holding back the idea of paying teachers based on how well they do their jobs may finally be weakening," announced *Education Week* in late 1999. In addition to Denver (see chapter 5), it referenced new initiatives in St. Paul; Cincinnati; Seattle; Coventry, Rhode Island; and the state of California.[59]

In the first decade of the twenty-first century, the idea of performance pay is once again alive and well, having been embraced by many states and communities. We should not think it is new, however, nor untried. It is neither. Instead, we should consider what we want to accomplish in our schools, what we may want to accomplish with a change in the compensation system, and what we can learn from history about what does and does not work. If it is true that those who don't study history are condemned to repeat it, anyone interested in changing teacher compensation should certainly consider the history of attempts to implement performance pay.

NOTES

1. Wade Nelson, "Timequake Alert: Why Payment by Results is the Worst 'New' Reform to Shake the Educational World, Again and Again," *Phi Delta Kappan* 82, no. 5 (January 2001): 386.

2. Wellford W. Wilms and Richard R. Chapleau, "The Illusion of Paying Teachers for Student Achievement," *Education Week* (19), 3 November 1999, 34, 48; Richard Bourne and Brian MacArthur, *The Struggle for Education, 1870-1970* (New York: Philosophical Library, Inc., 1970); W. H. G. Armytage, *Four Hundred Years of English Education* (Cambridge, England: Cambridge University Press, 1964).

3. Armytage, *Four Hundred Years of English Education*, 138.

4. Armytage, *Four Hundred Years of English Education*, 126.

5. Bourne and MacArthur, *The Struggle for Education, 1870-1970*, 20.

6. Nelson, "Timequake Alert," 385.

7. Bourne and MacArthur, *The Struggle for Education, 1870-1970*, 20; Nelson, "Timequake Alert," 385.

8. Armytage, *Four Hundred Years of English Education*, 124.

9. Nelson, "Timequake Alert," 385.

10. Bourne and MacArthur, *The Struggle for Education, 1870–1970*, 21.

11. Wilms and Chapleau, "The Illusion of Paying Teachers for Student Achievement," 48.

12. Bourne and MacArthur, *The Struggle for Education, 1870–1970*, 21.

13. Wilms and Chapleau, "The Illusion of Paying Teachers for Student Achievement," 48.

14. Nelson, "Timequake Alert," 386.

15. Wilms and Chapleau, "The Illusion of Paying Teachers for Student Achievement," 48.

16. Armytage, *Four Hundred Years of English Education*, 125.

17. Wilms and Chapleau, "The Illusion of Paying Teachers for Student Achievement," 48.

18. Nelson, "Timequake Alert," 387.

19. Nelson, "Timequake Alert," 386.

20. Bourne and MacArthur, *The Struggle for Education, 1870–1970*, 21.

21. Wilms and Chapleau, "The Illusion of Paying Teachers for Student Achievement," 48.

22. Nelson, "Timequake Alert," 388; Armytage, *Four Hundred Years of English Education*, 188.

23. Nelson, "Timequake Alert," 386.

24. Wilms and Chapleau, "The Illusion of Paying Teachers for Student Achievement," 48.

25. Jean Protsik, "History of Teacher Pay and Incentive Reforms," *Journal of School Leadership* 6 (May 1996): 266.

26. Protsik, "History of Teacher Pay and Incentive Reforms," 268–269; David B. Tyack, *The One Best System* (Cambridge, MA: Harvard University Press, 1974), 19.

27. Protsik, "History of Teacher Pay and Incentive Reforms," 268–269.

28. Tyack, *The One Best System*, 21.

29. Richard C. Wade, "Foreword," in *The Culture Factory: Boston Public Schools, 1789–1860*, Stanley K. Schultz (New York: Oxford University Press, 1973), v.

30. Tyack, *The One Best System*, 30.

31. Tyack, *The One Best System*, 22.

32. Stanley K. Schultz, *The Culture Factory: Boston Public Schools, 1789–1860* (New York: Oxford University Press, 1973), 229, 260; Tyack, *The One Best System*, 75.

33. Tyack, *The One Best System*, 75.

34. Schultz, *The Culture Factory: Boston Public Schools, 1789–1860*, 76.

35. Joel Spring, *The American School: From the Puritans to No Child Left Behind* (Boston: McGraw Hill, 2008), 152.

36. Herbert M. Kliebard, *The Struggle for the American Curriculum*, 2nd ed. (London: Routledge, 1995), 8–14; Protsik, "History of Teacher Pay and Incentive Reforms," 271.

37. Kliebard, *The Struggle for the American Curriculum*, 75.

38. Protsik, "History of Teacher Pay and Incentive Reforms," 271.

39. Protsik, "History of Teacher Pay and Incentive Reforms," 273.

40. Protsik, "History of Teacher Pay and Incentive Reforms," 275; Tyack, *The One Best System*, 267.

41. Richard J. Murnane and David K. Cohen, "Merit Pay and the Evaluation Problem: Why Most Merit Pay Plans Fail and a Few Survive," *Harvard Education Review* 56, no. 1 (February 1986): 2.

42. Cliff F. Grimes, "Historical Perspectives," in *Employee Motivation, the Organizational Environment and Productivity* (London: Accel-Team, 2006), 12.

43. Grimes, "Historical Perspectives," 16.

44. Grimes, "Historical Perspectives," 15, 18.

45. E. Brian Peach and Daniel A. Wren, "Pay for Performance from Antiquity to the 1950s," in *Pay for Performance: History, Controversy and Evidence*, ed. Bill L. Hopkins and Thomas C. Mawhinney (Binghamton, NY: Haworth Press, 1992), 5–26.

46. Gary P. Latham and Vandra L. Huber, "Schedules of Reinforcement: Lessons from the Past and Issues for the Future," in *Pay for Performance: History, Controversy and Evidence*, ed. Bill L. Hopkins and Thomas C. Mawhinney (Binghamton, NY: Haworth Press, 1992), 125–150.

47. David K. Cohen and Richard J. Murnane, "The Merits of Merit Pay," in *Research Report No. 85-A12*, National Institute of Education no. 80 (Summer 1985), 5.

48. Protsik, "History of Teacher Pay and Incentive Reforms," 275.

49. Fenwick English, "History and Critical Issues of Education Compensation Systems," in *Teacher Compensation and Motivation*, ed. Larry E. Frase (Lancaster, PA: Technomic Publishing, 1992), 3–25.

50. Dale Ballou and Michael Podgursky, *Teacher Pay and Teacher Quality* (Kalamazoo, MI: W. E. Upjohn Institute, 1997), 1; James D. Koerner, *Miseducation of American Teachers* (Cambridge, MA: Riverside Press, 1963).

51. Cohen and Murnane, "The Merits of Merit Pay," 6.

52. Wilms and Chapleau, "The Illusion of Paying Teachers for Student Achievement," 48.

53. English, "History and Critical Issues of Education Compensation Systems," 7.

54. Harry P. Hatry, John M. Greiner, and Brenda G. Ashford, *Issues and Case Studies in Teacher Incentive Plans* (Washington, DC: Urban Institute Press, 1994), 101.

55. National Commission on Excellence in Education, "A Nation at Risk: The Imperative for Educational Reform," April 1983, *A Nation at Risk*, U.S. Department of Education. Accessed 12 December 2004 at www.ed.gov.

56. Brad Goorian, "Alternative Teacher Compensation," *ERIC Digest* Number 142 (2000), Eric Clearinghouse on Educational Management. Accessed 6 September 2008 at http://search.ebscohost.com.odin.curry.edu/login.aspx?direct=true&db=eric&AN=ED446368&site=ehost-live.

57. E. Larry Frase, *Teacher Compensation and Motivation* (Lancaster, PA: Technomic Publishing, 1992).

58. Allan Odden, "New and Better Forms of Teacher Compensation Are Possible," *Phi Delta Kappan* 81, no. 5 (January 2000): 361.

59. Lynn Olson, "Pay-Performance Link in Salaries Gains Momentum," *Education Week* 19, no. 7 (13 October 1999): 1.

4

How Business, Unions, and the Public View Performance Pay

Business is probably the largest consumer of American education. . . . [The priority] is having people in the workforce who are capable and have the skills you need in the workforce today.

Charles Kolb (2006), President, Committee for Economic Development[1]

BUSINESS, SCHOOLS, AND PERFORMANCE PAY

Throughout modern history, business has tended to support educational accountability and to emphasize the connection between educational quality and business success. These attitudes date to the earliest days of performance pay in the 1800s in both Great Britain and the United States. In more recent times, business-dominated reports on education have almost always contained a statement in support of educational accountability and have often offered support for performance or merit pay for teachers. This support for increasing accountability through performance pay has been accompanied with increasing frequency by calls for an overall increase in teacher salaries.

A Nation at Risk was released in 1983 by the business-supported National Commission on Excellence in Education, the first major report of the current era to sound a series of themes that have become common today. Describing the economic and educational condition of the country as dire and the quality of the nation's teaching force as weak, it set forth a series of sweeping recommendations that are both substantive and insufficiently specific. The report lamented that teachers are poorly trained and come from the lower tiers of their college classrooms, that many teachers are not qualified for the jobs they hold (especially in math and science), and that teaching is not a competitive profession, with success dependent on outperforming others. It concluded that this cycle of poor jobs, lack of competitive drive, poor pay, and the related low opinion of the profession among the best college students have created a condition of chronic under-performance for the schools.

A Nation at Risk presents seven recommendations for teachers. These include higher entry standards into the profession, putting teachers on an eleven-month schedule, developing career ladders, and increasing pay. With regard to compensation and accountability, the report recommends that:

> Salaries for the teaching profession should be increased and should be professionally competitive, market-sensitive, and performance-based. Salary, promotion, tenure, and retention decisions should be tied to an effective evaluation system that includes peer review so that superior teachers can be rewarded, average ones encouraged, and poor ones either improved or terminated.[2]

As with many such reports, *A Nation at Risk*'s authors did not offer a way to pay for the proposals they promoted, nor did they provide a definition of "performance-based." Nonetheless, *A Nation at Risk* launched debate on a range of controversial ideas that had not received serious consideration in prior years (though most of the ideas were not new). Many of the reports that followed also questioned the quality of public schools, teacher accountability, and compensation.

As performance pay grew in popularity again in the 1990s, business leaders again supported a payment for results approach. Business was critical in funding and supporting the Denver experiment from the start, for example, and in keeping the school board focused on performance pay as one of its priorities at important points in the process.[3]

When they support performance pay, business leaders often promote the view that profits are the corporate bottom line and that schools' bottom line—student achievement—should be similarly clear and stark. In the late 1990s, the concept of paying teachers based on their performance was strongly endorsed by such groups as the Business Roundtable (BRT) and the National Alliance for Business (NAB), which together opined that the "quality of our education system has a direct impact on American business' ability to compete in the global marketplace, and on American workers' capacity to acquire the core knowledge and skills they need to be productive and secure in today's rapidly changing economy."

In 1999, the BRT and NAB endorsed "helping interested school systems develop ways of compensating teachers that reward increased student achievement"—including performance pay—as part of a three-part school improvement strategy that included high standards, rigorous standards-based assessments, and better accountability. In a brief for business leaders written in July 2000, the BRT/NAB alliance applauded Denver's pilot program, along with experiments in North Carolina, Cincinnati, Los Angeles, and other cities and states, some of which are no longer in existence. Two statements from this brief illustrate the business point of view:

> Used widely in the private sector, pay for performance is a strategic compensation system that ties financial and other rewards to increased performance. Many features of the current teacher compensation system are outdated and inadequate, and pay for performance can help heighten the focus on improving student achievement. An aligned system of standards, assessments, and accountability is essential to the effectiveness of our schools. Pay for performance can be an effective element of an aligned system.
>
> The benefits of pay-for-performance are well-known in the private sector, where compensation is frequently used as a management tool to achieve organizational goals. As part of a total compensation strategy, pay-for-performance is used in the private sector to reward individuals, groups and/or organizational performance in the form of bonuses and increased compensation for results. The vast majority of large US companies now use some form of performance-based pay with at least some portion of their employees—an increase of 50 percent since 1987, according to Ohio State University's Robert Heneman. And research suggests that roughly two out of three such efforts result in increased productivity or other measurable improvements.[4]

In 2000, NAB released *Improving Performance Competition in American Public Education*, a report which argued for more competition-related incentives, such as report cards for schools, schoolwide rewards for achievement and penalties for failure, and charter schools. It also advocated "gates" and graduation "hurdles" for students. Noting that the private sector "encourages hard work, innovation and high standards through the risks and rewards of competition," the report concluded that public school teachers and students "have faced few consequences for their failures and even fewer awards for their successes."[5]

By 2001, the Business Roundtable and National Alliance of Business joined with the National Association of Manufacturers and the U.S. Chamber of Commerce to publish *Investing in Teaching*. Among other recommendations, this report proposed tying pay to performance "with both group bonuses for improvement and monetary rewards for individuals based on demonstrated knowledge and skills and students' academic performance." This appears to have been a shift for the NAB—perhaps in response to experiments in Denver and elsewhere—in that it advocated both group and individual incentives, and included incentives for teachers to improve their skills and knowledge as well as results from unspecified measures of student achievement.

This report also proposed creating new career opportunities for teachers, decentralizing to provide teachers with greater freedom and flexibility, and raising salaries to as much as $100,000, but only if they were tied to results.[6] Though state plans rarely mention the need to raise salaries overall—an expensive proposition—many business and academic reports of the past decade have bundled the two ideas together.

As No Child Left Behind has intensified the focus on student test scores and more states have begun to look for strategies to increase those scores (and possibly for someone to blame if the scores don't rise), business has remained largely supportive of differentiated compensation. Before going out of business in 2006, the Teaching Commission, led for a number of years by retired IBM CEO Lou Gerstner, produced two final reports: *Teaching at Risk: A Call to Action* in 2004, and *Teaching at Risk: Progress and Potholes,* in 2006. The commission, comprised of prominent business and political leaders, sought to solve the problem of teaching—increasingly viewed as "a second rate occupation"—by professionalizing the teaching profession. It argued forcefully for putting a highly qualified teacher in every classroom, noting that NCLB requires states to develop a plan to reach that goal.

Typical of such business groups, Gerstner described the goal of the commission as attempting to address "the nation's dangerous achievement gap by transforming the way in which America's public school teachers are prepared, recruited, retained, and rewarded."[7] Among its proposals, the commission argued for replacing the current "rigid" system with "flexible, responsive systems that recognize and reward excellence and incorporate market incentives." While it describes its recommendations as "not overly prescriptive" and recognizes that there are promising experiments being tried, the commission sets forth a list of criteria that include both objective and subjective measures of performance, collaboration with teachers in developing the criteria, a "sustainable" funding stream, a career ladder for gaining status and responsibility, and market incentives for hard to staff schools and shortage subject areas.[8]

In releasing this report, the commission also acknowledged that neither the public nor teachers were fully behind its ideas, as a majority of both groups see standardized test scores as inappropriate measures of teacher performance. The commission's reports do not offer a solution to this problem, but in an interview at the release of the final report, Gerstner commented, "I'll accept that it's hard to measure student performance, but it's unacceptable to say the opposite, that you can't measure what students learn at all."[9]

Business Use of Performance Pay

Despite such statements of business commitment to performance pay in education, however, studies of business methods do not indicate wide success using performance pay (as differentiated from merit pay) except in situations where performance is clearly measurable and observable to both employee and employer. In fact, it is difficult to find proponents or practitioners of any strict form of performance pay in business—where pay is tied specifically to results—except in areas like sales or other forms of piecework. When quality of work is important, corporations do not generally evaluate college-educated employees by quantifiable goals, in part because it is hard to isolate the contributions of a single employee.[10]

While many businesses describe their compensation systems as built on merit, their definition of merit combines productivity and evaluations by superiors which are, at their root, subjective. The distinction is important. Business leaders often support test-related performance pay for teachers, arguing that these tests provide a measure of a teacher's value. In practice, however, businesses tend to reward those employees that supervisors think are doing the best job. This method may be partly objective, depending on the organization, but it is rarely data-based or completely objective.

For example, at Bain & Company, a Boston-based management consulting firm, managers spend about a hundred hours a year evaluating five employees. "When I try to imagine a school principal doing 30 reviews, I have trouble," observed director David Bechhofer in a 2000 interview. Regarding more objective measures, Bechhofer noted that "data-based measures of output can often be manipulated," and that it's unfair to reward employees for results they cannot fully control.[11]

In a situation where piecework is appropriate, some businesses pay a commission or bonus for higher production, but the criteria for these are narrow. Conditions must be equivalent, it must be clear to both worker and employer why one worker is earning more than another, and it must also be clear to the worker what he must do to earn more. These conditions are unusual enough in business, but rarer still in education.[12]

Politicians often fail to make this distinction. Pronouncements by the business community are sometimes taken to be the final word on productivity and efficiency. In these post-Enron, post-Worldcom, post sub–prime mortgage days, however, the meaning of corporate accountability is more nuanced. For example, airlines cannot simply generate profits at the expense of passenger safety or airline maintenance, and all parties—businesses, regulators, and the public—are now aware that quality and ethnical business practices are critical. Nor, we hope, will mortgage lenders focus strictly on the bottom line in the years to come. Even in business, it's not just the bottom line.

Unfortunately, the corporate view of school accountability espoused by politicians—enshrined in federal law through No Child Left Behind before the recent scandals hit—does not contain similar nuance. Rather, it is based on a simplistic concept of the educational bottom line and a simple formula: reward teachers for test scores and test scores will improve.

In 2000, for example, New York Mayor Guliani promoted merit raises for teachers with the statement that it was "how the private sector works." In a subsequent *New York Times* article, however, economist Richard Rothstein observed: "This, they say, is how the private sector works. But it is hard to find private sector examples for such proposals. True, stockbrokers and sales clerks are paid on commission. But the high pressure tactics this system can engender should be intolerable where children are concerned."[13]

In 2005 Massachusetts Governor Mitt Romney, a former Bain director, led the charge for performance pay for teachers in that state (perhaps with an eye on a presidential run) with the statement that closing the achievement gap is "the civil rights issue of our generation," and that performance pay "is the way to do it."[14] As noted above, however, performance pay was not the way they did it at Bain.

Many political leaders seem to favor a strict results-based model and business leaders often support them. When the business community comes together in groups like the Teaching Commission or the Business Roundtable, however, it often presents a more moderate point of view (though without detail), recommending that teachers' salaries be raised, that a dedicated funding stream be developed, that teachers be involved in determining what constitutes performance, and that a variety of plans—such as career ladders—be considered. The question these business recommendations raise is as much whether it is possible to implement such plans as whether they are desirable. Can communities or states find the money? Can they define teacher performance in a way that captures its complexity? Positions on this topic among business leaders have become more balanced and thoughtful in recent years, as complex issues have been raised and considered.

In contrast, political proposals—though they cite business as a model—tend to oversimplify both problems and potential solutions, and to overstate business use of similar plans. That is, they blur the distinctions among the different forms of performance and merit pay, and they leave out many of the complexities.

Thus, Robert Costrell, chief economist and education advisor to Massachusetts Gov. Romney (an interesting dual role) wrote in support of Romney's plan that performance pay "is a well-established principle in most fields. It's a tool both to attract high-caliber individuals and also to motivate higher performance." He noted that it was "commonplace" in higher education, including some unionized campuses, though in such settings (he did not note) it is usually a merit system in which individual professors are paid based on an analysis of the fields they come out of and whatever they can negotiate.[15]

Stanford business professor Jeffrey Pfeffer presents a different point of view, describing the argument that performance pay is motivational as one of the six "dangerous myths" of business. Pfeffer and his colleague Robert Sutton contrast business and education approaches in their most recent book, *Hard Facts, Dangerous Half Truths & Total Nonsense.* First, they observe, "The fact that an educational proposal comes out of a corporate world view does not make it a bad idea, of course, but it does not make it a good one either."

Educational proposals must be evaluated within the context of the educational enterprise. Proposals that emphasize efficiency may demand an approach that diminishes the individual differences among children. Those that emphasize effectiveness likewise demand individuation, and may be less efficient.

They also note obvious differences between the practices of education and business—differences which have frequently been described by educators as well: "Unlike the factory floor, which demands uniformity in its raw materials, education does not (yet) work that way."

Finally, they confirm that business leaders who have studied education have come to recognize those differences: "Despite political statements concerning the prevalence of performance pay in business, the opinions expressed by business groups that have looked at the educational enterprise go a long way toward recognizing the different goals and conditions that affect the industry of education, and offer a more balanced view of what is needed than is generally perceived."[16] (More on this in chapter 8.)

Although the business community does not speak with one voice, it seems fair to say that as more business leaders have become involved in education, many of them have come to recognize the complexities of the educational enterprise. Some segments of the community support strict performance pay, charter schools, and other strategies that attempt to mirror the competitive world of business, but more are open to working with teachers to find ways to strengthen teaching and learning, not just to impose solutions from the business world.

THE CHANGING ATTITUDES OF TEACHERS UNIONS

Since districts began adopting the single salary schedule in the early 1920s to rectify inequality in teacher pay, teachers unions have historically fought all forms of merit pay, and resisted most new forms of evaluation and accountability. As Cohen and Murnane observed in 1985, "Collective bargaining is now a fact of life in a very large fraction of America's school districts, and teacher unions have been notoriously allergic to pay for performance schemes."[17]

Starting late in the 1990s, however, the two major national unions and many of the locals began to embrace the concept of teacher accountability and to endorse various experiments to develop new compensation systems. In particular, members of the Teachers Union Reform Network (TURN) committed themselves to finding ways to improve teaching, and spearheaded efforts to negotiate innovative forms of teacher compensation that they believe provide both appropriate accountability and fair compensation. This network includes large cities such as Albuquerque, Boston, Denver, Los Angeles,

Memphis, New York, and Pittsburgh, as well as affiliates of both the National Education Association (NEA) and the American Federation of Teachers (AFT).

"Our members are more and more willing to take a look at some of these issues," Don Cameron, executive director of the National Education Association, observed in 1999. "The idea of incentives based on student performance and teacher performance is something I think we have to take an objective look at." And, according to Adam Urbanski, director of TURN and president of the Rochester Federation of Teachers at the time, "The question is no longer whether the traditional, lock-step salary schedule will survive. . . . It will not." Instead, he argued, teachers and their unions need to consider appropriate forms of accountability.[18]

Writing for TURN in 2000, Urbanski and Erskine, both local association presidents, offered the following:

> The teachers themselves must accept responsibility for change and see themselves as agents rather than mere targets of reform. Thus, the primary goal of TURN is to promote new union models that can take the lead in building and sustaining high achievement schools through improving the quality of instruction. The unions and union leaders must expand their view of themselves to include the role of leaders of reform.[19]

Several TURN districts were experimenting with new ideas for teacher compensation at that time, including school-based performance systems that provided bonuses either to the schools or to staff, and additional bonuses for meeting national board standards. This is the model of collaboration that took shape in Denver. In fact, teachers and the union played a strong leadership role in that highly collaborative effort. The willingness and ability of teachers to collaborate made Denver's success in developing and implementing its new compensation plan possible.

In addition to some local affiliates, the national associations have also embraced new compensation initiatives. In July 2000, the NEA narrowly defeated a resolution under which it would have endorsed pay plans based on factors beyond a teacher's length of tenure and level of education, after lobbying by members of the Denver delegation and others experimenting with such alternatives. NEA President Bob Chase, who expressed support for the resolution, said that the negative vote "reflected teachers' frustration with what they see as unfair accountability measures and the inappropriate implementation of state standards and high stakes tests for students."[20] Despite this defeat, however, it was significant that a national union even considered such a resolution, or that it came near to passing.

In early 2001, the AFT's thirty-nine-member executive council went even further, unanimously approving a resolution that "we must enhance the traditional compensation schedule using approaches that contribute to more effective teaching and learning." While the range of acceptable approaches did not include direct teacher pay for student performance, and while the AFT said it wouldn't accept all new compensation plans, a spokesperson noted that they were "willing to do incentives and differentials that make sense and that are not destructive to the educational process." Sandra Feldman, AFT president at the time, described the progress as "revolutionary."[21]

Over time, union leaders and other educators have become more open to the possibility of alternative forms of compensation. Writing in 2005, AFT president Edward McElroy noted problems with the current teacher compensation system: although it eliminates bias it does not reflect the professional nature of teachers' work, nor "the growing demands on teachers to help all students reach ever-increasing levels of achievement." While he did not endorse plans that pay teachers based on test scores, or experiments that have "opened the door to favoritism and discrimination" or have "bred harmful competition," he did support plans that include career ladder options, national board certification, schoolwide improvements, and classroom demonstrations of teacher skill and knowledge.[22] Similarly, New York City's United Federation of Teachers agreed on schoolwide bonuses in 2007, in exchange for other concessions.

Despite this moderation of views by both unions and business groups, a significant thread of the movement for performance pay (as well as for charter schools, vouchers, and various other reforms) is a pro-competition, anti-union stance. This position draws heavily on ideology. Its proponents often call for professionalizing teaching, but appear to define professionalization as teachers being willing to work without protection and with accountability measures that they believe are not accurate or fair.

In an Op-Ed article for the *Boston Globe* on the Massachusetts proposal, Hess and West of the American Enterprise Institute describe Gov. Romney's proposal as "noteworthy for [its] breadth and the size of the proposed bonuses." They quote the Mass. Teachers Association president denouncing the proposal as "inequitable, divisive, and ineffective . . . uniquely designed to destroy collegiality in a school" and complain that the union approach ignores the fact that "performance pay is routine in such other professions as medicine, law and engineering." Further, they say, union contracts deny principals the right to include student achievement in the teacher evaluation process. They urge taking on the unions, demanding higher student achievement, and changing the collective bargaining environment.[23]

This argument is popular and contains some truth, but it compares unlike circumstances to make its point. Few citizens use legal or medical services every day for many years, as students use schools, and society accepts the unequal distribution of resources in the legal and medical worlds. Both lawyers and doctors operate in an environment where they sell their services as individual entrepreneurs or partners, not as employees (though medicine is changing).

Law is performance related to the extent that people can choose a lawyer they want (and can afford). Legal aid lawyers help some citizens; others get no legal support at all. Medicine is similarly organized, except that most people have some sort of medical insurance plan. Still, the quality of service in both professions is directly related to a family's wealth, and many citizens are left uninsured. It is hard to imagine anyone seriously promoting either medicine or law as models for education.

At the same time, teachers know that a test-based accountability system—which most teachers and many parents recognize as unfair and inaccurate—could leave them at the mercy of conditions outside of their control. They also fear that a merit pay model in which principals determine raises is open to politics and favoritism. In essence, they're afraid that this approach to "professionalizing the profession" is really a plan to have teachers continue as labor (not independent practitioners) in an environment they can't control and without protections.

Control of circumstances is a significant issue. Bain's Bechhofer believes it's unfair to compensate workers based on conditions they can't control, but the premise of performance pay (and of No Child Left Behind) is that teachers control enough of the learning process to make a significant difference. Most teachers agree that they can make a difference, but student learning is affected by many factors, only some of which teachers can control. Far too many students spend more time watching television than attending school, for example, an activity that impedes learning.

Despite greater openness regarding accountability and new compensation plans, neither paying teachers based on the success of their students nor paying for teacher "merit" (as determined by principals) has been embraced either by AFT or NEA. In fact, according to Urbanski (in 1998), TURN's work on new performance pay structures might be "enormously helpful as an antidote to the goofy but persistent clamoring for merit pay. . . . Merit pay is not going away until there are some alternatives to it."[24]

In 2008, at twenty-one local district members plus the national unions and other affiliates, TURN is not a large network. Still, a number of its active unions are national leaders, and it continues to work towards mutually-agreed improvements. TURN members such as Denver, Minneapolis, and Rochester (New York) have helped to spur experiments, and the network includes improving student results as one of its core goals, affirming the responsibility of its members to collaborate to bring about higher student achievement and to improve the conditions under which adults teach and students learn.[25]

A 2007 Education Sector Report based on an interview of thirty union presidents from large and small districts in six states presents a good cross-section of the opinions and attitudes of teacher union leaders. Not surprisingly, these presidents agree on the importance of paying a competitive wage to attract and to retain teachers, and most appear to believe that that wage level has not yet been reached. "You support public education by making sure you have the best teachers," said one. "You do that by making sure that you have salaries and working conditions that entice them to come and make them stay."[26]

Union presidents' opinions on performance pay are mixed. Most support the idea of higher pay for additional duties—extra pay for extra work—such as mentor, math coach, or lead teacher, as this practice is already firmly ingrained in most districts through stipends for athletic coaches, club leaders, and various other additional duties. Some districts pay a substantial stipend for "consulting teachers" or "professional developers," which often involve summer work. One district—Montgomery County, Maryland—calls this a "career lattice" approach. It adds both additional pay and additional duties for more experienced teachers, and gives them "professionally rewarding opportunities" which help keep them in the classroom.[27]

Most of the union presidents also reject the idea of "merit pay" in which merit is based on supervisory evaluation. This is not only because of the dangers of investing this authority in a principal, but also because of the difficulty of judging merit. As an example, Education Sector describes Boston leader Richard Stutman asking sports fans to compare the New York Yankees' Derek Jeter to Alex Rodriguez. Rodriguez had the better statistics, but most fans would prefer to have Jeter on the team, he says. "If somebody is going to get the merit [pay], who is it?"

The presidents reject standardized test scores for similar reasons: these tests are inadequate measures of student learning and are therefore inappropriate for judging teacher performance. They may also lead to "perverse incentives" such as preventing teachers from sharing or collaborating, narrowing the curriculum, focusing too heavily on drills, and so forth. The presidents are somewhat more supportive of group incentives since these support teamwork and cooperation, and a few districts offer them.[28]

Although these union leaders do not reject all performance pay ideas, they are skeptical of the impact of such plans. Still, they recognize that the world is changing. Echoing Denver teacher leaders' remarks from its Pay for Performance Pilot, the presidents believe they must consider these ideas or worse ideas will be forced upon them. "I think we do need to look at pay for performance," said one, "but I think we have to decide what the performance is or how we measure performance. If we as a union are not engaged in the discussion, then it will be test scores."

Also similar to Denver's teachers, this group does not appear to see much connection between such incentives and teacher recruitment or retention. Instead, professional pay and good working conditions are the keys, they say. Most recognize that change is inevitable, but while some are experimenting with other changes, only Denver has so far abandoned the single salary schedule in favor of a new plan.[29]

As of 2008, AFT documents note weaknesses in the current compensation system—for example, when teachers get salary increases for earning college credits unrelated to their teaching. Though the AFT does not support abandoning the current system or narrow attempts to judge teaching solely on student test scores, it does support experiments in performance pay (not merit pay), as long as the plans are "part of an effort to support quality teaching and raise student achievement." The Milken Foundation's Teacher Advancement Program is cited as an example of this approach and the National Board of Professional Teaching Standards certification is an example of an alternative determination of teacher quality.[30]

The NEA website focuses more directly on ways to raise salaries for all teachers. It addresses concerns about merit pay—creating competition and undercutting collaboration among teachers—and the question of how to capture a teacher's performance.[31]

As with business, union attitudes have become more open and less adversarial. Union leaders agree on the goal of improved student achievement through appropriate forms of accountability and an effective learning environment. This change is led both by individual union locals, and by national leaders who recognize the growing national interest in accountability and who believe in effective teaching. These leaders are increasingly willing to experiment with forms of accountability that they believe will improve the teaching process. They also believe that teachers need protections from the arbitrary judgments of the bureaucracy and, it hardly needs saying, they support higher salaries for teachers across the board.

In addition to Denver, experiments have been launched in Minneapolis, where some teachers submitted proposals for funding in the state's program; Boston, where state and district union leaders have recommended incentives to encourage experienced teachers to teach in inner-city schools; and Chicago, where the teachers union has worked with administrators to design a program that will place "master teachers" and "mentor teachers" in struggling schools at significantly increased salaries.[32]

While these activities indicate more openness and cooperation around changes in teacher compensation, teacher perceptions remain mixed. Even those who support change are cautious, noting that teaching is not like manufacturing widgets or automobiles. Organizations such as the Education Trust and National Council on Teacher Quality also support teacher accountability if it is based on measures of student growth, but many teachers remain skeptical. Even a student-growth assessment model is far from comprehensive if it still relies on test scores and ignores other goals and factors that influence students. Where performance pay does seem to have teacher support, as in Denver and Minnesota, it is noteworthy that the programs were designed through partnerships between labor and management.

PUBLIC PERCEPTIONS OF TEACHER COMPENSATION

The public attitude towards state-level changes in teacher compensation may eventually be demonstrated at the ballot box. Denver's voters approved the new ProComp plan by a substantial majority (58 percent), but most such experiments remain highly controversial. Despite the mantra that schools are failing and in crisis, opinion polls demonstrate support for the public schools, particularly schools within the respondent's home community.

One of the oldest and most respected survey of public opinion on the public schools is the Phi Delta Kappa (PDK)/Gallup poll—an annual sampling of opinion that has been conducted since 1968. This poll consistently finds that parents and citizens give their local schools high marks, but have a less favorable view of public schools across the country. Further, support for the schools has risen substantially since the poll began. The results below are from the 2005, 2006, and 2007 polls, the most recent available at the time of this writing.[33]

In the 2007 survey, most parents approve of their children's schools (67 percent) and the schools in their communities (53 percent), a finding that has been largely constant for forty years. Among the public at large, 45 percent grade their community's schools with an A or a B. Breaking this down further, 53 percent of parents of public school students give their schools an A or B, and 43 percent of respondents with no children in school similarly rate their local schools highly. By contrast, only 16 percent of respondents award the nation's public schools an A or B (14 percent parents, 17 percent non-parents). These numbers are down a few percentage points from 2006, but up significantly over the life of the poll.[34]

This low opinion of schools nationally may reflect the barrage of criticism coming from some political and education leaders and the press, who constantly tie the word "crisis" to public schooling (see chapter 6). As the survey's authors note in the 2005 report, however, their results "should help destroy one of the myths surrounding the public schools": that they are losing public support. In fact, "the trend lines of the poll suggest the exact opposite," and are "truly impressive" when they reflect the opinions of parents whose children actually attend these schools.[35]

Because the public is more supportive of local schools than of schools nationally, the authors advise, "It seems fair to say it would be a mistake to shape public policy decisions on data regarding the nation's schools. The schools in their communities are the ones the public knows about and cares about."[36] Conversely, if policy makers act nationally without regard for the relatively low public perception of schools nationwide, they may be surprised when their ideas are not supported at the local level. That is, the authors clarify, "Gaining public support for school improvement will be more likely if proposals are based on the schools in the community and not on the nation's schools."[37] Most respondents think that if a school's performance is to be judged on test scores, it should be improvement in those students' scores (82 percent) rather than proficiency or the percentage that passes the test (16 percent).[38] This finding is significant, as most states judge students on a single proficiency standard.

Although the public tends to support testing in the schools, it is divided on whether these tests should be used for high-stakes decisions; 52 percent say tests should be one measure of teacher proficiency in the 2005 survey, while 44 percent say they should not. In 2007, when the question was asked which incentives for teachers would be the most beneficial, 87 to 95 percent of respondents supported all of the measures proposed: smaller class sizes, financial incentives based on teacher performance, additional professional development, and higher salaries for beginning teachers.

Similarly, the public supports a range of factors identified for possible use in determining teacher pay. The percentage of people who believe that each of the following indicators is very or somewhat important is indicated in parentheses: seniority (73 percent), student performance on state tests (81 percent), college credits or degrees (87 percent), the difficulty of finding a teacher to teach in a particular school (89 percent), and the difficulty of finding a teacher in a subject area (91 percent).[39] The question asks whether testing should be "one measure," not whether it should be "the measure" of teacher quality. It is fair to assume, I believe, that support for any of these factors as *the* measure of teacher quality would be considerably lower.

Each of the past several years, the PDK/Gallup poll has asked people their opinion of standardized testing—whether there has been too much, not enough, or the right amount. The percentage of people who believe there has been too much emphasis on these tests has gone up every year, from about 30 percent (2002) to about 40 percent (2007).[40] Opinions on No Child Left Behind are polarizing, with increases in both those who view the law favorably (31 percent) and unfavorably (40 percent). While respondents still support current levels of testing, the more they have come to understand NCLB, the less they like it.[41] Similarly, the Teaching Commission's surveys of public opinion indicate that the public wants to give teachers raises but does not want to tie those raises to teacher performance. Similarly, rather than give principals more power over teachers, the public prefers to reduce class sizes.[42]

The PDK/Gallup polls consistently find that the public considers lack of financial support to be the biggest problem facing the public schools, regardless of whether the respondents have children in the schools. In identifying the biggest problem, twice as many respondents cite lack of funding (22 percent) as the next highest item, lack of discipline (10 percent). Only 5 percent believe that finding good teachers is the most important problem. These results taken together—the perceptions that local schools are doing well, that the main problem schools face is a lack of funding, and that a variety of factors should determine teacher pay—suggest that more communities might support complex measures like Denver's and perhaps locally devised plans in states such as Minnesota, but would not support plans too heavily dependent on test scores or any other single factor.

Other surveys have found somewhat different results, depending on how they posed the questions. An ETS poll in 2007 asked respondents whether they support NCLB, but this poll has been criticized for describing the law in a positive light without mentioning the critiques, and for mentioning the promise of additional funding twice. The result was 56 percent favorable, 39 percent unfavorable. A survey by the Scripps Survey Research Center indicates that states are required to test students "to determine if schools do a good job teaching," and mentions critiques about an overemphasis on testing. Asked whether Congress should renew, change, or cancel the law, 23 percent of its respondents say the law should be renewed; 48 percent, changed; and 14 percent, cancelled.[43]

Regarding the skills of the twenty-first century, a survey commissioned by the Partnership for 21st Century Skills finds that a majority of respondents are concerned that the United States is not preparing students for the twenty-first century with skills that they will need to compete. According to this study, 88 percent of respondents believe schools can and should incorporate "critical thinking and problem solving, communication and self direction, and computer and technology skills" into their curricula. The authors of the study identify collaboration, communication, and cultural knowledge as essential today, differentiating these skills from the "back to basics" approach of ten to fifteen years ago.[44]

The public has so far shown mixed support for test-based accountability measures used for teacher compensation or for making decisions about students. Although most states have high-stakes tests, and although these tests tend to have a majority of public support, that majority is often slim and the resistance is active. Continued support for testing is by no means assured, however; in fact, it appears to be diminishing. Respondents in the PDK/Gallup poll oppose reporting children's test scores separately by 54 to 43 percent, and they oppose including the scores of special education students in a school's total by 62 to 33 percent. An overwhelming majority of 81 to 17 percent favor a growth model of student achievement, which measures student progress, over a proficiency model in which students must reach a certain level regardless of their starting place.[45] (See chapter 10 for a discussion of these models.)

On the other hand, where citizens have been asked if they would be willing to spend more for the schools, they have often answered yes. This has occurred not just in local funding votes, but also in surveys of the general public.

Finally, the authors of the 2006 PDK/Gallup poll note two questions that have been asked for several years—whether the fault for problems at the schools lies primarily with the schools or with society (asked since 1990), and whether the achievement gap is a result primarily of the schools or of society (asked since 2002). In 1990, 73 percent of respondents thought that the schools' problems were mainly the fault of society, while 16 percent lay the blame with the schools. In 2006, those figures were 70 percent and 22 percent.

Similarly, in 2002, 66 percent believed that the achievement gap was primarily due to factors outside of the school, while 29 percent attributed the gap to the quality of schooling. In 2007, the figures were 77 percent and 19 percent, respectively. "This," conclude the authors, "is near-consensus support for the belief that the problems the public schools face result from societal issues and not from the quality of schooling."[46] Given this public opinion, it is hard to imagine that public support of a test-based compensation system aimed at addressing the achievement gap will gain great traction with the majority of citizens.

Although the public has rarely been able to vote on a specific plan for teacher compensation, it did have that opportunity in Denver in 2005, where teachers and administrators had worked together to present a multifaceted plan. The next chapter describes some of the issues involved in Denver's migration from an initial proposal for test-based performance pay to a complex realignment of teacher compensation. The plan was ultimately approved by a substantial majority of the school board, teachers, and voters.

Denver's progress so far in piloting and adopting a new compensation plan provides an example of trends shown above—that both business and the unions are interested in working together on raising salaries and supporting accountability if appropriate means can be found. It also appears that the public, while remaining skeptical of NCLB and wary of over-testing, is open to such experiments. Given these trends towards moderation and collaboration among these three critical parties, the time appears right for changes in teacher compensation. Clearly, however, success will require more balanced proposals and greater collaboration than have yet been seen in most states and districts.

NOTES

1. David J. Hoff, "Big Business Going to Bat for NCLB," *Education Week* 26, no. 8 (18 October 2006a): 1, 24.

2. National Commission on Excellence in Education, "A Nation at Risk: The Imperative for Educational Reform," April 1983, *A Nation at Risk*, U.S. Department of Education. Accessed 12 December 2004 at www.ed.gov.

3. Donald B. Gratz, William J. Slotnik, and Barbara J. Helms, *Pathway to Results: Pay for Performance in Denver* (Boston: Community Training & Assistance Center, 2001); William J. Slotnik et al., *Catalyst for Change: Pay for Performance in Denver, Final Report* (Community Training & Assistance Center, January 2004).

4. Business Roundtable, "Pay-For-Performance: An Issue Brief for Business Leaders," *Publications*, July 27 2000. Accessed 28 May 2004 at www.businessroundtable.org/publications.

5. Mark Walsh, "More Incentives Would Drive Schools to Improve, Business Alliance Argues," *Education Week* 19, no. 23 (16 February 2000): 8.

6. Jeff Archer, "Businesses Seek Teacher 'Renaissance,'" *Education Week* 20, no. 21 (7 February 2001): 1; *Investing in Teaching: A Common Agenda* (National Alliance of Business, Business Roundtable, National Association of Manufacturers, Chamber of Commerce, 9 January 2001).

7. Louis Gerstner et al., *Teaching at Risk: Progress & Potholes* (New York: The Teaching Commission, 2006), 5.

8. Gerstner et al., *Teaching at Risk: Progress & Potholes*, 27.

9. Aaron Bernstein, "Lou Gerstner's Classroom Quest," *Business Week Online* 7 April 2005: Daily Briefing. Accessed 6 June 2006 at http://web.ebscohost.com.odin.curry.edu/ehost/detail?vid=4&hid=102&sid=96a0c182-9e45-4839-865401d0f25d7157%40sessionmgr108&bdata=JnNpdGU9ZWhvc3QtbGl2ZQ%3d%3d#db=aph&AN=16756070.

10. Richard Rothstein, "Lessons: Arguing Against Merit Pay as Incentive for Teachers," *New York Times* 26 April 2000: Section B, page 11. Accessed 6 June 2006 at www.nytimes.com.

11. Rothstein, "Lessons."

12. Richard J. Murnane and David K. Cohen, "Merit Pay and the Evaluation Problem: Why Most Merit Pay Plans Fail and a Few Survive," *Harvard Education Review* 56, no. 1 (February 1986): 2.

13. Rothstein, "Lessons."

14. Michael Janofsky, "Teacher Merit Pay Tied to Education Gains," *New York Times*, 4 October 2005, 12.

15. Robert Costrell, "Governor Romney's Differential Pay Proposals," *Rennie Center E-Forum* 1, no. 1 February 2006, *Rennie Center for Education Research & Policy*. Accessed 13 February 2006 at www.renniecenter.org.

16. Jeffrey Pfeffer and Robert Sutton, *Hard Facts, Dangerous Half Truths and Total Nonsense: Profiting from Evidence-Based Management* (Harvard Business School Press, 2006).

17. David K. Cohen and Richard J. Murnane, "The Merits of Merit Pay," in *Research Report No. 85-A12*, National Institute of Education no. 80 (Summer 1985), 2, 5.

18. Lynn Olson, "Pay-Performance Link in Salaries Gains Momentum," *Education Week* 19, no. 7 (13 October 1999): 1.

19. Adam Urbanski and Roger Erskine, "School Reform, TURN, and Teacher Compensation," *Phi Delta Kappan* 81, no. 5 (January 2000): 367.

20. Jeff Archer, "NEA Delegates Take Hard Line Against Pay for Performance," *Education Week* 19, no. 42 (12 July 2000): 21, 22.

21. Jeff Archer, "AFT to Urge Locals to Consider New Pay Strategies," *Education Week* 20, no. 23 (21 February 2001b): 3.

22. Edward J. McElroy, "Teacher Compensation: What Can Be Done to Maintain (and Improve) Teachers' Wages and Benefits?" *TeachingK-12*, 8, August/September 2005. Accessed at www.TeachingK-8.com.

23. Frederick M. Hess and Martin R. West, "Taking on the Teachers Unions," *Boston Globe* 29 March 2006: Op Ed. Accessed 11 April 2006 at www.boston.com.

24. Ann Bradley, "A Better Way to Pay," *Education Week* 17, no. 24, 25 February 1998. Accessed 8 May 2000 at http://www.edweek.org/ew/articles/1998/02/25/24pay.h17.html?qs=A_Better_Way_to_Pay.

25. Teachers Union Reform Network (TURN), 2008. Accessed 13 July 2008 at www.gseis.ucla.edu/hosted/turn/turn.html.

26. Susan Moore Johnson et al., *Leading the Local: Teachers Union Presidents Speak on Change, Challenges* (Washington, DC: Education Sector Reports, June 2007), 9.

27. Johnson et al., *Leading the Local*, 9–10.

28. Johnson et al., *Leading the Local*, 10.

29. Johnson et al., *Leading the Local*, 12.

30. Sandra Feldman, "Rethinking Teacher Compensation," *American Teacher* (2004), *American Federation of Teachers*; accessed 2 January 2008 at www.aft.org/pubs; "Professional Compensation," *American Federation of Teachers*, Hot Topics Statement, n.d. Accessed 2 January 2008 www.aft.org/topics/teacher-quality/comp.htm.

31. "Professional Pay: Myths and Facts," *National Education Association*, n.d. Accessed 2 January 2008 at www.nea.org/pay/teachermyths.html.

32. Sam Dillon, "Long Reviled, Merit Pay Gains Among Teachers," *New York Times* 18 June 2007. Accessed 18 June 2007 at www.nytimes.com; Maria Sacchetti, "Extra Pay Urged at Poorest Schools: Teachers' Unions Propose Incentives," *Boston Globe* 30 November 2006. Accessed 30 November 2006 at www.boston.com; "Merit Pay a Start to Building Better-Performing Schools," *Chicago Sun-Times* 6 November 2006: Editorials. Accessed 6 November 2006 at www.suntimes.com/news/commentary.

33. Lowell C. Rose and Alec M. Gallup, "The 37th Annual Phi Delta Kappa/Gallup Poll of the Public's Attitudes Toward the Public Schools," *2005* 87, no. 1 (September 2005): 41–57; Lowell C. Rose and Alec M. Gallup, "The 38th Annual Phi Delta Kappa/Gallup Poll of the Public's Attitudes Toward the Public Schools," *Phi Delta Kappan* 88, no. 1 (September 2006): 41–57; Lowell C. Rose and Alec M. Gallup, "The 39th Annual Phi Delta Kappa/Gallup Poll of the Public's Attitudes Toward the Public Schools," *Phi Delta Kappan* 89, no. 1 (September 2007): 33–48.

34. Rose and Gallup, "The 39th Annual Phi Delta Kappa/Gallup Poll of the Public's Attitudes Toward the Public Schools," 39.

35. Rose and Gallup, "The 37th Annual Phi Delta Kappa/Gallup Poll of the Public's Attitudes Toward the Public Schools," 42.

36. Rose and Gallup, "The 39th Annual Phi Delta Kappa/Gallup Poll of the Public's Attitudes Toward the Public Schools," 40.

37. Rose and Gallup, "The 38th Annual Phi Delta Kappa/Gallup Poll of the Public's Attitudes Toward the Public Schools," 42.

38. Rose and Gallup, "The 39th Annual Phi Delta Kappa/Gallup Poll of the Public's Attitudes Toward the Public Schools," 34–35.

39. Rose and Gallup, "The 39th Annual Phi Delta Kappa/Gallup Poll of the Public's Attitudes Toward the Public Schools," 43–44.

40. Rose and Gallup, "The 39th Annual Phi Delta Kappa/Gallup Poll of the Public's Attitudes Toward the Public Schools," 37.

41. Rose and Gallup, "The 37th Annual Phi Delta Kappa/Gallup Poll of the Public's Attitudes Toward the Public Schools," 47.

42. Bernstein, "Lou Gerstner's Classroom Quest."

43. David J. Hoff, "To Know NCLB Is to Like It, ETS Poll Finds," *Education Week* 26, no. 42 (20 June 2006): 29.

44. Meris Stansbury, "Voters Urge Teaching of 21st Century Skills," *ESchoolNews* 15 October 2007. Accessed 30 November 2007 at www.eschoolnews.org.

45. Rose and Gallup, "The 38th Annual Phi Delta Kappa/Gallup Poll of the Public's Attitudes Toward the Public Schools," 51–52.

46. Rose and Gallup, "The 38th Annual Phi Delta Kappa/Gallup Poll of the Public's Attitudes Toward the Public Schools," 43.

5

Lessons from Denver— The Pay for Performance Pilot and ProComp

If other districts simply adopt ProComp, as some will probably do, they are doomed to failure. The story of Denver's success is about the process of organizational change, not what this process eventually produced. It's about how ideas were developed and tested, how the pilot was supported, how labor-management collaboration facilitated progress, how teachers developed means to assess their own progress, how the pilot was vetted by an outside agency, how its lessons were communicated through the district and many other details. This story needs to be understood . . . because policy makers across the country are diving into various performance pay schemes, sometimes citing Denver's lessons, with little idea of what those lessons are.[1]

In March 2004, teachers in Denver approved a historic revision to the teachers' contract in which compensation is linked, in part, to student success in the classroom. In November 2005, the voters of Denver agreed to fund the proposed contract in the amount of $25 million, including an escalator clause that would increase taxes according to inflation. This unusual contract marked a new era in Denver, in which teachers can earn more than before but in which they will face an increased level of accountability. For the rest of the country, Denver could be the leading edge of a new kind of agreement between teachers and the communities they serve, an agreement including greater pay and increased accountability. In fact, with many states and communities already engaged in or seriously discussing performance pay arrangements, Denver may be simply be the first in a series of contractual dominoes ready to fall.

But wait. How much are the states and communities experimenting with or considering performance pay emulating Denver? To what extent are they attempting to learn from its experience? The answer to these questions appears to be: not much. While leaders interested in performance pay cite

Denver as a prime example, few of the major programs appear to have learned—or even attempted to learn—the lessons the Denver experiment has to teach.

Denver began with a Pay for Performance pilot jointly run by the district and teachers association, supported by the business and philanthropic community, seriously implemented (though not without problems), and thoughtfully reviewed. One component of the pilot was technical assistance and research on the pilot conducted by an outside agency. The Community Training & Assistance Center (CTAC) was selected for that role. (I was involved in the pilot as a principal in the research effort for the first half of the project.)

Two major reports by the CTAC in 2001 and 2004[2] and a 2007 book by key actors in the project[3] describe the entire process and the resulting compensation program in great detail, and will not be repeated here. Denver's experience does offer some lessons, however, and this chapter briefly describes the development of the Pay for Performance Pilot, and the Professional Compensation system that grew from it, to highlight some of these lessons.

The pilot caused significant improvements in the way the district does business—improvements demonstrated both in aggregate student achievement and in the opinions of participants—and led to a new plan for teacher compensation, approved in 2005. This system is not primarily a test-based pay for performance plan, but rather a comprehensive amalgam of successful teaching and service to the school community—a much broader assessment of performance that includes many of the different components of performance pay plans described in earlier chapters.

Denver's new Professional Compensation system, known as ProComp, addresses problems identified through the pilot as well as longstanding issues and concerns felt in Denver and many other communities regarding teacher and district accountability. In fact, Denver's experience demonstrates why, even with thoughtful leadership and broad support, a strict performance pay system—where performance is defined as student achievement and measured by standardized test scores—is an inappropriate model for education.

Denver's pilot was a success not because it proved the efficacy of Pay for Performance in education but because of how it was managed, what was learned, and the highly significant vote of teachers to abandon the common "steps and lanes" approach to compensation for a new four-point strategy. Moreover, the pilot demonstrates how attempts to gauge student achievement with precision, or to tie teacher performance to student achievement, can create reverse incentives and negative consequences for all parties. Thus, Denver's experience provides powerful information both as to what is useful and to what is not, thereby opening up new possibilities as it closes the door on others.

THE PAY FOR PERFORMANCE PILOT

The core concept of the Denver pilot was to pay teachers directly for their students' results. It was a substantial effort involving many people and stretching over four years. The pilot provided small bonuses for teachers who met either one or two objectives for student achievement that they themselves set ($750 per met objective). These objectives had to be approved by their principals, who also confirmed that they had been achieved. A joint labor–management Design Team developed and implemented the pilot and provided leadership from its inception.

The plan was initiated by the Board of Education and administration in the mid-1990s, and proposed by an outgoing superintendent and board member in 1999. Board president Laura Lefkowitz described the proposal in an Op-Ed column in the *Denver Post* as "an idea whose time has come." Teachers would "no longer receive automatic pay raises each year. Instead, all raises would be earned."[4]

Lefkowitz also indicated that a "cornerstone" of the proposal was to raise salaries for starting teachers by 20 percent, to $30,000. The plan was to take student differences into account and support teachers, and she acknowledged that some students' limited English proficiency and inadequate home support were factors. But, she observed, "We also know that all children can progress over the course of a school year with the instructional guidance of a high-quality teaching professional." In responding to criticism that the entire plan was based on a "hunch" that linking compensation to achievement would improve outcomes, she responded:

> What's wrong with this picture? Should the widget salesman whose job is to sell widgets be rewarded for how many sales calls he makes or for how many widgets he sells? In the real world, students don't earn an "A" for effort alone. In most workplaces, this type of pay structure is hardly considered radical; it is the norm.[5]

The teachers' association was not initially in favor of the plan, though some teacher leaders had already been discussing potential changes in the salary structure. Andrea Giunta, president of the Denver Classroom Teachers Association, described the reasons teachers were opposed. "Perhaps the most important is that teachers have no control over what happens to students outside of the classroom." This was important because, according to the National Commission on Teaching and America's Future, "the home environment is responsible for 49 percent of the factors influencing student achievement."[6]

However, having endured several years of contentious bargaining and a fairly recent strike, trust between teachers and the administration was low. Union leaders did not trust administrators to treat teachers fairly; they were also not anxious to do battle again. Instead, they won three important concessions. The first was that teachers would be judged based on "teacher-set objectives" (with principal approval) such that teachers' discretion and knowledge of their students would be a significant factor in determining the results they would be expected to achieve. Second, they insisted that a study be conducted by an outside agency to determine the effectiveness of the pilot. And third, it was agreed that the idea was to be piloted first, after which any future plan would be subject to a vote.

The deal initiating a two-year pilot was finally completed over the summer of 1999, to be started immediately. By the time the Design Team was formed, the school year had already started. With little time for planning or orientation, the Design Team began by soliciting schools to join the pilot, a process that yielded just enough elementary schools able to muster the required faculty vote. While teachers' reasons for joining varied, two sentiments expressed frequently at the pilot schools from the start are captured in the following statements. First, that teachers could simply get paid for what they were already doing:

> "As far as PFP goes, it's easy money. I was doing it, and I'm still doing it."
> "I like PFP. It's a nice little benefit for doing what we are already doing."
> "We were setting goals even before PFP, so why not get the $1,500?"
> "We're here early and stay late. We're that kind of school. We thought, 'We're doing this anyway; we may as well get paid for it.'"

Second, teachers felt these changes would be imposed on them anyway, so they would be better off being involved from the start.

> "We wanted a part of this [PFP]. We wanted a voice, or they'll say that we sabotaged it [when it doesn't work]. Now we have two members on the design team who are leaders and who help teachers. We want to be a part of reform instead of just being the object of it."
> "Oregon has imposed PFP through legislation. If the [Colorado] legislature imposes it, we'll be glad that we tried it out on our own and that we have data."
> "It seems that PFP will be instituted district-wide, whether or not we participate, but participating may give us some advantage in shaping it."

Thirteen schools signed up for initial participation in the pilot, which required an 85 percent vote of the faculty in favor of participating (later lowered to 67 percent). These included elementary schools from across the district, among both the wealthiest and poorest sections of the city. Middle and high schools were added in subsequent years, but the participation of elementary schools remained stable (only one change). Following a positive vote, all teachers in the pilot schools were required to participate, from art and gym teachers to nurses and counselors.

The pilot started with three schoolwide approaches: the Iowa Test of Basic Skills, criterion-referenced or teacher developed assessments, and teacher skill and knowledge. The basic work of the pilot for teachers was to set objectives and try to meet them. While teachers participated in training as the pilot proceeded, the pilot did not substantially change day-to-day activity at the school or within the classroom, according to teachers and administrators. Parents tended to be unaware of it for the first few years. Principals knew of the pilot, especially if they had been in office when it started at their schools, and many came to see the use of objectives as an important management tool over time. During the first two years, however, principals reported that their supervisors were engaged in other priorities and rarely asked about the success of the pilot or brought it up during supervisory or other meetings.[7]

The Design Team visited schools and trained teachers regularly, and also attempted to negotiate the administrative bureaucracy. Successful implementation of the pilot required additional effort from departments such as Assessment and Testing, Curriculum and Instruction, Human Resources, and Technology Services. Because it created more work for these departments, some resisted or ignored requests for assistance. Weak and changing district leadership contributed to the confusion and lack of response. Some administrators were heard to say, regarding the Design Team's requests for help, "Just because they don't have anything else to do doesn't mean I don't."[8]

By its nature, the pilot faced a series of challenging district-wide issues. Linking student performance to teacher performance required linking teachers to students in various databases—something that had never been done before. Systems for reporting student results according to a teacher identification number simply did not exist. There was insufficient baseline data from which to measure growth. Means to assess nonacademic teachers were also lacking. For example, one Design Team member met with nurses and related professionals for more than a year to determine appropriate standards and assessments for nursing.

Unlike a controlled experiment, the pilot went through many modifications and addressed many "real world" implementation issues, which are captured in CTAC's 2001 and 2004 reports. In fact, extraneous factors and mandates—many imposed by these same governmental bodies that champion charter schools for their freedom from such mandates—pummel schools every day, rendering the results of controlled experiments at the system level largely irrelevant, and explaining why so few laboratory-tested ideas are successfully implemented on a larger scale. Denver's experiment took place in the real world of an urban school district—a large teaching force and bureaucracy, a highly diverse student population, a high-stakes testing environment, and the range of problems and concerns that confront all urban school districts.

Among the extraneous factors, Denver experienced a tumultuous turnover of superintendents in the early stages (five in two years). Also, partway through the pilot the state began to identify schools as low performing based on the newly developed Colorado Student Assessment Program (CSAP)—which used set proficiency scores rather than the indications of student growth provided by the ITBS. This confused the public and many teachers, since teachers whose students showed growth could receive PFP bonuses even if the state had labeled their school as low performing.

The district sometimes also created its own confusion through hastily developed initiatives and conflicting priorities. An administrative performance pay plan angered principals and sapped support for the pilot when most central administrators received bonuses while less than half of the principals did. That initiative was soon abandoned. At another point, a district-wide literacy initiative was launched, requiring a different approach to goal-setting and undermining objectives set for the pilot.

LESSONS LEARNED: PREMISE AND PRACTICALITY

Test-based pay for performance plans are built on two conceptual pillars: (1) that student achievement can be assessed with sufficient rigor, breadth, validity, and reliability that it can be used to make decisions about teacher pay, and (2) that teachers can be motivated to achieve better results for their students through pay incentives. Denver's pilot identified several flaws in this simplistic approach, and provided lessons from which it could draw in designing a new plan. These lessons informed the eventual development of ProComp, and the new plan is substantially different from the pilot as a result. Some of the lessons are presented below. Although ProComp is now in operation (and although its leaders doubtless have identified problems), it is still early to draw conclusions. Lessons can be drawn from the pilot, however, and include the following:

Learning and Assessment

The pilot began by dividing schools into three approaches, with the idea that the success of the different approaches would be compared. All teachers were required to participate in the approach chosen, including art, gym, and music teachers, special education teachers, nurses and counselors, and other specialists. The approaches were:

1. *Norm-Referenced Tests:* Approach One schools were to use the Iowa Test of Basic Skills (ITBS) as their measurement. (This was in the years before most states had developed their own statewide tests, and the ITBS was already given citywide each year from third through eighth grade.) For the most part, the schools that chose this approach were inner-city schools.
2. *Criterion-Referenced Tests:* In Approach Two, also frequently described as teacher-developed tests, teachers sometimes used prepared tests like Six-Trait Writing or DRA (Developmental Reading Assessment), but often used tests of their own devising, either by choice or necessity. Whatever measures were used, the Design Team insisted that they had to be *growth* measures—assessments that measure the amount a student has learned from one grade to the next rather than whether the student has reached a fixed standard.
3. *Teacher Skills and Knowledge:* Approach Three schools chose to have teachers set objectives related to increasing their own skills, but these teachers were also supposed to demonstrate the impact of their increase in skill through some measure of student achievement. The schools that chose this approach frequently had a professional development program they were already engaged in and a measurement for it. For example, one school was involved in a business-sponsored improvement program, and several were focusing on writing and used Six-Trait Writing for assessment along with a separate professional development program. In these instances, the professional development was already in place. Schools that chose this approach tended to be in the more affluent areas.

It became apparent almost immediately that this division would not work for the reasons described below. The pilot rapidly migrated to a mixture of the three approaches, depending on the teachers involved. In the second year, the union and district agreed to abandon the attempt to have whole schools use a single approach.

Including All Teachers

One of the most persistent problems plaguing the pilot was how to measure results for the many different kinds of teachers. The starting point was individual objectives. Approach One schools focused on the ITBS, but neither this test nor other obvious measures were appropriate for many teachers; these included kindergarten through second grade teachers; gym, art, and music teachers; and counselors, nurses, librarians, special education teachers, and academic support specialists.

In some schools, gym, music, and art teachers incorporated elements of reading or math into their objectives. In others, individual teachers created objectives based on the subjects they taught. Neither of these was satisfactory, since it would be hard to believe (and harder to show) that even the most conscientious integration of reading into physical education classes would be likely to show up on a child's reading scores on the ITBS. Teachers tried, but objectives based on standardized tests were inappropriate for nearly two thirds of the teachers at any given schools.

Nor were there consistent district-wide measures of success in art, music, or physical education even in the schools not focused on the ITBS. Special education teachers, as another example, set objectives according to their populations and often achieved them. But these could not be measured objectively, weren't comparable from one class to the next, and had nothing to do with any standard measure. Some schools and teachers used criterion-referenced tests or teacher-developed tests, a flexibility that provided opportunities for many more teachers to create testable objectives.

The schools that emphasized teacher skills and knowledge were also required to demonstrate student achievement. These schools had generally adopted some schoolwide training that they then incorporated into their objectives; they were "already doing it," so why not get paid for it? The schools that were working on writing were able to use pre- and posttests to show both that teachers received training and that the training resulted in particular skills the children could demonstrate.

Assessing a Teacher's Contribution to Learning

Gauging an individual teacher's contribution to the achievement of a student or group of students requires that we know how much that achievement has changed during the time the students have studied with that teacher—student *growth* or *gain*. The standards approach to testing promoted nationally and in most states is not based on student growth (though that is changing). Instead, absolute standards are established, and cut-off scores are set on state tests and labeled with words such as "advanced," "proficient," and "needs improvement." The further a student is from these goals, the more he or she must improve.

The Design Team adopted the stance early on (prior to school rankings based on the state test) that growth rather than absolute achievement would be the benchmark for showing student success. In a district that ranges from inner-city to highly suburban, this decision was essential to successful implementation, since it was the only way to assess how much a teacher might have contributed to a student's growth, and since no other method would have been fair to the teachers in diverse schools. When the state began rating schools based on CSAP partway through the pilot, many teachers and parents were confused. The emphasis on student growth taken by the Design Team seemed more fair to participants, as indeed it was. The norm-reference ITBS allowed for a measure of growth (though norming has its own issues). The Iowa test was administered once a year, so growth was measured from one spring to the next. In most other instances, however, growth was measured within a given year (pre- and posttests of various types).

In the first two years of the pilot, teachers recorded using 116 different assessments to reach their objectives.[9] In the last year of the pilot, 422 different assessments were used, including "166 identifiable assessments" and another 256 teachers who listed "teacher-made test," "criterion-referenced test" or "pre/post" as their measurements."[10]

Testing for Learning or Testing for Comparing

This experience demonstrates a conflict between two competing purposes for assessment. Accountability is about comparing results, either across teachers or against a set standard, or both. Focusing on a single test that every student would take is a method designed with the goal of accountability in mind: the results can theoretically be compared from one teacher to the next. But such an approach could not be implemented in Denver even at the schools that selected it for a range of reasons. Conversely, more complex assessments, such as those involving rubrics or designed for specific students or topics, may measure learning in specific situations but cannot be used for broad comparisons (see chapter 9).

The pilot continued to use the Iowa test for broad comparison purposes, but the plethora of different assessments described above shows how many teachers needed other ways to assess the progress of their students. Whether they used well-known assessments such as Developmental Reading Assessment (DRA) and Six-Trait Writing or designed their own, teachers chose assessments that were applicable to their own classrooms. These assessments were also formative, in many cases, providing quick feedback and helping the learning process. It was not possible for many teachers to use the Iowa test (or the state's CSAP) to measure the progress of their students. In fact, only 35 percent of Denver's teachers are covered by the state's tests.[11] The other teachers used the more than four hundred measures already described, addressing the issue of student progress but making direct cross-district comparisons of teachers impossible.

In following this path, Denver's pilot chose to emphasize student learning over comparative accountability. It allowed individual objectives and many different measurements, and relied on teacher and principal professionalism to assure that the results were meaningful. This path was motivational and effective, but did not produce a compensation system of sufficient clarity and objective fairness to support anything beyond the small bonuses in the pilot. Recognizing this, members of the Joint Task Force developing the new plan did not propose this system as its basis. Instead, it departed sharply from this single basis for compensation, and added several additional professional factors to the mix.

In addition, the pilot was based on having teachers set two objectives, which did not begin to cover the range of expectations teachers and students must meet. All of the parties understood this. At the same time, the pilot only added small bonuses to teacher pay for meeting the two objectives; it constituted only a very small part of their compensation. In this way, the pilot provided a limited test of some aspects of performance pay, from which the parties could learn in designing the final plan.

High Stakes

One of the most critical results of tying compensation to student achievement is to raise the stakes on measures of achievement. The impulse to narrow the curriculum is heightened, for example, as it has been in urban schools across the country. In addition, all of the issues of accuracy and comparability across students, classrooms, and teachers—including the validity and reliability of the results—are exacerbated. Any test that will significantly influence teacher pay will have to meet a high standard of accuracy.

Teachers agreed that the bonuses paid in the pilot did not have the effect of pushing them too far towards activities that would be rewarded but which might have overly narrowed the curriculum or otherwise diminished the educational experience. This remains a concern in the new plan, however, and in others proposed around the country. To the extent that standards and tests have narrowed the curriculum or produced any other negative (or positive) results, those results will likely be heightened if significant financial incentives for teachers are tied to them. This is the point of incentives, of course, but the incentives do not distinguish between intended and unintended consequences, as the elimination of recess and increase in cheating at many schools have demonstrated.

Teacher-Set Objectives

The teachers' right to set their own objectives was a central component of the union's initial bargaining posture, for several reasons. First, teachers feared that the board would impose both a form of measurement and a specific goal such as five percentile points on the Iowa Test of Basic Skills. They believed that such an approach would be inappropriate for children and unfair to teachers—specifically, that a single goal would work to the disadvantage of the struggling children in urban neighborhoods and the teachers who taught them. Given the absolute standards set by many states and the rush to make tests more rigorous, this fear seems justified. Perhaps more important, some teachers feared that board members were looking for a means not only to reward some teachers but to punish others. If they were correct, a single testing system could remove job protections from teachers based on unrealistic expectations—not only might the measures be inappropriate or unfair, they could also lead to teacher dismissal.

Teacher-set objectives were therefore a cornerstone of Denver's PFP pilot, becoming both a major strength and a significant cause of confusion. In the beginning, teachers set objectives with little guidance. Most of the requirements for objectives that the Design Team developed in the first few years were aimed at measurement: what would be measured and how. For example, teachers had to include some form of pre- and posttests, they weren't responsible for students who had not been in their classes for a set length of time, one of the two objectives had to be classwide, and so forth. These arose partly in response to objectives that—often unwittingly—were unreasonably narrow or vague. For instance, when the objective was that "50% of the bottom quartile of my class will gain three points," this would represent, in a class of twenty, two and a half children.

Over time, the emphasis moved increasingly towards the use of *learning objectives* with a measurement component, rather than objectives based on measurement. This distinction was critical. Early objectives were often based on test scores or percentile gains on standardized tests, largely content free. The Design Team stressed to teachers that their objectives had to be measurable, so that teachers could demonstrate that their students had made specific achievement gains.

Later objectives were designed to be content-driven—so that teachers were focusing on teaching specific content or skills rather than simply raising scores—and appeared to be more successful in increasing learning. This approach was championed by CTAC, which devised a rubric for assessing objective quality in the project's second year, so that it could examine the relationship between the quality of the objective and student learning. Over time, the Design Team developed comprehensive training for teachers in how to set learning objectives.

CTAC's midpoint report identified a correlation between teachers with the highest-quality learning objectives and student success in those teachers' classrooms. Though the main tests CTAC used to measure results were the ITBS and CSAP—not, in most cases, the specific target of the objectives—there was a modest correlation between teachers who knew how to formulate high-quality objectives and overall classroom success. Since objectives addressed many topics and broad-scale measurement could only be conducted with a nonspecific test, the link between the two, while logical and suggestive, is not conclusive.

In its final report, CTAC found that higher-quality objectives "are associated with higher average NCE scores on independent measures; and . . . meeting two objectives is associated with higher average student achievement than meeting only one objective."[12] Still, this does not tell us whether better teachers write better objectives, whether better objectives lead to better teaching, or something else.

Teacher-set objectives relied on the professionalism of teachers—since they had a financial incentive to set *low* objectives—as well as the principals, who reviewed and approved teacher objectives. The evidence suggests that professionalism was maintained in Denver. Teachers did not generally set low objectives (possibly because the bonuses were small) and at least some principals used reviewing objectives as an opportunity to coach, guide, and support teachers. In addition, CTAC observed significant improvement in objective setting and the ways in which teachers and principals used data in the planning of instruction—even among new teachers and those not directly involved in the pilot—as the district learned to support these efforts.[13]

The advantage of strong learning objectives for teachers is that they clearly identify goals and tap into teachers' sense of their own professionalism. In Denver and elsewhere, such objectives have proven motivational and effective, and teacher professionalism won out in Denver. Teachers appreciated the autonomy provided by the process. As the Design Team got better at describing quality and providing training around objectives, teachers got better at writing them. At the same time, most teachers met their objectives. Over the four-year span, 89 to 93 percent of teachers met at least one objective and received compensation.[14]

Still, any system where substantial salary adjustments are made on individually devised measures of growth will be subject to abuse or suspicion, and may not be trusted. The easier the objective, the more likely the pay increase. How is it possible to manage such an undertaking without having teachers "rush to the bottom" with easy-to-achieve objectives? So while it appears that teacher-set learning objectives, with support, are beneficial to student learning, providing a bonus could encourage teachers to keep these objectives low, as the bonus could be a *disincentive* to higher standards. Teacher-set objectives remain a feature of ProComp because of the advantages they clearly provide, but those involved recognize that this potential problem, along with others, still exists.[15]

Motivation and Incentive

The assumptions on which performance pay are based have already been discussed: that teachers aren't trying hard because they have no financial incentive to do so; that they know what to do to increase student achievement but aren't doing it simply for lack of that incentive; and that they have the skill, resources, and support to be more successful if only they would try harder.

But surveys and interviews of Denver teachers throughout the pilot showed that even the strongest supporters of the pilot did not believe it caused them to work harder. Teachers dismissed this idea for two reasons.

First, they were already working as hard as they could, they said, putting long hours into preparation. Second, even if this had not been the case, the small amount of money involved would not have been sufficient incentive to work harder. "Money is not an incentive, it's an insult," said one teacher in an interview. "Teaching is what I chose to do, and I do it well."

Despite this reaction to the financial incentive, teachers in the pilot came to believe that both they and their schools were more focused on student learning, that this focus had led to better results for students whether these results showed up on standardized tests or not, and that the pilot's emphasis on content-based learning objectives, data, and individual growth had improved their success.[16]

Respondents at all levels agreed that the emphasis on learning and achievement and the increasingly sophisticated support offered by the Design Team spurred schools to focus on issues of achievement, provided a tool that principals could use to discuss achievement with teachers, and created a more focused schoolwide effort on reading, writing, and math. The improved results, according to teachers, had less to do with rewarding higher performance and more to do with providing focus, support, data, and specific techniques for applying what is known about learning at the school and classroom level.

The district's increased support for the schools—particularly on setting learning objectives in the context of school goals—yielded a more focused effort at many of the pilot schools. In fact, after CTAC developed its rubric for objective setting and the Design Team developed a training program, the district adopted the process for all schools (without bonuses). Thus, improvement came about primarily for three reasons: individual teachers learned new skills, schools focused on teaching and learning, and the pilot led to substantial improvement in the district's curriculum alignment, school support, and assessment.

Even though PFP was the vehicle for these changes, the steps that appear to have brought about improvement did not require incentive pay. CTAC concluded that the pilot was:

> . . . a catalyst for changing the district so that it could become more focused on student achievement in a more coordinated and consolidated way. . . . The changes required to identify, strengthen and reward individual student growth and individual teacher contributions under pay for performance have the added effect of stimulating other parts of the school system to improve the quality of support and service.[17]

Nowhere does it conclude that teacher motivation based on increased compensation was a vital factor; instead, it was the new skills gained, along with the organizational focus and support, that brought about improvement.

FROM PFP TO PROCOMP

Developing a New Plan

Halfway through the pilot, a Joint Task Force was created to consider what was being learned and to develop a new plan for teacher compensation. It was, like the Design Team, a joint labor–management team. It had a representative from the Design Team, but functioned independently. Even at the midpoint, it seemed likely that the proposed plan would differ substantially from the plan being tested in the pilot, and the JTF spent a year studying lessons from its own pilot and other compensation systems and developing a "theory of learning" on which to base its actions.[18] In the end, the draft plan that the task force put forth in April 2003 derived lessons from the Pay for Performance pilot but was far from a pay for performance plan. The approved plan is built on the four components described below: teacher skill and knowledge, professional evaluation, market incentives, and student growth (teacher-set objectives).

The task force was clear on the relationship between the new Professional Compensation System (ProComp) and the pilot. "ProComp is not merit pay," proclaimed a section of the ProComp brochure. "Denver's new teacher compensation system should not be confused with 'merit pay' and 'performance pay'—which have been used to describe earlier experiments in teacher compensation plans that were not successful." Instead, they described the new plan as "results-based pay," using multiple criteria to assess teachers' performance. Teachers would receive increases only if they demonstrated results, but these results could be demonstrated in several different areas.[19]

Building a Constituency

In April 2003, the Joint Task Force issued its initial plan. In announcing the plan, the district emphasized the role of the Joint Task Force and described "four distinctions from the current salary system":

1. Teachers who meet and exceed rigorous expectations in a fair system will have uncapped annual and career earnings.
2. The district will pay annual and sustained bonuses for demonstrated student growth. It will eliminate guaranteed increases for years of service.
3. Teachers can receive salary increases and bonuses for demonstrated acquisition of additional knowledge and skills related to student growth and their instructional discipline.
4. The district will offer incentives to teachers of demonstrated accomplishment who choose to work in schools and teaching assignments with high teacher turnover and a poor track record of student growth.[20]

As the pilot wound down, the internal and external players who had been instrumental in creating and running the pilot turned to implementing Pro-Comp. With no pilot to run, the effort was focused first on convincing teachers that a system with accountability but without the traditional steps and lanes would work to their benefit (and their students), and later on convincing the voters that such a plan would be worth higher taxes. These campaigns, described in detail by Gonring, Teske and Jupp, required substantial energy and effort, but were crucial in the eventual acceptance of the plan.

The draft plan the task force put forth in April 2003 derived lessons from the Pay for Performance pilot but was far different. Discussion and feedback were part of the rollout process, and based on this discussion, that plan was modified to include four primary features. Teachers approved the plan in March 2004 and the public voted to commit $25 million to fund it in November 2005. It contains the following components.

- Knowledge and Skills: Teachers can earn Professional Development Units (PDUs) in various ways, including advanced degrees, to achieve additional compensation. However, these skills must be closely linked to the classroom. Teachers must demonstrate the application of their skills in the classroom and consider their impact on children.
- Professional Evaluation: A supervisory evaluation is conducted using standards for effective teaching. Teachers must present a body of evidence including student work, and must meet all standards to earn a small increment.
- Market Incentive: Teachers may be eligible to receive bonuses for serving in hard-to-staff assignments and/or hard-to-serve schools. Definitions of these categories are data-based, and are agreed to annually by the district and the union.
- Student Growth: Teachers set two student growth objectives annually, in collaboration with their principals or supervisors. Teachers who meet both will receive a 1 percent addition to their base salaries, while teachers who meet one objective will receive a 1 percent bonus.[21]

Denver benefited from the professionalism of the association's leadership, the steadfast backing of the Board of Education, the support of business, substantial financial support from the philanthropic community, the visibility of a pilot in which teachers had been actively involved, and the absence of organized opposition—a combination of highly favorable conditions. Even so, proponents recognized that much misinformation and resistance to change existed across the district and in the community, and that the support neither of teachers nor of the public was guaranteed. They worked hard to build this constituency, without which the entire effort might now be over. Even with these positive conditions, leaders did not take approval for granted. A significant lesson for districts thinking of this kind of system change (or any other) is the need to build a constituency for that change.

Denver's Professional Compensation system has much to offer other districts in terms of how to think about teacher compensation, but the process may offer the most important lesson. ProComp would not have passed —or even come close—without the years of effort leading up to the final vote. It's difficult to see how other districts, without this history, will be able to implement similar plans. The Denver story, while successful to date, reminds us of a truism in organizational change: a good idea is not enough. Without the constituency of support for the proposal that was a long time in the making—and that was constantly and consciously nourished by the Design Team, Rose Community Foundation, and other supporters—it would have been just another interesting idea that couldn't gain enough support to be tried.

IMPLEMENTATION: COMPLEX CHANGE IN A COMPLEX ORGANIZATION

Beyond the lessons about teacher motivation and the impracticality of test-based incentives, Denver's experiment also provides a series of organizational lessons, mentioned briefly below.

Implementing Systemic Change

Even without the seemingly insurmountable problems of accurately and broadly assessing student learning, or the perverse disincentive of the motivational aspects of the pilot, or the finding that better organizational alignment and greater focus rather than pay incentives led to the improvements and popularity of the pilot, Denver's pilot provides significant lessons for any district attempting to implement such a complex and far-reaching change.

One point is that pilot activities required a full-time Design Team of four people to develop and implement it, as well as considerable activity in many other central departments and the schools. Collecting data, linking student data to teacher data, and providing technological support to teachers and schools were huge issues for the district, requiring time, effort, and funding. Changing professional development activities and instituting new training also required significant institutional effort. The work involved in implementing this or any change across a district will undermine any district effort where the initiative is not a high priority and the support is not widespread.

Perhaps the most important point, stressed by Denver's leadership and CTAC, is that changes in teacher compensation are not *the* reform. At best, such changes are an attempt to align the organization in pursuit of its goals. Further, none of the parties involved think that the incentive value of the bonuses provided to teachers made much difference in improving teaching and learning in Denver. Instead, teacher-set learning objectives and the district's new focus on teaching and learning made the difference in the pilot. The district's ProComp plan attempts to bring together many lessons regarding teachers, but this ground-breaking compensation plan is still just a tool in service of the district's goals. Brad Jupp, a former union official and Design Team leader who is now a district administrator, describes ProComp as "the servant to the district's broader initiatives." He and his colleagues do not believe it can be "the engine that drives the train."[22]

"Pay for performance is miscast as a financial or programmatic reform," observes Slotnik, who has worked in Denver and other districts. The focus on teacher pay is "what catches the public's attention," but it's the focus on student learning that makes the difference.[23]

Linking Individual Student Results to Individual Teachers

Implementing pay for performance in the Denver schools produced a range of needs for data, coordination, and funding. One of the cardinal successes of the pilot was that it showed that coordinated support for the schools could produce better results. At the same time, the enormous demands for data capacity, training, coordination, focus, and funding hampered the project and suggest areas where the possible may be so complex and costly that it isn't practical. In short, training teachers in objective setting, improving the focus on core areas of learning, and creating better alignment between curriculum, instruction, assessment, and professional development are possible and desirable (though not easy). Linking all students to all of their teachers may be neither.

The difficulties of linking art, music, and gym teachers, along with special education teachers, counselors, and others to individual students have already been noted. Add to these problems the complexity of secondary schools, where an individual student may have seven or eight teachers and a teacher may have more than one hundred students. Without using teacher-set objectives, the school would need pre- and posttests capable of being used in all related courses across a district in every art, history, or government class, every English class on drama or mythology, every class on acting and theatrical history, every music class on theory or composition, and every math, science, or computer class on a particular subject. It would also need the capacity to collect and analyze these data. This might be possible, but it would not be practical or desirable.

Motivation and Constituency Building

Despite the success of the pilot, test-based PFP with the goal of broad comparability didn't work in Denver. This is not just because it is a flawed concept with regard to teacher motivation (though it is) but also because it simply couldn't be implemented effectively. Such a simplistic model doesn't reflect the complexity of teaching and learning and schools, and doesn't make sense for too many teachers and classrooms. Conversely, the opportunity for teachers to shape the learning environment and establish learning goals for their students engages teachers.

What did work in the pilot was largely incorporated into ProComp. School and district focus and clear priorities (good management) are critical. A focus on learning that can be assessed, not simply test scores, is also critical. Engaging and motivating teachers, and providing them with the skills they need to do the best job they can are all essential factors in teacher and student success. Pay is an important component of this calculation, but motivation is considerably more complex in a profession that people have chosen for reasons other than pay. Involving teachers in setting and reaching goals with their students proved to be a pivotal component of the pilot, and is now a central part of ProComp.

For any organizational change to succeed, many people need to be involved. Thus, building a constituency in support of the change is essential. The Denver story would have had a different ending if leaders inside and outside of the district had not focused great effort on this task. Finally, schools exist in a district context. District focus and support were important factors in Denver. When the district was focused on teaching and learning, and on supporting the pilot, it made a difference. When the district focused elsewhere or was unfocused, school leaders and teachers were distracted.

The Importance of Piloting

The original pay for performance plan discussed in Denver was too rigid and complex to implement. One of the modifications that came out of negotiations between the district and the union was that there would be a pilot, and that a component of that pilot would be an outside study of results. The pilot was originally scheduled for two years, but later extended to four. Even at the two-year mark, however, as the pilot got ready to take on secondary schools and the Joint Task Force was formed to develop a plan, many lessons had already become clear. The three-approach strategy had been abandoned; all parties could see that the idea of using standardized tests for all teachers could not work, and recognition of the importance of teacher-set objectives was growing.

Had this plan been attempted without a pilot, however, it would almost certainly have failed by this point. The schools that joined initially were supportive of the effort and willing to learn as they went along. The Design Team became increasingly sophisticated and skillful at training and supporting schools. The district slowly learned to change its focus in ways that supported teaching and learning. Technology and assessment tools were developed by the district in support of the pilot's activities. New methodologies for objective-setting, assessment, and supervision were developed and implemented.

None of this was in place in the early stage, and there is no shred of doubt that had the pilot not been conducted—had a new program simply been implemented without the experimentation, the study, the constituency building, and the willingness to learn and change that the pilot exemplified—the entire program would have collapsed within the first few years. Organizational change is complex, particularly in large organizations. The willingness to start slowly, learn from problems and errors, and build a change rather than simply announcing it, are critical elements of change.

Organizational Focus

At the organizational level, Denver's pilot allowed the district to build capacity around such skills as data use, objective setting, and classroom observations at the schools. It forced the district to realign around support for the schools, over an extended period of time, and to develop its own capacity to assist the development of principal and teacher leadership and professionalism across the district. The pilot also provided critical outside expertise to examine results and develop new pathways to success, at times proposing solutions that those in trenches couldn't see, and at other times identifying inconvenient but critical issues. The pilot succeeded in creating change at the district level, and that change led to the development of ProComp. Had this organizational change not taken place at the district level, however, it is doubtful that classroom results would have improved or that a new plan would now exist.

Considering Costs

One final factor that needs mentioning is cost. It is unlikely that a performance pay plan will ever save money. In fact, the plans recommended by the many business and governmental commissions already described almost universally call for increased salaries to accompany the new forms of accountability they propose. But teachers are wary of giving up job protections if there is a chance the funding for promised incentives may run out. Further, if a district were to promise incentives for people who took on certain tasks or achieved certain goals but then have to back off that promise—or to award compensation to some but not all of the people who had earned it— the entire plan would be undermined.

Denver's plan included a trust fund provision in the public vote, through which funds will be made available in subsequent years if teacher performance warrants them. This is a positive and fortunate arrangement which many districts may not be able to repeat. But districts should consider the impact of changes in the compensation system, and determine sources of future funds that may be needed. In addition, there are costs to the institutional change itself, both financial and nonfinancial. These include, according to CTAC, "the institutional costs of reordering district priorities, functioning with higher levels of inter-departmental coordination, operating with a greater sense of urgency and reallocating existing funds."[24]

The impact of these factors should not be underestimated. Organizational change is not about adopting new policies, but rather about setting a new direction and building capacity to implement that new direction over time. A district that simply attempts to adopt Denver's plan without building the constituency and capacity to make it work will not succeed in creating positive and lasting change.

THE CONTINUING SAGA

As this book goes to press, Denver teachers and the district are involved in a contract dispute over ProComp. Administrators want to increase starting salaries for teachers by $9,000, and to double the incentive for teaching in hard-to-serve inner-city schools. Teachers want to wait to make such changes until results from an ongoing study are complete in a year, and to award a 3.5 percent increase across the board in the meantime.

Though this dispute is not resolved at the time of this writing, the nature of the dispute yields some additional lessons for those who would pursue performance pay. Potential lessons from this ongoing dispute appear to reinforce upcoming discussions of teacher motivation, district goal-setting, and assessment. These lessons are presented in the final chapter.

NOTES

1. Donald B. Gratz, "Pay for Performance Teacher Compensation: An Inside View of Denver's ProComp Plan," *Teachers College Record* 22 February 2008, Book Review. Accessed at http://www.tcrecord.org, ID Number 15022.

2. Donald B. Gratz, William J. Slotnik, and Barbara J. Helms, *Pathway to Results: Pay for Performance in Denver* (Boston: Community Training & Assistance Center, 2001); William J. Slotnik et al., *Catalyst for Change: Pay for Performance in Denver, Final Report* (Community Training & Assistance Center, January 2004).

3. Phil Gonring, Paul Teske, and Brad Jupp, *Pay-for-Performance Teacher Compensation* (Cambridge, MA: Harvard University Press, 2007).

4. Laura Lefkowitz, "Pay for Performance Teachers Should Earn Their Raises," *Denver Post*, 27 June 1999, Perspective: H-01.

5. Lefkowitz, "Pay for Performance Teachers Should Earn Their Raises," H-01.

6. Andrea Giunta, "Pay for Performance Plan Ignores Kids' Outside Influences," *Denver Post*, 27 June 1999, Perspective: H-01.

7. Gratz, Slotnik, and Helms, *Pathway to Results*.

8. Gonring, Teske, and Jupp, *Pay-for-Performance Teacher Compensation*, 60.

9. Gratz, Slotnik, and Helms, *Pathway to Results*, 44.

10. Slotnik et al., *Catalyst for Change*, 119.

11. Gonring, Teske, and Jupp, *Pay-for-Performance Teacher Compensation*, 143.

12. Slotnik et al., *Catalyst for Change*, 62.

13. Slotnik et al., *Catalyst for Change*, 62, 106; William J. Slotnik, bslotnik@ctacusa.com, Discussion of Denver Pilot and PFP (Boston, 10 July 2008).

14. Slotnik et al., *Catalyst for Change*, 57.

15. Gonring, Teske, and Jupp, *Pay-for-Performance Teacher Compensation*, 114.

16. Gratz, Slotnik, and Helms, *Pathway to Results*, 106; Slotnik et al., *Catalyst for Change*, 106.

17. Slotnik et al., *Catalyst for Change*, 11.

18. Gonring, Teske, and Jupp, *Pay-for-Performance Teacher Compensation*, 70.

19. Denver Public Schools, *ProComp: A Collaborative Project of Denver Public Schools and Denver Classroom Teachers Association* (Denver, CO: Denver Public Schools, 2005), 3.

20. Denver Public Schools, "Denver Considers Bold New Teacher Compensation Plan," *Press Release* (Denver, CO), 18 April 2003, 2.

21. Joint Task Force on Teacher Compensation, "At a Glance . . . Professional Compensation for Teachers, Tentative Agreement," 2004. Accessed 28 March 2004 at www.denverteachercompensation.org; Gonring, Teske, and Jupp, *Pay-for-Performance Teacher Compensation*, 14–20.

22. Phil Gonring, Paul Teske, and Brad Jupp, *Pay-for-Performance Teacher Compensation* (Cambridge, MA: Harvard University Press, 2007), 114.

23. William J. Slotnik, "Mission Possible: Tying Earning to Learning," *Education Week* 25, no. 5 (28 September 2005): 32–33, 40.

24. Slotnik et al., *Catalyst for Change*, 140.

II

THE ASSUMPTIONS OF PERFORMANCE PAY

Introduction to Part II

Do these assumptions seem plausible? Think about it. Can you imagine a person saying, "I am motivated a lot by money, so I think teaching first graders is the career for me." We have found that a thoughtful consideration of the assumptions that underpin interventions is often sufficient to reproduce the insights gained from piles of empirical research. That doesn't mean you shouldn't try to access such research or gather your own data, but it does mean that . . . sometimes careful, structured analysis can get you almost to the same place.[1]

Having laid out a basic case for performance pay, discussed its history, considered the views of business, labor, and parents, and looked at Denver's nationally recognized pilot, it is time to return to the fundamental assumptions on which most state and district plans are based. The case for test-based performance pay in education rests on assumptions about the economy, the historic effectiveness of the schools, human motivation, and the purposes of education. Some proponents also seem to assume that announcing a policy or program is the same as implementing it—that institutional change is easy.

Each of these assumptions has been introduced previously, and most are deeply flawed. They are stated briefly below, and addressed in detail in subsequent chapters. While teachers, business leaders, and parents in some districts have begun to discuss differentiated compensation plans for teachers that they might agree on, these fundamental assumptions still drive most of the public policy discussion—and still present thorny issues to consider.

ASSUMPTION #1: THE CRISIS IN EDUCATION

Public education is in crisis. This crisis is demonstrated by the achievement gaps on tests of academic proficiency between different groups of American children, and between American children and those from other countries. Demonstrating our inability to compete in the world economy, these gaps will lead to dramatic negative economic consequences for the country, for the American lifestyle, and for American children left unprepared to compete in the twenty-first century. This major societal problem is caused substantially, if not entirely, by poor-quality teaching: we are unable to recruit qualified teachers (especially in math and science), we are unable to retain good young teachers, and current teachers are not working hard enough for lack of a financial incentive to do so. High-stakes tests, though they don't measure everything, are sufficiently accurate to indicate this need and to measure the proficiency of students, schools, and teachers.

ASSUMPTION #2: THE ECONOMY AND EDUCATION

The education crisis is closely linked to a looming economic crisis in four primary ways. First, the education level of workers is directly linked to their productivity, which in turn is linked to the country's economic success. Higher levels of education lead to higher productivity and better economic results for all. Second, individual productivity leads to economic success for productive individuals. Third, because of these links, schools have always been a major route out of poverty for low-income Americans, and remain a major driver of individual success today. Fourth, if states apply high standards and hold schools, teachers, and students accountable, they can substantially reduce the achievement gap and largely overcome the pernicious effects of poverty on families. If the policy of high standards and accountability is implemented seriously, it will raise future generations out of poverty even as it stimulates the economy, improving the lot of all Americans.

At the same time, an economic crisis looms because the American economy has changed and its schools have not kept pace. Manufacturing jobs have been lost to knowledge-based jobs, particularly in science and technology. Competition from countries around the world is challenging America's dominance in these and related fields. Global competition and the widening income gap between rich and poor have led to serious concerns about the future economic health of the country. These growing economic threats give urgency to the need for schools to educate students to higher levels of achievement, both for their own success and for the country's. Standards in the academic subject areas must be maintained or raised, particularly in math and science, as international tests show American students falling behind their peers. This is the primary purpose of the public schools.

ASSUMPTION #3: MOTIVATING WORKERS

The problem of motivation has two components: motivating current teachers to do a better job, and attracting new teachers from among the top tier of college graduates. Retaining the best teachers from both of these groups is a related issue. Much of the teacher quality problem, in this assumption, is caused by a compensation system that fails to attract good new teachers, fails to differentiate between good teaching and bad, and fails to hold teachers accountable for the results they produce. Such a system does not motivate teachers to give their best. Because they get paid the same regardless of student results, teachers simply don't try as hard as they could—even though they have the knowledge, skill, resources, and time to do so.

Districts can resolve this problem by designing a differentiated compensation system that attracts, retains, and motivates teachers to do a better job, as often happens in business. Higher financial incentives for student achievement (test scores) and the ability to earn more over time based on this performance will attract better-quality college graduates and motivate good teachers to excel.

ASSUMPTION #4: IMPLEMENTING INSTITUTIONAL CHANGE

An individually based system in which teachers earn a significant portion of their income based on the success of their students can be developed economically and implemented fairly, again as has been done in business. The struggle with regard to performance pay has more to do with confronting unions and entrenched interests than with issues of implementation. Unintended consequences, while they may occur, will be minimal.

ASSUMPTION #5: DEFINING AND ASSESSING PERFORMANCE

It is possible to measure student performance and define teacher effectiveness with sufficient accuracy, validity, and reliability to make high-stakes decisions based on the results, as is already done for students in most states. No Child Left Behind has increased the stakes tied to tests, but linking teacher compensation to desired results will enhance the performance of both teachers and students. Performance must be defined if it is to be measured, and the premise of performance pay is that performance can be defined and assessed with sufficient accuracy to justify life-changing decisions.

Unfortunately, most of these assumptions are misleading or incorrect. Even so, while proponents of alternative forms of differentiated compensation such as group rewards, career ladders, and "market-based" approaches are working from different assumptions and looking at different plans, the assumptions above provide the logic for the policies being developed and discussed by the leaders of most states and the federal government, by many business supporters, and by that wing of the education establishment that supports the current standards and testing approach to accountability.

The remaining chapters address each of these assumptions, as well as alternative forms of differentiated pay for teachers. Building on issues introduced previously, chapter 6 reviews the nature and extent of the perceived crisis in education, as well as the economic basis for that perception. What are the links between school results, economic productivity, and the health of the economy? Will higher standards lead to better jobs and higher productivity, improving the results for future workers and the economy? Are students in other countries outperforming American students? If they are, what does it mean? Continuing with the economic arguments, chapter 7 explores the relationship between poverty and school success, including the much-discussed academic achievement gap.

Since motivation is a key assumption of performance pay, chapter 8 reviews what is known about motivation in the world of work, including the extent and nature of performance pay in business and the extent to which principles of business apply in an educational setting. What motivates teachers, and how can teacher effectiveness and recruitment be improved?

Since performance-based programs must define performance in service of organizational goals, chapters 9 and 10 look at the goals of our educational system and how those goals can best be measured. If the purpose of changing the pay structure is to motivate behavior and enhance results, what behavior and what results are we seeking as citizens and as parents? What skills will be needed in the twenty-first century, and what can we do to prepare students with them? How can these skills be assessed? What do we mean by student and teacher performance?

Chapter 11 summarizes the critical points and lessons learned, and briefly considers the various alternative performance pay plans—proposals such as group rewards, career ladders, market-driven compensation, and broadening teaching duties to include mentoring, curriculum leadership, and other important educational tasks. All of these plans are in place in some form in one or more places, and each may present attractive alternatives to a school district or a state considering changes. The chapter concludes with principles for districts to consider in pursuing possible approaches to teacher compensation—how to get from here to there.

NOTES

1. Jeffrey Pfeffer and Robert Sutton, *Hard Facts, Dangerous Half Truths and Total Nonsense: Profiting from Evidence-Based Management* (Harvard Business School Press, 2006), 23–24.

6

Schools and the Economy: A State of Crisis?

When Japan was in the ascendancy, we experienced much hand-wringing about American schools, and much government and public pressure for American educators to learn from the Japanese. But a decade later, when Japan's economy had collapsed, the reverse was not true. One might have supposed that the country's remarkable new economic success would have led to a revision of the view that the public schools were in crisis. If schools were responsible for the devastating economy of the late 1980s, they might also be assumed to bear some credit for the boom of the 1990s. But that was not the case.

THE ROOTS OF CRISIS

Despite a rose-tinted view of simpler times, Americans have rarely experienced an era when the public schools were not in crisis and the subject of a struggle. From the founding of the country's first public schools in Boston in the early 1800s, citizens and leaders have fought over which children should attend which schools, where minority students should be sent, the quality of teachers, school conditions, the curriculum, assessment, accountability, patronage, local versus central control, and the effectiveness of both schools and teachers. One or more parties have regularly proclaimed a crisis in the schools and/or a crisis in society to be solved through the schools, and used that crisis to justify and build support for their particular proposal. Words like *crisis, scandal, deplorable, wretched,* and *disgraceful* have never been far from the public schools, but they are most often employed in describing the current school system, not the idyllic schools of the past.

Sputnik and the Math/Science Gap

There were many battles about purpose, structure, and control of the schools through the beginning of the twentieth century, but by 1920 the current structure and operation of public education had been established. Through the end of the Second World War, schools were much as we see them now, though more relaxed, focusing on a balance between life skills and academics, and including a vocational track for many students.

Starting late in 1949, perhaps driven by the growing concern about communism that fueled the witch-hunts of the McCarthy era, several major books and a series of attacks on the "anti-intellectual" character of American schools launched "a period of criticism of American education unequaled in modern times."[1] The president of Phi Beta Kappa, among others, proclaimed a crisis in the public schools because of "godlessness and moral relativism" on the one hand, and anti-intellectualism on the other.

In 1955, psychologist Rudolf Flesch[2] caused a national stir with his book *Why Johnny Can't Read*, which accused the schools of ignoring phonics in favor of a "whole word" or "look and say" method. This book was reprinted several times, and by 1981 (*Why Johnny Still Can't Read: A New Look at the Scandal of our Schools*), Flesch estimated that 85 percent of schools were still not using his phonics-based method: "I said in my book that phonics-first worked splendidly and should be used in all schools, while 'look and say' was wretchedly poor and should be abandoned at once. . . . The results of this mass miseducation have been disastrous. America is rapidly sinking into a morass of ignorance."[3] Today, some fifty years later, the country has almost universally adopted a phonics-based approach to reading, but student reading skills are often described as worse than ever.

A few years later, in 1957, Russia successfully launched its Sputnik satellite, the first man-made object to orbit earth. This dramatic feat alarmed the nation, prompting leaders to look for someone to blame, and set off a frenzy of recrimination about the presumed poor quality of math and science taught to school children. The postwar emphasis on "life adjustment" was already under attack as both anti-intellectual and undermining the quality of education. Sputnik assured its demise.

With the success of Sputnik, the Russians had "beat us into space" and launched, in addition, a national crisis with education at its core. The satellite was seen as proof that Russia had become superior to the United States in science, math, and technology. A massive effort was needed to catch up and, by implication and sometimes direct statement, to protect our democracy. In 1958, Congress passed the National Defense Education Act, declaring that "the defense of this Nation depends upon the mastery of modern techniques developed from complex scientific principles."[4]

In fact, the United States had developed a satellite before the Soviets launched Sputnik—the U.S. Explorer I satellite was launched less than four months later—but President Eisenhower was interested in using satellites to spy and had kept quiet about his plans. As we can now see, therefore, the attacks on American schools for failing to teach students enough science to produce a satellite were not well-founded. But the American satellite was not known to the public at the time (nor, apparently, was Congress informed). The schools were an easy target, and the perception of crisis was widespread.[5]

The particular significance of the Sputnik crisis was that it created the first strong perceptual link between America's public schools and those in other countries, and between education and national security. This comparative view of education is still prevalent today. By the end of the decade the quietude of the pre-1950s era had been destroyed. American children were widely described as deficient in reading, math, science, and technology.

A Failure to Learn

The 1960s and 1970s were a time of dramatic societal change, including the Vietnam war, the civil rights and women's movements, and several assassinations and riots in many cities. The differences of race, poverty, and special needs were "discovered" and addressed in education policy, and individual freedoms were championed in many ways throughout society.

The 1960s also saw the essential discovery that family background matters in student achievement, as described more completely in chapter 7. The Coleman report, released in 1966, was expected to demonstrate the primacy of teaching but instead concluded that family background overwhelmed every other factor in predicting education success.[6] Rosenthal and Jacobson's *Pygmalion in the Classroom*[7] demonstrated the impact of teacher expectations on young children, and connected low teacher expectations for black and poor children with lower performance. Jonathan Kozol's *Death at an Early Age*[8] chronicled the systematic exclusion and under-education of black children in the Boston Public Schools, a condition that was mirrored in many other school districts and revealed in many other books.

A new set of critiques also emerged regarding the basic practices of education. Long-time teacher John Holt published his first book, *How Children Fail*, in 1964. In it, Holt describes how bright children are patient, resilient, able to address repeated failures, and creative in solving problems. He observes that almost all infants demonstrate those same attributes in exploring their environments. But he also notes that many children don't behave that way in school. What happens to this "extraordinary capacity for learning and growth?" he wonders. "What happens is it's destroyed, and more than by any other one thing, by the process we misname education."[9]

One major critique of the approach to public education at that time was prepared by Charles Silberman (*Crisis in the Classroom*), who believed that children were being educated for docility. "The most important characteristic schools share in common is a preoccupation with order and control," observes Silberman. The rigid timetable, the "tyranny of the lesson plan," the "slavish adherence to routine for the sake of routine," all conspire to keep the schools from actually performing their primary educational mission.[10]

These two concerns—the dullness and one-size-fits-all nature of public education, and the growing awareness of the ways in which children of color or who had special needs were treated—led both to legislation and changes at the school level. The Elementary and Secondary Education Act (ESEA) was passed in 1965 to begin to address the needs of poor and minority children, and the first act to address the newly identified category of children with disabilities was passed in the 1970s, later to be named the Individuals with Disabilities Education Act (IDEA).

The movement towards open education and the concern with the individual student that spurred these legislative initiatives also brought about some significant changes to the schools. Elementary schools became more activity centered, with more group work and individual exploration. A variety of alternative programs and course electives were created in junior and senior high schools across the country. The more child-centered approach at the elementary level has remained the norm, at least in suburban districts where worries about state tests are not as great, but most of the alternatives in middle and high schools have long since disappeared.

Though many of these innovations haven't survived, they did address the country's understanding of significant problems at the time. These conditions identified in the 1960s remain in place today—the "tyranny of the lesson plan" and "slavish adherence to routine" still exist in many schools—but by the end of the 1970s the country's mood had changed again. A new problem was identified.

Standards and High-Stakes Tests—The Current Educational Crisis

Most observers date the beginning of the current era in public education in the United States to the 1983 publication of *A Nation at Risk*. This previously discussed report was developed by the business-sponsored National Commission on Excellence in Education and embraced by President Ronald Reagan. Its conclusions—which promoted a more business-oriented view of education and which has framed the debate for a generation—dramatically advanced its view of impending collapse. The language of crisis is worth repeating:

> Our Nation is at risk. Our once unchallenged preeminence in commerce, industry, science, and technological innovation is being overtaken by competitors throughout the world. This report is concerned with only one of the many causes and dimensions of the problem, but it is the one that undergirds American prosperity, security, and civility. We report to the American people that

while we can take justifiable pride in what our schools and colleges have historically accomplished and contributed to the United States and the well-being of its people, the educational foundations of our society are presently being eroded by a rising tide of mediocrity that threatens our very future as a Nation and a people. What was unimaginable a generation ago has begun to occur—others are matching and surpassing our educational attainments.[11]

As with many such documents, *A Nation at Risk* looks nostalgically at past eras, but it's important to note that the "generation ago" it describes so glowingly is the same generation in which the Sputnik crisis convinced the country that the Russians were surpassing Americans educationally—the one in which students were seen, at least at that time, as unable to read and deficient in math and science.

In the decades following *A Nation at Risk*, the message of crisis in the public schools has been persistent. Schools are failing to prepare students for jobs in the global economy; the United States cannot produce the workers it needs; and the country may be heading for an economic collapse. For example:

- Teaching Commission (2004): "Just over two decades ago, the National Commission on Excellence in Education published *A Nation at Risk,* drawing widespread attention to the sorry state of American schools. . . . Yet for all these efforts to fix our schools, academic achievement is still disappointing. While we have seen a welcome rise in recent national math scores, overall test scores are still at about the levels they were in 1970. Less than one-third of U.S. fourth-graders meet the 'proficient' standard on the National Assessment of Education Progress (NAEP). High school graduation rates have actually declined. . . . And international comparisons show that American teens continue to lag behind high school students in many other industrialized nations in math and science. . . . Perhaps most troubling, large discrepancies persist between poor and minority students and their peers."[12]
- Teaching Commission (2006): "A fiercely competitive global information economy, powered as never before by innovation and intellect, demands that American's young people be well educated. It is not only their individual potential that hangs in the balance; it is the nation's economic future."[13]
- Heritage Foundation (2006): "The battle over who should control America's schools is a battle for the future of our nation. For decades, the quality of our schools has declined as the demands of special interests have trumped the needs of children and the dreams of parents." (However, the tide is slowly turning, the foundation says, because of the increase in parent choice programs, charter schools, open enrollment, vouchers, tax credits, and home schooling.)[14]

- The Conference Board et al.: "At the high school level, well over one-half of new entrants are deficiently prepared in the most important skills—*Oral* and *Written Communications, Professionalism/Work Ethic,* and *Critical Thinking/Problem Solving.* College graduates are better prepared, with lower levels of deficiency on the most important skills, but too few are excelling. Only about one-quarter of four-year college graduates are perceived to be excellent in many of the most important skills, and more than one-quarter of four year college graduates are perceived to be deficiently prepared in *Written Communications.* . . . How can the United States continue to compete in a global economy if the entering workforce is made up of high school graduates who lack the skills they need, and of college graduates who are mostly 'adequate' rather than 'excellent'?"[15]
- The College Board: ". . . The nation was declared to be 'at risk' in 1982 [sic], and the fact is that it is still at risk. As this document makes clear, the risk extends well beyond the classroom. It includes challenging social and global trends that are accompanying the aging of America and the entry of the United States into a global economy. The peril is not solely, or even principally, a failure of American schools, but a failure of American vision and leadership."[16]
- The National Center on Education and the Economy (2007), in *Tough Choices or Tough Times:* "While our international counterparts are increasingly getting more education, their young people are getting a better education as well. American students place anywhere from the middle to the bottom of the pack in all three continuing comparative studies of achievement in mathematics, science and general literacy in the advanced industrial nations. . . . In this environment, it makes sense to ask how American workers can possibly maintain, to say nothing of improve, their current standard of living. . . . This is a world in which a very high level of preparation in reading, writing, speaking, mathematics, science, literature, history and the arts will be an indispensable foundation for everything that comes after for most members of the workforce. It is a world in which comfort with ideas and abstractions is the passport to a good job, in which creativity and innovation are the key to the good life, in which high levels of education—a very different kind of education than most of us have had—are going to be the only security there is."[17]

It is interesting to note that several of these reports and many others identify schools as only one of the problems, but all focus exclusively on schools as the solution.

The Reagan and Bush I eras (1980–1992) saw a large escalation in the annual deficit and national debt. America's economy plummeted while Japan's soared, prompting a new wave of concern that Japan's educational system was far superior to our own. As the George H. W. Bush years gave way to the Clinton era, however, a remarkable thing happened: the economy improved. It improved a great deal. From a budget deficit of $290 billion in the early 1990s (and the Japanese famously buying New York's Rockefeller Center in 1989) to the first national surplus in decades, the country moved into one of the longest periods of growth in the history of the world.

When Japan was in the ascendancy, we experienced much hand-wringing about American schools, and much government and public pressure for American educators to learn from the Japanese. But a decade later, when Japan's economy had collapsed, the reverse was not true. One might have supposed that the country's remarkable new economic success would have led to a revision of the view that the public schools were in crisis. If schools were responsible for the devastating economy of the late 1980s, they might also be assumed to bear some credit for the boom of the 1990s.

But that was not the case. When the economy improved dramatically in the 1990s, a different view of schools emerged. Discussion of a close connection between schools and the economy disappeared. The public schools were still in crisis, still inadequate, still failing, according to critics. But the *nature* of that crisis—the ways in which the crisis was defined—had changed. Instead of the need for "world class standards" to compete in the global economy, the crisis became the "achievement gap" between the best and the worst students, between rich and poor students, between whites and Asians on the one hand and Blacks and Hispanics on the other.

While the description of the *problem* had changed significantly, however, the proposed *solution* changed little: high standards measured by standardized tests, with the teeth of sanctions for students, teachers, and schools if the standards were not met. Whereas in the 1980s the primary crisis had to do with lack of global competitiveness, the 1990s crisis was about internal comparisons among American students. World-class standards gave way to the achievement gap, but the crisis continued.

In a normal planning process, problems are identified, the causes of these problems are explored, and solutions are devised to address the particular causes behind the problem. New problems demand new solutions. In the ongoing cycle of educational critique over the past several decades, however, the solution has remained constant while the problem has changed. This might be called "a solution in search of a problem," and may lead us to suspect that the solution exists not to solve the educational problem identified but to serve some other end—political, social, or economic.

This approach to planning has also been recognized in studies of business. In his *Primer on Decision-Making*, for example, Stanford management professor James March[18] describes it as "garbage can" decision making, in which a solution with political salience or timeliness becomes a kind of garbage can into which all kinds of problems are thrown. When this happens, solutions often end up attached to problems that they don't actually address.

THE EDUCATION–ECONOMY LINK

The connection between education and the economy is not as strong or direct as often perceived. Just as it's not possible that the 1950s were both the golden era of educational success referenced in *A Nation at Risk* and a period of abysmal failure in math, science, engineering, and reading, so it is not possible that the schools were responsible for the failing economy of the 1980s but had nothing to do with the booming economy of the 1990s. In fact, the connection between education and the economy is at best indirect; researchers find little evidence of a cause-and-effect relationship. Nonetheless, many of the claims of school crisis are predicated on economic concerns, so we will explore that topic in the balance of this chapter.

Four economic issues bear on this discussion, as shown in the assumptions above. First, productivity: the links between education, worker productivity, the worker's economic success, and the country's economic success. Second, the extent to which schools are or have ever been the route to success for poor and minority children. Third, whether American students are actually lagging behind students in other countries, and what that means. And finally, the connection between family background, factors such as poverty and parental income, and school success—the achievement gap. The first three of these were introduced previously in chapter 2 and will be discussed below. The final topic is presented in chapter 7.

Education and Economic Productivity

As we've seen, the productivity of the American worker is higher than it's ever been, even if most workers do not reap the rewards of this labor. While American workers are substantially more productive than ever before, this productivity is not significantly improving either their lives or the strength of the economy. In fact, the income gap between rich and poor is rising dramatically, as businesses appear to be skimming profits to support skyrocketing executive compensation packages (largely unrelated to performance) plus mergers, acquisitions, and other opportunities for the rich to get richer.

No one disputes that worker productivity has increased, or that the economic gap between rich and poor is widening despite this productivity. But these facts demonstrate that productivity does not directly drive either an individual's economic success or the nation's. Distribution of the fruits of that productivity—something schools are not involved with—is a key factor.

These facts also weaken the argument that a crisis of worker underperformance based on weak educational attainment is looming. Workers are performing better than ever before, as measured by productivity. Either the schools are responsible for this productivity or they are not; either way, however, lack of productivity is not a cause of current economic problems.

Mishel and Rothstein provide the following commentary with regard to the *Tough Choices* report cited above:

> This new report is a sequel to one that the first Commission issued in 1990. Then, as now, it made some reasonable recommendations about educational improvement, but its economic analysis was spectacularly wrong, as events have proved. Like the new one, the earlier report saw skill development as virtually the *only* lever for shaping the economy. The earlier report charged that inadequate skills, which resulted from flawed schools, had caused industrial productivity to 'slow to a crawl' and would, without radical school reform, lead to a condition of permanently low wages for the bottom 70% of all Americans.
>
> Yet within a few years of the 1990 report's publication, Americans' ability to master technological change generated an extraordinary leap in productivity. This acceleration, exceeding that of other advanced countries, was accomplished by the very same work force that the first Commission said imperiled our future. And it created new wealth that could have supported a steady increase in Americans' standard of living.
>
> Indeed, for a brief period, it did so . . . the late 1990s saw broad-based wage growth increasing the living standards of all families, including both those headed by high school graduates and those headed by college graduates. Even the wages of high school dropouts climbed. But then, after 2000, wage growth stopped, and living standards fell. Yet the skills of the work force continue to boost productivity. In the last four years, wages of both high school- *and college-*educated workers have been stagnant, while productivity grew by an extraordinary 11.5%.[19]

So much for the link between productivity and worker success.

The link between education and productivity is also more fiction than fact. Although the economy was in turmoil by the end of the 1980s, it is likely that this downturn was driven more by the supply side economic policies of the Reagan administration than by anything the schools had or could have done. Certainly the anguished cries of alarm from *A Nation at Risk* looked different by the 1990s, when the country experienced the longest sustained period of economic growth in the history of the world.

It should take little more to indicate the weakness of this connection than to look at the economic cycle from the problems in the 1980s, to the boom in the 1990s, to the economic downturn of the first decade of the twenty-first century. It is generally true that a well-educated workforce is important to productivity and overall economic success, and current levels of productivity indicate that American workers have sufficient education to be productive. What is not true—and what can't be true if we think about it—is that short-term economic changes have much to do with schooling.

Education takes a long time, after all, and schooling changes slowly. If schools were to change this year, next year's graduates would have one year under the new system. A complete change would take twelve years before students would fully be products of a new approach. Short-term changes in the economy, by contrast, are caused by short-term economic decisions made by business and the government, along with external events. If education were closely linked to these events, economic conditions—good or bad—could not change so quickly. Thus, though the schools produced graduates capable of the increase in productivity described by Mishel and Rothstein above, it wasn't that the schools ramped up their technological training at this particular moment, only to let it drop off a few years later. The more appropriate conclusion is that the graduates of the public and private schools in this country are ready to produce, if economic and corporate conditions allow.

Since productivity has increased dramatically from the 1990s into the 2000s without workers seeing the fruits of these labors, and since the distance between the rich and the poor has increased, and since education cannot have been responsible for the economic swings of the last three decades, it is time to stop claiming that the quality of workers that schools prepare is a major factor in the country's economy, or that they are not productive. The problems that may be contributing to the economic downturn at the end of the decade are not driven by anything the schools have done. Workers, by and large, are doing their jobs well. If they weren't, productivity would not be so high. Rather, the decisions made by businesses and the governments around the world—along with the weather, war, famine, terrorism, and other unpredictable events—drive these local economic conditions.

Eliminating Class Differences

One of the myths of America is that the schools have provided a route to success for generations of immigrants. While basic educational skills are needed for most people to succeed, and while some individuals have used academic success to advance, the evidence suggests that economic success *precedes* educational success for most people. That is, entrepreneurs and successful businesspeople seek an education for their children beyond what they themselves received.

The discussion in chapter 3 shows why this would be so. While teaching children to read, write, and compute was always a goal of the public schools, the larger goal was to maintain order and perpetuate society as it was constructed at the time. Schools and other bureaucracies developed during the nineteenth century were created primarily to protect and support an American society its leaders believed to be under attack, *not* to change it. And while our goals may have evolved since that time, the structure of schools has changed little. The policy bureaucracy that controls schools—more stringent at the beginning of the twenty-first century than ever—was not designed to create innovation or bring about change, but rather to promote order and uniformity.

Colin Greer argued in 1972 that schools have not historically been the route to economic success. "Rarely, if ever, have the public schools become channels of substantial change either within their own structure or in the structure of society at large. But we have believed that they have, and we continue to believe it."[20] Instead, he contends, while blacks faced discrimination in both schooling and jobs, immigrants and poor people from the farms found economic success before educational success. "The white poor found jobs, which did for them what the schools claimed they would do, move them upward, slowly, as a result of their own efforts."[21] The schools were not the drivers of this change.

The situation has not changed, as the Brookings Institute's *Opportunity in America: The Role of Education* (2007) confirms. "It takes about five generations for the advantages and disadvantages of family background to die out in the United States. People do go from rags to riches—or riches to rags—in a single generation, but only rarely. Americans need to pick their parents well. Circumstances of birth matter a lot, and the advantages and disadvantages of birth persist."[22]

Part of the reason is that America does not provide much opportunity for social mobility compared to other countries. "In fact," according to Brookings, "measures of inter-generational income mobility place it near the bottom of the pack." And, while the distribution of income is roughly the same in Europe as in American, "the U.S. social welfare system is far less generous than those of its European counterparts. The distribution of earned incomes in Europe does not differ greatly from that in the United States. But Europeans do a lot more to redistribute income." So we should not expect schools to be major engines of economic equality, since they have not been in the past. If more equitable distribution of income is our goal, we should look at redistributing income equitably.

The Brookings report suggests that "in both U.S. culture and history" the schools have been used "to enhance opportunity." This is a common belief, but the evidence seems to suggest otherwise. Schools *have* helped immigrant cultures assimilate—they have taught immigrant children literacy plus the culture and values of America—but schools have not contributed broadly to the economic success of the poor. That was not the original intent of schools in America (or anywhere else), and it has not been the result. Today, according to the Brookings report, "at virtually every level, education in America tends to perpetuate rather than compensate for existing inequalities."[23]

In this vein, one of the constant laments of education reformers has been that schools, as they have been organized for more than a century, are "a vast sorting and selecting machine" which creates winners and losers as it winnows the field for colleges and future success. Look at this from the perspective of our grading system. While it has always been possible for any student to get A's in school, it has never been possible for all students to get

A's. If that happens, a teacher is accused of being "too easy." It makes sense that in any given class, some students will do better than others. But as long as we use comparative judgments, we will be creating winners and losers—an achievement gap.

A stated goal of the standards movement has been to overcome this problem. Students are theoretically given as much time as they need to complete their studies and are all expected to succeed. In practice, however, it does not work this way. When all students succeed, standards are raised. Testing is used to keep students back and even to fail them, and tests of young children tend to reinforce their self-image as deserving whatever status they earn in their early school experience, long before the extra opportunities kick in.

The point, however, is that while schools have provided a route out of poverty and into success for some students, they have not done that for large numbers. Families and immigrant groups have taken several generations to succeed, and school has been only a small part of that success. If this were not the case—if schools really were the route for large numbers of people out of poverty and into economic success—American society would demonstrate more economic equality than it currently does.

While the growing income gap between poor and rich Americans is a serious problem for our country, therefore, this gap cannot be eliminated by the schools alone. The important distinction is between the individual Horatio Alger rags to riches story and the broader leveling of society. Schools have provided the route to success for some individuals, but these individuals were the exceptions rather than the rule. More often, immigrants or others in the lower classes worked hard and became successful financially before they expanded their education. Even Horatio Alger's young heroes—true to life in this respect—rise in life through hard work, a positive attitude, business cleverness, luck and "pluck," but rarely if ever through education.

Educational Attainment and Individual Success

What about the claim that much higher levels of educational attainment are needed for today's students to be successful working adults in our increasingly technological society? Although many people make this claim, there is disagreement concerning the level of technological skill needed. Some of the reports cited above and in chapter 2 predict a great need for highly skilled workers in a technological society, but others see most jobs in the low-paying service sector, as more and more engineering and technology jobs go to lower-paid professionals in foreign countries.

In addition, while educational attainment often correlates with income, the stronger correlation is between the parent's income level and the education and eventual income level of the child. In the Economic Policy Institute's comprehensive biennial view of the economy, *The State of Working*

America 2006/2007, Mishel, Bernstein, and Allegretto show that children seldom move more than one income band away from the income of their parents. That is, 65 percent of children from the least wealthy quintile ended up in the bottom 40 percent of the wealth scale.

Similarly, 36 percent of children whose parents were in the top quintile of family wealth remained in the top quintile themselves, with another 24 percent in the next highest quintile; only 7 percent ended up at the bottom.[24] This finding supports the Brookings conclusion that it takes five generations, on average, "for the advantages or disadvantages of family background to die out in the United States."[25]

With regard to educational opportunities, Mishel and his colleagues also observe that "unequal educational opportunities and historical discrimination play a role," but that "children from wealthy families have much greater access to top tier universities than kids from low-income families, even once their innate abilities are taken into account."[26]

The conclusion suggested, once again, is that educational attainment is more likely to be a result of family wealth than wealth being a result of education. Further, according to Mishel and his colleagues, "The jobs of the future will require greater educational credentials, but not to any great extent." From 2004 levels, the share of the workforce requiring a college degree "will rise by just one percentage point, to 28.7%, by 2014."[27] If less than 30 percent of the workforce will require a college degree in 2014, an educational crisis does not appear to be looming.

GLOBAL COMPETITIVENESS AND INTERNATIONAL TESTS

Despite this analysis, most people assume that workers' education levels are directly linked both to their individual economic success and to the future of the nation's economy. Given this assumption, it is not surprising that reports of American students lagging behind foreign students alarm the public. Instead, it is these comparisons themselves that should be cause for concern.

First, because they are newsworthy, the problem areas for American students are frequently emphasized, while their successes are just as frequently ignored. In the past, some have raised concerns about the validity of the test comparisons—for example, that only elite (and older) students in some countries are compared to a broader span of younger students in this country. Some of these problems have been addressed but, as Bracey notes, politicians and the press are selective about the international comparisons they emphasize.

In 2003, for example, the press paid more attention to the U.S. scores on PISA (Programme for International Student Assessment) than to more favorable scores on TIMSS (Trends in International Mathematics and Science Study)—quite possibly because the PISA scores were less favorable and therefore made more dramatic news stories. Similarly, the press largely ignored a broader assessment by the World Economic Forum (WEF) in Switzerland, which ranked the United States first in the world in global competitiveness in 2004–2005. In this report, education was considered as a part of "human capital" which, along with eleven other "pillars," made up the overall competitiveness score. This may be a more balanced way of considering the impact of education on the economy. The factors that comprise global competitiveness also include *creativity* and *innovation*, which the WEF considered the most important, and in these areas it also rated the United States as number one.[29]

These traits are not measured by standardized tests, nor supported by most of the test-related "solutions" promoted by NCLB. But they do align with most studies' conclusions as to the skills workers need in the twenty-first century. Can it be, given the record-setting productivity of American workers today and the broad ratings of the WEF regarding global competitiveness, that the crisis of American education is not quite as bad as it's portrayed? It is common to read today that student test scores went up in several areas and down in others but that "we are very concerned" about the area where they went down. This makes for good news copy but bad public policy.

On the international tests themselves, the reports of U.S. students doing poorly are misleading in several respects. First, as Boe and Shin[29] point out, "U.S. students have generally performed *above average* in comparisons with students in other industrialized nations," and in almost all instances score no lower than average. Further, the countries where students score higher include Iceland, New Zealand, Portugal, and Finland. When compared against the other G7 nations (Canada, France, Germany, Italy, Great Britain, and Japan)—a better match to conditions in the United States—our students are consistently "better than average."

Second, anomalies remain in many of the tests, such as TIMSS, which measures students in grade 8 and in "the final year of secondary school." The problem here, according to Boe and Shin, is that the final year of secondary school can be anywhere from three to almost eight years after eighth grade, depending on the country. Since better scores on tests are associated with more years of schooling, this once again sets up a false comparison. In some countries, students specialize early, and may be expected to score higher due to more schooling in a particular area. There is no indication that this should be cause for alarm.[30] In fact, according to Rotberg, the problem is often one of sampling. Which students, schools, and regions of the country are selected? Are vocational schools included? What percentage of youth, and what segments of society, continue through high school? Are children with disabilities included? Differences in these factors skew results.[31]

The various test results do not indicate that American students are "performing poorly" in any statistical sense. Their performance can only be considered poor if we believe our students should be best in the world (as often proclaimed). Boe and Shin consider this aspiration "unreasonable." "The U.S. is not 'first in the industrialized world' in minimizing the percent of its population living in poverty or in minimizing its infant mortality rate," they observe. "So why should anyone expect the U.S. to be first in the world in educational achievement?"[32]

Tufts University provost Jamshed Bharucha has concluded that despite the higher test scores some other countries obtain, the U.S. approach to education is more likely to improve retention and particularly to develop skills like critical thinking. Many Asian countries force students to specialize at a relatively early age, increasing the depth of content coverage, but not providing a breadth of knowledge or encouraging them to ask questions, engage with the material, or debate the relevance and application of their fields in the world. This is why many of the top Asian universities are looking to emulate our methods even though Asian students may surpass ours on tests.

It turns out, according to Bharucha, that the American approach produces better workers—workers who have investigated many topics and understand how the world works, who are more willing and able to ask questions, who can think for themselves, and who can solve problems. U.S. colleges "encourage class participation, original thought and intellectual risk-taking." A deep investigation of a narrow topic, and the recall of facts about that topic, is of considerably less value—test scores notwithstanding.[33]

Finally, consider the analysis developed by Keith Baker, a retired researcher for the U.S. Department of Education. He proposes a hypothesis based on the expectations in the press and the reports above: that high scores on international tests are directly correlated with national success. He applies this hypothesis first to the FIMS test, the First International Mathematics Study conducted in eleven nations in 1964. The twelve-year-olds who took that test are now of the generation of leaders in their respective countries. He compares their test scores by country with eight indicators of national success: wealth, rate of growth, productivity, quality of life, livability, democracy, and creativity.

In all but one instance, Baker finds a negative correlation. That is, high scores on the tests predicted a poor showing on the indicators. Only one factor—creativity—produced a weak positive correlation ($r = .13$). A similar approach using the more recent PISA produced similar results. "Mediocrity in test scores is, for nations, a good thing!" he concludes.[34]

Since this analysis produces results that are "highly counterintuitive," Baker offers the following explanation:

> Among high-scoring nations, a certain level of educational attainment, as reflected in test scores, provides a platform for launching national success, but once that platform is reached, other factors become more important than further gains in test scores. Indeed, once the platform is reached, it may be bad policy

to pursue further gains in test scores because focusing on the scores diverts attention, effort, and resources away from other factors that are more important determinants of national success.[35]

Quoting Einstein's observation that "the true sign of intelligence is not knowledge but imagination," Baker says that the public has been "barraged" by claims that the American schools are "disaster zones," but that such a claim is "flat out wrong. It is wrong in fact, and it is wrong in theory. For more than 40 years, those who believe this fallacious theory have been leading the nation down the wrong path in education policy."[36] As the World Economic Forum concluded, Americans excel in creativity and innovation, factors more closely aligned with success than test scores.

While the reports and newspapers continue to harp on the danger of disaster associated with the failure of U.S. students to be first in the world on these measures, therefore, most of the evidence seems to point in the other direction. In searching for an explanation of the mismatch between public perception and the testing reality, Boe and Shin propose three possibilities: that observers of these tests results "are simply not aware of the results of the full array of surveys that have been conducted in recent years," that people who understand the results simply view anything short of first as "poor performance," or that "some observers might pick and choose from among existing surveys only the results that support their belief that American education is inadequate, disregarding evidence to the contrary."[37]

Whatever the reason, international test results should not be used to drive perceptions about failure, disaster, or crisis in the public schools, since they are not linked with indicators of success for the countries involved, and since they tend to show American students as average or above average as compared to their peers.

This conclusion also makes the most sense with regard to the economy, according to Rotberg. In a recent commentary, she asks, "Did the United States lose the leather, textile, and steel industries because of its ranking on test-score comparisons? Did General Motors lose sales to Toyota in the U.S. market because of American students' math performance?" Further:

> Even if some of our software and innovation come from other countries, is it because our education system has produced insufficient numbers of high-quality scientists, mathematicians, and engineers? Is there a shortage of U.S. scientists, as some firms have reported, or is there a shortage at the wages the firms would prefer to pay? Are companies outsourcing jobs to China and India because Americans are not qualified for them, or because the firms can pay much lower wages to workers in these countries?[38]

THE NATURE OF THE CRISIS

None of the above should suggest that all students leave school well-prepared or that there is not room for improvement. Many tests of basic reading, writing, and math given to high school graduates—whether by corporations or the testing companies—find that their skills are often considerably lower than desirable. In some instances, particularly in large urban districts, school bureaucracies are dysfunctional to the point where incompetents are protected at all levels, positive changes are squashed, and few students receive the education they need or deserve. These are not the norm, however. According to Slotnik, the majority of failing schools may be found in just twenty-nine districts out of the thousands of districts across the country.[39] This means there is work to be done in certain districts, not that there is a nationwide crisis.

Accusations of crisis are pernicious because they can lead to unnecessary and extreme change. Change in teacher compensation could dramatically alter where teachers place their time and effort, for example. In fact, that is the intent. But if these changes are based on poorly defined or incorrect analysis, or are not linked to the aspirations we have for our children, there will be little meaningful improvement. And if there is little improvement, there will also be more hand-wringing and accusation. While this could benefit future politicians and commentators, it will not benefit children or society.

Because inaccurate perceptions such as those above can fuel significant policy change it is important to carefully consider the problems and challenges facing the country, the extent to which the two are connected, and the goals we want to pursue through the schools. Only by considering these connections and goals—only when we have reached some level of agreement on what results we want—can we expect to bring about any improvement in these results. This consideration should take place with urgency, perhaps, but calmly and analytically, without the "sky is falling" attitude that permeates so much discussion of education.

Can schools be improved? Yes, and some need to be improved dramatically. But neither the increasing income divide nor changes in the job market are primarily the result of anything the schools are or are not doing. Discussions of school improvement, including teacher compensation, will be most effective if they take place in this context.

The perceived crises outlined above and in chapter 2 are based on a few major premises stated earlier: the school–economy connection, the supposed crisis of academic achievement (test scores), and the associated crisis of teaching. But these arguments are based on assumptions that do not bear up under scrutiny. In addition to the above, consider the following propositions, which will be explored in the remaining chapters of the book.

The Achievement Gap

The achievement gap is real, but is not wholly (or even largely) the result of poor teaching or schooling. Test score gaps are found between urban and suburban schools, as well as between different racial and economic groups, but the strongest links are economic and social. To say that schools are responsible for eliminating the achievement gap is to say that the conditions of poverty that affect children don't matter. As the income gap between rich and poor families increases, it may be convenient to believe this, but it is not true.

Almost all children can learn, and many can learn more than they do, but a number of factors enhance or impede that learning. Those factors are economic, social, physical, and motivational as well as instructional, but student results track family income more closely than any other factor, including teacher quality. Student results relate to the entirety of each student's world, including school and classroom environment, home environment, the quality of teaching, and family support. These factors are complex, and many are not within the control of the school or teacher. Improvement strategies are not likely to be effective unless all of the relevant factors are addressed, not just a few.

Good teaching and a positive school environment are extremely important, and there is much to be done in this realm. Good teaching can help students make great strides, as can good health care and a stable home situation. A well organized school can provide a productive learning environment, and promote high expectations and good habits in students. An excellent teacher can inspire the most troubled child to rise above his situation. But in the aggregate, it takes more than teaching and schooling to overcome all the obstacles of poverty. Better teaching in better-run schools will help, and the drive to improve some urban schools is badly needed, but better living conditions are also required. Some schools do face serious teaching (and leadership) issues, particularly in the cities, but this is not true at all urban schools, nor are these issues the whole story. The achievement gap is much more complex than any single factor.

Testing

Test scores are useful in many ways, but are weak indicators of the preparation of our students to work or succeed in life. Nor do they adequately reflect the goals that society has for its children. For tests to have "construct validity," they must fairly and accurately represent the universe they are attempting to describe. Thus, an algebra test may accurately represent the concepts of algebra, but a test or even a series of tests hardly represents the universe of learning and growth we expect for our children in our schools.

As Deborah Meier has observed with regard to NCLB, "The very definition of what constitutes an educated person is now dictated by federal legislation. A well-educated person is one who scores high on standardized math and reading tests. And ergo a good school is one that either has very high test scores or is moving toward them at a prescribed rate of improvement. Period."[40] As the growing disenchantment with NCLB demonstrates, most people do not accept this definition.

For changes in teacher compensation to lead to improved results for students, we must carefully consider the breadth and depth of our goals and shape incentives to address the full range of these goals. It seems unlikely that we will abandon the kinds of tests most people are now familiar with but—as almost all testing experts agree—these should be only a part of the overall assessment.

Teaching and Testing

While it has been shown in some studies (and is intuitively obvious to many) that good teaching makes a large difference in student growth, these conclusions are often based on test scores as a surrogate for educational success. Further, if we *define* the best teachers as those whose students get the highest test scores, we create a tautology—of course the best teachers will have students with the highest test scores.

But the impact of teachers on students is variable and extremely difficult to quantify. The teachers whom students remember years later are most often those who were confident in the student's ability, who allowed the student to pursue interests inside and outside the curriculum, who supported the student during a difficult time, and, yes, who held the student to high standards. They are not necessarily the ones whose classes got the highest test scores. Just as with business, focusing on a short-term bottom line in teaching may undercut long-term planning and growth. Assessments of teaching should reflect this complexity.

This is not to say that we should not seek to identify and promote quality teaching. It does mean, however, that we should carefully identify the results we want. We should build an agreement on what constitutes teacher and student performance—both at the district level and as a nation—before we start tying compensation to that performance. The willingness to build that kind of agreement is what separates Denver from most previous experiments, and explains why their final plan was approved by teachers, the district, and the voters with little opposition.

As shown above, researchers find no clear evidence that differences in international test scores are primarily caused by low-quality teaching. Teaching may be a factor, but these results may also have to do with school organization, a curriculum that is too broad and shallow, the control of instructional materials by a few large publishers, a grade-segregated and passive learning environment, or the country's exploitive pop culture. They may also be due, in part, to the inadequacy of tests as a measure of learning, or to the culture, language, and economic advantages of different groups of students. And it may be, as Baker concludes, that good test scores don't predict success in other areas.

Teacher Quality and Teacher Shortages

The problems of teacher quality and the impending shortage of teachers are often raised in the context of the academic crisis described above. Most of these reports note that new teachers tend to come from the bottom third of college graduates, and proclaim that we need to do better. Others predict an impending shortage of teachers—given upcoming baby boomer retirements and the fact that many new teachers do not stay in the profession. As the College Board warned in 2006,

> A problem of epic proportions looms on the horizon. It has yet to register fully with the nation. Amazingly, 46 percent of the new teachers who enter elementary and secondary schools will leave the classroom within five years. Nearly half of the current teachers have already served for 20 years or more and may be looking at retirement. Where will we find replacements? How will we pay for them? What does the future for the teaching profession look like?[41]

Most of these groups advocate higher salaries across the board, from the Teaching Commission reports and the recent *Tough Choices or Tough Times*, reaching as far back as *A Nation at Risk*. In these reports, the authors believe that higher salaries are needed to attract better teachers. Most also believe that some form of performance pay is required, including higher pay for better performance, for additional duties, or for "teachers willing to work the same hours per year as other professionals do."

Whether this shortage is a true crisis remains to be seen. There is substantial evidence that it may be, though some think the problem is overblown. We already recognize a need for teachers in the cities, however, and it is likely that the need for urban teachers will also grow. The question is how best to address these needs.

Regarding teacher quality, a late 2007 study by the Educational Testing Service indicates that teacher quality, as measured by the test scores and college grades of new teacher candidates, may be improving. The study looked at 153,000 prospective teachers who took the Praxis exams between 2002 and 2005, and found that both their SAT scores and college grades were significantly higher than those of similar candidates a decade ago, though candidates for elementary positions, special education, and physical education lagged behind the others.[42] This improvement in teacher test-taking skills and grades in college may or may not be significant, but it has so far not changed the general perception that teachers are often academically weak.

Nothing in the arguments above should be construed to suggest that schools do not need to change and improve. Instead, the purpose of this discussion is to lower the volume on the cries of crisis, not to stop consideration of teacher quality. There is evidence of a growing teacher shortage, at least in some areas, and there are issues of teacher recruitment and teacher accountability. Educational and political leaders need to consider the nature of the problems and to address their causes, but without the exaggeration and school bashing. To the extent that we have a need to recruit more (and better?) teachers, are the causes most often blamed—lack of motivation, lack of the perceived ability to get ahead—the real causes? Are performance-based financial enticements what potential teachers really desire? Are people attracted to teaching and other helping professions by the chance to compete for more money, or are working conditions and the support to succeed more important factors?

Despite the barrage of criticism, members of the public—particularly parents—still tend to support the schools in their communities, as reported in chapter 4. And yet, concerns persist regarding the structure and impact of the public schools, and there are compelling reasons for reviewing and changing the teacher compensation system. Unfortunately, the language of crisis does not help in finding substantive solutions. Changes in the practice of schooling and teacher compensation will be effective only if they address the real goals and problems of education—goals developed and agreed to by all of the affected parties—without the hype and hand-wringing.

NOTES

1. Herbert M. Kliebard, *The Struggle for the American Curriculum,* 2nd ed. (London: Routledge, 1995), 220–222.

2. Rudolf Flesch, *Why Johnny Can't Read* (New York: Harper & Brothers, 1955).

3. Rudolf Flesch, *Why Johnny Still Can't Read* (New York: Harper & Row, 1981), 1.

4. Kliebard, *The Struggle for the American Curriculum,* 227.

5. Owen Edwards, "Explorer I Satellite," *Smithsonian* 38, no. 10, January 2008: 36, Curry College. Accessed 11 March 2008 at http://web.ebscohost.com.odin.curry.edu/ehost/detail?vid=12&hid=102&sid=96a0c182-9e45-4839-8654-01d0f25d7157%40sessionmgr108&bdata=JnNpdGU9Z Whvc3QtbGl2ZQ%3d%3d#db=aph&AN=28023368; Gerard J. DeGroot, "Sputnik 1957," *American History* 42, no. 5, December 2007: 34–39. Accessed 11 March 2008 at www.ebscohost.com..

6. James S. Coleman et al., *Equality of Educational Opportunity* (Washington, DC: U.S. Department of Health, Education and Welfare, Office of Education, 1966).

7. Robert Rosenthal and Lenore Jacobson, *Pygmalion in the Classroom* (New York: Holt, Rinehart, 1968).

8. Jonathan Kozol, *Death at an Early Age* (Boston: Houghton Mifflin, 1967).

9. John Holt, *How Children Fail* (New York: Dell Publishing Co., 1964), 167.

10. Charles Silberman, *Crisis in the Classroom* (New York: Random House, 1970), 54, 122–126.

11. National Commission on Excellence in Education, "A Nation at Risk: The Imperative for Educational Reform," April 1983, *A Nation at Risk*, U.S. Department of Education. Accessed 12 December 2004 atwww.ed.gov.

12. Louis Gerstner et al., *Teaching at Risk: A Call to Action* (New York: The Teaching Commission, 2004), 12–13.

13. Louis Gerstner et al., *Teaching at Risk: Progress & Potholes* (New York: The Teaching Commission, 2006), 12.

14. Heritage Foundation, *Where We Stand: Our Principles on Improving Education* (Heritage Research, 2006).

15. *Are They Really Ready to Work?* (The Conference Board, Partnership for the 21st Century, Corporate Voices for Working Families, Society for Human Resource Management, 2006), 7.

16. Center for Innovative Thought, *Teachers and the Uncertain American Future* (New York: The College Board, July 2006), 5.

17. *Tough Choices or Tough Times: Executive Summary*, New Commission on the Skills of the American Workforce (Washington, DC: National Center on Education and the Economy, 2007), 4–6.

18. James G. March, *A Primer on Decision-Making* (New York: The Free Press, 1994).

19. Lawrence Mishel and Richard Rothstein, "False Alarm," *Phi Delta Kappan* 88, no. 10 (June 2007): 737.

20. Colin Greer, *The Great School Legend: A Revisionist Interpretation of American Public Education* (New York: Viking, 1972), 29.

21. Greer, *The Great School Legend*, 141.

22. Isabel Sawhill, *Opportunity in America: The Role of Education* (Princeton, NJ: Brookings Institute, 2006), 2.

23. Sawhill, *Opportunity in America*, 1–3.

24. Lawrence Mishel, Jared Bernstein, and Syliva Allegretto, *The State of Working America 2006/2007* (Ithaca, NY: Economic Policy Institute, Cornell University Press, 2007), 95.

25. Sawhill, *Opportunity in America*, 2.

26. Mishel, Bernstein, and Allegretto, *The State of Working America 2006/2007*, 94.

27. Mishel, Bernstein, and Allegretto, *The State of Working America 2006/2007*, 112.

28. Gerald W. Bracey, "15th Bracey Report on the Condition of Public Education," *Phi Delta Kappan* 87, no. 28 (October 2005): 141.

29. Erling E. Boe and Sujie Shin, "Is the United States Really Losing the International Horse Race in Academic Achievement?" *Phi Delta Kappan* 86, no. 9 (May 2005): 688–695.

30. Boe and Shin, "Is the United States Really Losing the International Horse Race in Academic Achievement?" 693–694.

31. Iris C. Rotberg, "Quick Fixes, Test Scores and the Global Economy," *Education Week* 27, no. 41 (11 June 2008): 32.

32. Boe and Shin, "Is the United States Really Losing the International Horse Race in Academic Achievement?" 694.

33. Jamshed Bharucha, "America Can Teach Asia a Lot About Science, Technology, and Math," *Chronicle of Higher Education* 54, no. 20 (25 January 2007): A33.

34. Keith Baker, "Are International Tests Worth Anything?" *Phi Delta Kappan* 89, no. 2 (October 2007): 102–104.

35. Baker, "Are International Tests Worth Anything?" 104.

36. Baker, "Are International Tests Worth Anything?" 104.

37. Boe and Shin, "Is the United States Really Losing the International Horse Race in Academic Achievement?" 694.

38. Rotberg, "Quick Fixes, Test Scores and the Global Economy," 27.

39. William J. Slotnik, Discussion of Denver Pilot and PFP (Boston, 10 July 2008).

40. Deborah Meier, "NCLB and Democracy," in *Many Children Left Behind*, eds. Deborah Meier and George Wood (Boston: Beacon Press, 2004), 67.

41. *Teachers and the Uncertain American Future*, 5.

42. David H. Gitomer, *Teacher Quality in a Changing Landscape: Improvements in the Teacher Pool*, Policy Evaluation & Research Center (Princeton, NJ: Educational Testing Service, 2007); Bess Keller, "New Teachers Outdo Peers of Last Decade on Academic Scales," *Education Week* 27, no. 16 (19 December 2007b): 1, 14–15.

7

Education, Poverty, and the Achievement Gap

Even if policy-makers choose to ignore the differences among children, good teachers will not. They will not work in schools where they believe the expectations are unrealistic, and will certainly not risk lower pay or other sanctions for failing to advance some kids to the level of their better prepared peers. If we are to achieve the goals of a revised teacher compensation system, it is critical to understand how standards and expectations for students interact with student and school demographics. Teachers certainly understand this dynamic, and no performance pay scheme will be successful unless it finds a way to address the realities of American society that enter the classroom.

The achievement gap is the most consistently cited problem that education reform efforts are supposed to address, but despite many attempts, the gap remains. The latest initiatives—standards, high-stakes tests, and performance pay—are supposed to eliminate this gap by taking on two factors identified in the past as holding students back—low expectations (standards) and poor teacher quality (performance pay). But there are many more factors beyond these, where they exist, that affect a child's success in school.

Three points are central to any consideration of the "achievement gap" between middle- and lower-class students in this country, and between students of various ethnic backgrounds. The first of these is that the factors that most closely track student performance in school are not school factors—as important as those are—but family and community factors. Of these, the most important are conditions associated with poverty and the education of the parent or parents. These conditions—poor environmental conditions, poor health care, lack of time and resources, lack of language and other growth experiences—work against a child's success in school. No discussion of the achievement gap is complete without considering the environment in which students spend most of their time.

Second, it is important to remember that the United States does less to mitigate the results of this income gap than most advanced countries—even as that gap has been growing. Supports for poor parents and children—from health care to unemployment income to job training—tend to be less generous in the United States than in most European countries. Since the income gap is growing, and since less is being done to support children and families in poverty, there is no reason to expect that the conditions of poverty will soon be eased.

Third is the historic role of schools, which are commonly perceived as having provided the route to success for the lower classes. Rags to riches stories have always been a part of the American myth, as noted in the previous chapter, and are as common among successful people today as in the past. Senator Edwards, Presidents Clinton and Obama, and Massachusetts Governor Deval Patrick, to name just a few, all rose from poverty to places of prominence, and many such successful people credit part of their success to the education they received, often from the public schools.

Given this perception, it is easy to see why the persistent "achievement gap," which tends to separate poor from middle-class students and minorities from whites, is dismaying. The continued existence of this gap suggests that the public schools are no longer fulfilling their historic role—that they no longer help the poor climb into the middle class, or provide young black and Latino children with hope and a chance at a better life.

In fact, it does not appear that schools have ever filled this role. While education has provided a route to success for some individual students, and while basic skills such as reading and writing are undeniably a part of the foundation of success for most people, the schools have never served as a broad social equalizer for the poor. Instead, schools have tended to perpetuate the status quo—both historically, and in our present day. This is not because of individual teachers or schools, but because schools in all societies serve to pass on the values and structures of those societies. It is because schools are structured to sort children into different levels, because school success is closely linked to family background and resources, and because of the stratification of society along social and economic lines.

School teachers and administrators understand better than most that expectations and standards alone will not eliminate the achievement gap because they do not address all of its causes. The persistence of the conditions of poverty, and the impact of those conditions on the academic success of students, continue to fuel that gap—as they have throughout American history, and as they do in other countries throughout the world.[1] If eliminating the achievement gap remains a primary educational goal, and if performance pay for teachers is tied to that goal without addressing the external factors that lead to that gap, the achievement gap will not go away and the performance pay plan will not succeed.

To understand how we might address this gap, we need to understand its causes. These include both school practices and the effects of family background, especially poverty—the most closely linked condition. This chapter looks at the nonschool causes.

THE REDISCOVERY OF INCOME AND RACE

In 1964, Congress commissioned James S. Coleman and a team of researchers to conduct a study on educational opportunity as part of the Civil Rights Act (Equality of Educational Opportunity). This team was expected to demonstrate conclusively that what matters most for student learning is the quality of the teaching they receive. This massive study came to be known as the Coleman Report; Coleman and his team drew on data from 570,000 students, 60,000 teachers, and 4,000 schools across the country.

The conclusion that Coleman and his colleagues arrived at challenged expectations. Instead of finding that teacher quality was the primary factor in determining student success, the researchers concluded that a student's family background was the most important. In a country largely divided along black–white lines, both economically and socially, they described how black children started out behind their white peers and never caught up, even when the schools had equivalent teachers and resources. Further, they determined that the next most significant factors in student success after family background were the students' sense of control over their own destiny, and whom they went to school with. Black students who went to schools with more white, middle-class students did better. They also found that the impact of having "good" teachers was greater for black students than for white, but did not overcome other factors.[2]

Some critics used the Coleman report to recommend defunding the schools: schools make no difference, so why should we fund them? However, most observers now view the results as the first credible demonstration of the impact of family background and circumstances. David Armor, one of the original researchers, describes the study as opening up a question that remains unanswered: "No one has found a way, on a large-scale basis, to overcome the influence of the family."[3]

Critics of the study have also questioned some of Coleman's conclusions and methods. For example, a recent reanalysis of Coleman data by Geoffrey Borman using more modern techniques posits that as much as 40 percent of the achievement differences among students may be attributable to school factors, a higher figure than Coleman's. Despite such critiques, however, the basic premise of the Coleman study—that family background and school population are two of the most significant factors in student success—remains unchanged.[4]

At about the same time as the Coleman Commission was doing its work, Rosenthal and Jacobson[5] were conducting a study of teacher expectations that was also to become famous. As described in *Pygmalion in the Classroom,* these researchers arranged a study of teacher expectations at a small elementary school they called the Oak School, a school in a mixed community serving lower-earning but not poor families. In their experiment, they randomly identified certain children to teachers as likely to "spurt" or "bloom." Neither the children nor their parents knew of this designation, but the teachers apparently believed the researchers, expecting the identified children to do better than their peers. After a year, these students had gained significantly on their IQ tests, and teachers described them as "more intellectually curious, as happier, and, especially in the lower grades, as less in need of social approval."[6] This effect continued to be visible, though less pronounced, among children through fifth grade.

This study produced some important findings. First, the children whom teachers expected to do better did better. The critical point here is that the children were no different from their peers except in one respect: their teachers expected more from them. As the authors point out:

> There was no crash program to improve [the students'] reading ability, no special lesson plan, no extra time tutoring, no trips to museums or art galleries. There was only the belief that the children bore watching, that they had intellectual competencies that would in due course be revealed. What was done in our program of educational change was done directly for the teacher, only indirectly for the student.[7]

Second, the authors observed that teachers reacted favorably when students performed as expected, and unfavorably when students performed against expectation. That is, "[t]he more the upper-track children gained in IQ, the more favorably they were rated by their teachers." Conversely, "[t]he more the lower-track children of the control group gained in IQ, the more unfavorably they were viewed by their teacher."[8] Thus, children who did not live up to higher expectations or down to lower ones were viewed less favorably.

Rosenthal and Jacobson conclude in their book that their findings could lead to a "new expectancy" regarding children: "The new expectancy may be that children can learn more than had been believed possible. . . . The new expectancy, at the very least, will make it more difficult, when they encounter the educationally disadvantaged, for teachers to think, 'Well, after all, what can you expect?'"[9]

Both of these studies have had their critics, but they have also been influential over the years. It was no coincidence that these and similar studies began to appear as the national civil rights movement was gaining momentum, and as recognition of the impact of racism fueled a national awakening. Just as the National Defense Education Act in 1958 recognized the national defense importance of a good education, the Elementary and Secondary Education Act (ESEA) of 1965, part of Lyndon Johnson's Great Society initiative, recognized for the first time the impact of poverty on students, and the difficulties schools had overcoming this impact. The forerunner of No Child Left Behind (which is the name given to the current iteration), ESEA sought a new way to address the longstanding achievement gap between students of different socioeconomic and racial groups.

During this period, the civil rights movement exploded into the national consciousness, school busing was instituted in cities across the country to achieve racial balance, and a series of exposés of urban schools were printed. Stark descriptions of urban schools such as Kozol's *Death at an Early Age* (1967), which detailed the deprivations faced by his students in an inner-city Boston school and uncovered a substantial difference in funding and support for black and white schools, were common.[10]

Sociologist William Ryan's *Blaming the Victim* (1971) describes how society tends to blame the poor and weak for their predicament. Ryan rails against the belief that some students are "culturally deprived" and the "folklore of cultural deprivation," saying that these phrases carry a "not so subtle prejudice," and that the belief that such children can't learn much assures that they won't.[11] In particular, Ryan claims that while middle-class children may be more adapted to school, the reverse is also true—that schools are better designed for middle-class students.

Ryan disputes two "additional elements of cultural deprivation folklore," that "Negroes are not interested in education, and Negro children are 'nonverbal.'"[12] In fact, he offers evidence that the education level of African Americans climbed dramatically between 1920 and 1960, and that they have demonstrated "an enormous commitment to learning." The differences, he claims, are stylistic or cultural rather than substantive. He notes that black children who are highly verbal on the playgrounds and in nonschool settings use more slang than white, middle-class children, and have a different worldview, while middle-class children are "wordbound"—inclined to define rather than use words relating to action and feelings. "A middle class child says a rock is a stone; a lower class child says a rock is hard and you throw it."[13]

Ryan complains that Coleman treats the relationship between family background and school success as a cause and effect relationship. Instead, he says, the central question is why the gap exists. He insists that we consider the organization of the schools, their funding, and the expectations they have for their students.[14]

These works are useful as anchors of the positions taken by different camps today. As is frequently the case, too little consideration is given to the possibility that all points of view are correct in different measures or situations, and that the reality varies by student, family, and context. Clearly, poor children do not do as well as middle- and upper-class children, and blacks and Hispanics, who are often poor, do not do as well as whites. Thus, we have what has come to be known as the achievement gap. We should also remember that the achievement gap is a creation of today's standardized tests, which speaks to Ryan's point, and exists because of schools' focus on academics. If we measured student achievement in different ways and more broadly—even if we measured it in terms of student growth—the gap might cease to exist.

Ryan's statement that the central question hasn't changed is as true today as it was in 1971—why does the achievement gap exist? Because this gap is so important to the discussion of school accountability and public education policy, it is particularly germane in discussions of teacher performance and effectiveness.

CURRENT VIEWS ON POVERTY AND THE ACHIEVEMENT GAP

The conventional wisdom today is that children of all races are endowed with the same natural abilities (in the aggregate) and that they should all be expected to perform and be held to the same standards. If schools and teachers raised expectations for their students, according to this view, the achievement gap would disappear. The policy superstructure of education in the last decade has been built on forcing schools to have higher expectations for all children. Thus, in promoting No Child Left Behind, George W. Bush decried the "soft bigotry of low expectations."

The Education Trust, an advocate for higher standards and sanctions for underperforming schools, attributes much of the problem to teacher quality, addressing this point in a 2006 report entitled *Teaching Inequality: How Poor and Minority Students are Shortchanged on Teacher Quality.* The report's finding, citing an Illinois study, is this: "Teacher quality turns out to matter a lot."[15] The report concludes that a teacher's level of literacy and academic skill (test scores), mastery of content, experience, and pedagogical skill all make a difference, and that urban schools serving poor and minority children tend to have teachers with lower levels of all of these attributes. The report also claims, based on a Tennessee study using value-added measures, that "students who have three highly effective teachers in a row score more than 50 percentile points above their counterparts who have three ineffective teachers in a row."[16]

Teaching Inequality's recommendations seem reasonable. They include treating teachers more like professionals, changing the structure of teaching, and "re-thinking" teacher compensation and tenure, among a list of others. The report concludes with the "simple truth" that "public education cannot fulfill its mission if students growing up in poverty, students of color and

low-performing students continue to be disproportionately taught by inex-
perienced, under-qualified teachers."[17] Like many such reports, however,
this one mentions the effects of poverty but only addresses the issue of
teacher quality, holding teachers and schools accountable for seeing that all
children meet the same standards at the same time, regardless of background.

While few would doubt that good teachers are more effective than bad
ones, the Education Trust's analysis raises questions. The Chicago research
regarding teacher quality that it cites (IERC) is based on applying a particular description of quality teaching—the Teacher Quality Index (TQI)—to
teachers at both high- and low-performing schools as determined by the
state test. Not surprisingly, it finds that there is an inverse relationship between teacher quality as measured by its index and high-poverty schools.

Unfortunately, while we may not be surprised that the poorest schools
have the least academically prepared teachers, and while we may agree
that teacher preparation makes a difference, these facts do not support
the conclusion—embodied in the high standards and sanctions the trust
supports—that recruiting better qualified teachers will reverse the achievement gap. That conclusion would be justified only if teacher quality were the
only factor, or the dominant factor—a conclusion the study does not support, and one that the original researchers do not draw.

In fact, the National Center for Fair and Open Testing (Fairtest) calculates,
using the IERC data presented in the Education Trust report, that teacher quality would only account for six percentage points on the achievement gap. That
is, if all of the students had weak teachers, the achievement gap between poor
and middle-class students who achieved proficiency would be 34 percent; if
all of the students had strong teachers, the gap would be 28 percent.[18]

The original IERC study on which the Education Trust based its report believes teacher quality is important but not defining: "TQI matters, and matters most for the most disadvantaged schools . . . but [it] does not level the
playing field with regard to challenges that schools with high poverty
face."[19] Thus, while we should certainly take steps to provide good teachers
for all students, and should make extra efforts to place good teachers in
high-poverty schools, such steps do not remove the difficulties of circum-
stance that students bring with them.

A Tennessee study also cited by the Education Trust shows large test score
gains for students taught by the most effective teachers, with the greatest gains
made by the low-achieving students.[20] This finding echoes Coleman's conclusions and once again supports the goal of bringing the most effective teachers
into the classrooms of low-achieving students, but such steps do not come close
to eliminating the achievement gap. Further, the trust laments that the most effective teachers are more likely to teach white than black students, and the least
effective teachers are more likely to teach black than white students. However,
if the Tennessee teachers labeled most effective were found primarily in more

middle-class schools as the report suggests, the culture of the school may also have had an impact in the achievement of students and the categorization of teachers—including the mix of middle-class and low-income students and their feelings of control over their own lives.

This proximity of middle-class and low-income students—the nature of the population of the school—was one of the three factors Coleman identified as most important, and is also identified by Rothstein, Barton, and others as a significant predictor of student success (see below). While the teacher skill and experience are important to student success, other factors must also be considered.

The third problem with studies of teacher quality is that most of the student measures in these studies—and many of the teacher measures—are based on standardized test scores. A definition of teacher quality or student success based solely on such limited measures will be a very narrow definition. Early definitions of good teaching were sometimes circular. If good teaching is defined by recording the test results of each teacher's students, the best teachers will produce kids who get the highest test scores—by definition. If middle-class children are more "wordbound," to use Ryan's term, and are thus better at standardized tests, a measure based on those tests may not be accurate.

The Teacher Quality Index used by the IERC in Chicago contains six factors: teachers' ACT Composite and English scores, whether they failed the Basic Skills test on the first attempt, whether they had emergency or provisional teaching certificates, the competitiveness ranking of their undergraduate colleges, and whether they had three or fewer years of experience.[21] While these scores may indicate a teacher's academic proficiency, they may also indicate test-taking ability, native language, and family income as well. They do not encompass the full range of teacher quality (nor does the IERC claim that they do). They can be useful, but to the extent that we are defining both teacher inputs and student outputs in terms of standardized tests, we should be careful of the conclusions we draw.

While there is little doubt that teacher quality is important and that better teachers tend to opt for more suburban districts, therefore, there are two pernicious assumptions that should not be allowed to creep into discourse around education policy (as they often do). If these assumptions are allowed to dominate, education policy will ignore significant factors about the lives of children they are supposed to help, to the detriment of all.

First is the implied assumption that poverty and other home conditions aren't important—that they can be overcome by the school. Implicit in much of the discussion about standards is that all children can learn at the same levels, period. It wasn't that long ago that some poor and minority students were regularly segregated into inferior classrooms where little was offered to them or expected of them. These children were too often "warehoused" in remote classrooms (or sometimes in whole schools), where nothing much was expected and nothing much taught. Some students were identified as special needs or, before that, retarded or slow. The poor conditions in these schools have been described in numerous books and reports dating back to the 1960s.

We no longer believe (if we ever did) that these children are incapable of or uninterested in learning. Neither family background, nor particularly race, conclusively determines a child's future. But this doesn't mean that family background has no effect. To maintain that all children can learn to the same standards at the same time if only the schools would do their job is equally dangerous. If it were true, poverty would not matter, nor would culture, nor would health care, nor family expectations or access to resources, nor any of the many other factors that separate different groups of children living in different circumstances.

The pendulum has swung from low or no expectations in the middle of the 1900s—when race and poverty were seen as destiny and children were not expected to overcome them—to an equally extreme position that considers these factors immaterial. But to imply that family conditions aren't a factor in student success is harmful to children and the educational process. To say that these conditions matter but act as though they don't is little better. Such expectations hurt children who struggle and make progress, but who nonetheless do poorly on tests. Plenty of evidence shows that poverty and other home conditions matter a great deal. They do not determine a child's future—they can sometimes be overcome by the family or the school or the child with help—but they certainly matter.

The second assumption, which too often follows on the first, is about blame. Today's educational mantra insists that if all groups of children are inherently equal in ability, and if all children can therefore learn at the same high levels, someone must be at fault if they don't learn at high levels— either the school, the teacher, or the student him- or herself. This is the logic of No Child Left Behind when it proposes sanctions on students and schools for underperforming. Since all children can learn, and since standards have been set for what they should learn and when, there is no excuse for their not learning—not language, not health, not poverty, not cultural expectations, not family differences. There is no excuse; there is only blame.

From a policy point of view, it is convenient to believe that poverty, housing, health care, and safety don't affect educational attainment, and that educational attainment is the route out of poverty for students who are willing to work hard. This is a wonderfully useful political philosophy. It absolves leaders of the need to address poor nutrition, inadequate housing, lack of health care, and related issues. It provides substantial cover for some of the most vociferous supporters of standards, high-stakes tests, and sanctions as accountability measures, as well as for those who support charter schools and various forms of privatization. Blame the schools, teachers, and kids for something they can't universally achieve; diminish any talk of the complex issues of poverty; undercut the unions, and take credit for being tough and holding people accountable—all in one easy policy position.

This may not represent the *intent* of many thoughtful policy makers and caring educators who recognize the problems of poverty. But the logic of standardization implies this view. If all students are to meet the same standards with little regard for these factors—if students are all to learn to the same high levels at the same time, and if schools, teachers, or students are to be blamed if this doesn't happen—the result is an implicit statement that the problems of poverty don't matter. If teachers are held similarly (and unfairly) accountable, no performance pay plan will work.

On the one hand, it appears to be true that standards and tests have improved instruction for some children who might previously have been ignored or forgotten, underchallenged and undereducated, and that many of these children are either low income and/or minority. And it's also true that some effects of poverty can be overcome under certain settings, as has been demonstrated by well-publicized urban schools across the country. On the other hand, it is clearly the case that poverty and related factors make a difference in children's lives, and that not all of the difference can be addressed by the single institution of the school.

The purpose of bringing up the impact of poverty is not to blame the victim once again. Quite the opposite. Poverty and related conditions are not destiny, but they are conditions that matter. They cannot be ignored or wished away. In fact, to pretend that these factors don't exist and to punish those who fail to achieve at the expected levels, largely because of these factors, is itself a form of blaming the victim. Expecting two groups to perform at the same levels when they start with vastly different backgrounds is neither realistic nor fair.

Similarly, expecting urban teachers to bridge this gap entirely is to expect much more from some teachers than others—hardly an expectation that will attract good teachers to the schools where they are most needed. In either instance, ignoring the impact of a student's background is to say that background doesn't matter and to fail to treat these children as the individuals they are. Nobody should be "off the hook" for improving student success. Not school teachers and administrators, not civic and political leaders, and not the families themselves. Given the close connection between the achievement gap and the income gap, all segments of society are part of both the problem and the solution.

THE CONDITIONS OF POVERTY

"Research ties fourteen factors to student achievement," according to Barton, "and low income and minority children are at a disadvantage in almost all of them."[22] Drawing from hundreds of studies on these issues, Barton's meta-analysis identifies the life experiences and conditions that are associated with school achievement, and examines the extent to which these factors differ according to race/ethnicity and income. He concludes that a gap exists in terms of race for all fourteen factors, and in terms of economic status for eleven of the twelve factors for which data by income were available. Barton's factors are identified in table 7.1.[23]

Barton's research clearly identifies a set of school factors where poor children and racial minorities tend to receive less. These include the need for experienced teachers, an appropriately rigorous curriculum, and reasonable class sizes. In addition, however, he finds that home factors from parent availability and support, to health care, to preschool television viewing, all play a role in student achievement.

In another widely cited study of the effect on class and the classroom, Rothstein describes the conditions of poverty and race that affect student success in school. The premise of his 2004 book, *Class and Schools,* is that we must undertake social, economic, and educational reform if we truly want to eliminate the achievement gap. "For it is true," according to Rothstein, "that income and skin color themselves don't influence student achievement, but the collection of characteristics that define social class differences inevitably influences that achievement."[24] He also considers housing and economic resources, health differences, and a range of cultural differences between groups. These involve communications, expectations, and social values, all of which play a role in developing a child's interests, attitudes, and aptitudes. Rothstein describes health, reading, language, and enrichment experiences that differ sharply between economic classes.

Below is a summary of issues affecting poor and minority children as identified by Barton, Rothstein, and others.

Health Issues

It should be easy to understand that students who are less healthy—who are hungry or tired or whose diets are inadequate—will have a hard time focusing on learning. This is why school lunch and breakfast programs are in

Table 7.1.   Barton's Fourteen Factors Related to Student Achievement

Before and Beyond School	*In School*
• Birth weight	• Rigor of curriculum
• Lead poisoning	• Teacher experience and attendance
• Hunger and nutrition	• Teacher preparation
• Reading to young children	• Class size
• Television watching	• Technology-assisted instruction
• Parent availability	• School safety
• Student mobility	
• Parent participation	

place in many schools (though these vary in quality), but the problems often begin at birth. Children born of parents who themselves are not healthy—who are born at a low birth weight or whose mothers were smoking, drinking, or taking drugs while pregnant—can start off with a cognitive disadvantage that may be hard to overcome. While these problems are not exclusive to low-income communities, they are more prevalent there.

Poor and minority children are also less likely to have the appropriate visual and hearing screening, and therefore may not hear instructions or see the board as well as others. They are more likely to have high levels of lead in their bloodstreams from inadequate housing that still has lead paint, and/or to have diabetes or asthma. Each of these conditions is significant; each is related to substandard living conditions, and each can have a negative effect on student learning. For example, children with asthma—an increasingly common condition in the inner city—may miss sleep and are less likely to exercise and be fit.

In addition to conditions that exist at birth, poor and minority children are more likely to live where high-sulfur heating oil and diesel fuel are prevalent, to eat poorly, and to watch television from an early age. These factors may lead to children who have weak visual acuity and more difficulty reading. Rothstein speculates that "a good part of the over-identification of learning disabilities for lower-class children may well be attributable to undiagnosed vision problems that could be easily treated by optometrists and for which special education placement then should be unnecessary."[25]

Another area where poor and minority children fare poorly compared to their middle-class peers is in dental care, where toothaches and related problems may distract children or lead to more serious conditions. In an extreme example, one homeless twelve-year-old recently died from an infection that started with his lack of dental care.[26]

Reading and Language

Though too often ignored, the health issues above may be the most obvious of the problems facing many inner-city children. Less well known are the language and reading gaps that often leave these children with reduced vocabularies and diminished belief in their own ability to use language. Children from poor and minority households are likely to watch more TV at a young age, and to be read to less. Both of these conditions are negatively associated with reading ability, vocabulary development, and success in schools. In addition, Barton finds that "each hour of television a child watches on a daily basis between the ages of 1 and 3 years old increases by 10 percent the risk that the child will have attention problems. Forty-two percent of black forth graders watch six hours or more of television per day—more than three times the percentage of white fourth graders who watch that much."[27]

Further, in a study that has received too little attention, Hart and Risley identified the dramatically different nature of conversation between children and their parents in different economic classes. In middle- and upper-class homes, an average three-year-old has a vocabulary of about 1,100 words, while a welfare child's vocabulary is about 525 words. (These children's IQs are similarly divided: 117 for the professional-class children, 79 for the welfare children, possibly based on their language skills.)[28]

These starkly different vocabularies are related to two other factors in the conversation between adults and children in these two different kinds of household. One is the number of words spoken to the child at home. In 1995, Hart and Risley found that children in professional homes hear an average of 487 "utterances" each hour (from a simple command to a long statement), while working-class children hear 301 utterances per hour and children in welfare households hear only 178. Extrapolating to a three-year-old child, the professional-class child will have heard some thirty million more words in his or her household than a welfare child of the same age.

Second, the nature of these verbal exchanges is also starkly different. In dividing the nature of the discussion between encouragements (words of praise or approval) and discouragements (words of prohibition or disapproval) the researchers found that the average three-year-old in the professional household had heard 500,000 encouragements and 80,000 discouragements in his lifetime, while the same-age child in the welfare home had heard 75,000 encouragements and 200,000 discouragements. The average working-class child would have heard 186,000 encouragements to 108,000 discouragements.

Another way to look at this is that middle-class children hear roughly six encouragements for every discouragement. Welfare children hear only one encouragement for every 2.5 discouragements. In addition to limiting a child's vocabulary, this difference is likely to encourage one set of children to think for themselves and have confidence in their own ability much more than the other set. (Remember Coleman's conclusion about the importance of a child's sense of control over his or her destiny.) Since the complexity of the words and sentences also increased with income level, the children of professionals gain another advantage in language acuity.[29]

"All the families nurtured their children and played and talked with them," according to Hart and Risley. "They all disciplined their children and taught them good manners and how to dress and toilet themselves. They provided their children with much the same toys and talked to them about much the same things. Though different in personality and skill levels, the children all learned to talk and to be socially appropriate members of the family with all the basic skills needed for preschool entry." But, a thirty million word disadvantage by age four for the welfare child seems extremely difficult to completely overcome, especially when a greater percentage of the words heard have been discouragements.[30]

Cultural Differences

Another factor that is often used to predict student success is the educational attainment of parents. That attainment may be related to the parents' own social and economic status, and in turn may affect the aspirations and expectations parents have for their children. Communities of working-class parents may value education for their children but may still have lower expectations as to what those children will accomplish in school.

Rothstein calls this the "role model gap." Both parents and children in middle-class families see a professional role as a natural expectation for the children. Working-class parents present a different model, even if they try to maintain high expectations for their children's education. Although the stated expectation of attending college is similar for eighth graders of all races and economic classes, many fewer blacks actually enroll in college or, if they do, persist on to earn a bachelor's degree. The intent is the same for all groups, but black and lower-class students find less peer or parental pressure and support to keep them going when conditions become difficult.

Even middle-class black children appear less likely to study hard and succeed in school. This may be the result of many factors: health and language factors mentioned above, a culture of underachievement in the black community based on past and present discrimination in the labor market, and possibly media depictions of black culture as well. If even educated blacks have a harder time than whites getting a job, black teenagers may see little point in school. To the extent it exists, this culture discourages black teenagers from reaching their educational potentials. The more any group perceives that there is little reward for the work required to get an education, the less likely the members of that group may be to put forth the effort. It is true that finishing high school is not a road to the middle class for too many young, urban blacks, as shown in the last chapter. Unfortunately, this perception is often glorified and promoted by music and pop culture.

Resources

Many of the conditions mentioned above relate directly or indirectly to money. Middle-class families can afford better health care and homes. They can provide healthy meals, and can usually avoid unhealthy air and unsanitary conditions. They are often more stable than poor families, for whom moving from house to house and school to school disrupts everyone involved. They can also provide transportation to events and to school, giving their children more time for other activities.

Beyond basic needs, the supplemental resources that middle-class parents can afford create another divide between their children and the children of poor parents. Middle-class children have more books in the home, more art and educational toys, more access to computers and electronic resources, and many more opportunities to participate in sports, art, music, dance, travel, and other activities. Not only do poorer children not have access to this variety of stimulation, some are also forced to remain inside for safety reasons while their middle-class peers can either play outside or participate in other activities. These differences in opportunity dramatically increase the divergence in the amount of television children watch. Watching television is an activity with few redeeming qualities—it decreases vocabulary and creativity, increases attention disorders, and can lead to poor health by encouraging too much snacking and too little exercising.

Summers present the same problems as school afternoons for poorer families, particularly those headed by single parents, in that middle-class children have opportunities denied to the poor. Both single-parent and dual-parent families who work full time and who can't afford a summer camp may end up leaving their children to their own devices for long stretches during the summer. This may lead to too much television watching, too few positive and stimulating activities, and too many opportunities to get into trouble. But middle-class families are more likely to have a parent available to stay at home or to have the wherewithal to put their children in camps, which provide both a safe environment and stimulating activities for the children. Even for teenagers, jobs and social activities are more available in the suburbs and in more affluent city areas.

Finally, Rothstein notes a phenomenon documented by Coleman and mentioned above: that the population of a school is also correlated with student success. "Ambitions make a difference. . . . Lower-class children achieve less if the share of low-income children in their schools is higher. The drop is most severe when the subsidized lunch population exceeds 40%."[31] Racial integration attempted to address this concern, among others, but led in too many instances to white flight and the resegregation of communities by both race and income. The economic segregation of our communities in particular—the poor getting poorer, the rich richer, and many in the middle class struggling not to slide backwards—may portend increases in the achievement gap rather than decreases.

ADDRESSING THE PROBLEMS OF THE ACHIEVEMENT GAP

A long-circulating truism holds that the number most likely to predict a child's success in school is his zip code. Good schools exist in many places, but the schools with the highest test scores tend to be located in the wealthiest communities. Many of the challenges behind the achievement gap that urban schools face are not within the purview of schools to address, let alone solve. Schools alone cannot solve a problem that involves substandard housing, low wages, poor health care, and generations of family interactions that leave some children less prepared for school than their peers.

At the same time, as Barton and Rothstein point out and as Rosenthal and Ryan identified in a previous era, school factors must also be addressed to eliminate the achievement gap. These include the distribution of qualified teachers, the development of rigorous and relevant curricula, the use of growth measures of academic achievement, and the development of academic expectations based on each student's individual abilities and interests rather than on the basis of group membership.

Nothing in the argument above or the ones to follow should be construed to justify inequitable or wasteful practices at the schools. It is the case, however, that no school has the ability to solve all of the problems identified. If society wants to solve these problems, it will have to broaden its understanding of the factors behind student achievement and address the issues that prevent families from improving their lot. These include housing, health, safety, and opportunity as well as support for parents in creating a positive home environment.

Though some of this research is fairly new, or has quantified what was only suspected in the past, most of these factors have been well known for many years. Given this knowledge, it's hard to believe that anyone involved with education policy could take the official public position that all students should achieve at the same level and at the same time. Or that, if this success does not take place, the schools and teachers are accountable. Expectations are important, but they are not the only factor. Unfortunately, the implication of No Child Left Behind, and the stated belief of some policy makers, is that raising expectations will eliminate the achievement gap. It will not.

Poverty is not destiny, as many individuals and some schools have helped to demonstrate. Nearly all children can learn. It is also true, however, that each child is an individual—made up of interests, talents, emotions, and desires, and strongly influenced not only by the circumstances at school, where she spends a portion of her life, but also by her circumstances at home and in her community, where she spends much more of her life. Programs to help each child succeed must take all of these factors into account. One size of expectation will not fit all.

DEMOGRAPHICS AND TEACHER COMPENSATION

These differences among children are critically important when we design a teacher compensation system. Teachers in Denver and other cities have shown that they are willing to teach in inner-city schools. Denver's teachers and community have agreed that this willingness is worthy of consideration in the new compensation plan. Denver's teachers, district leaders, and voters have also agreed that individual teachers will set their own goals within their individual classrooms, a significant departure from the one size fits all model.

As with most other professions, teachers are as interested in their working conditions as in their level of pay, as described more completely in the next chapter. If children in inner-city schools don't come to school ready to learn and if, at the same time, teachers are expected to advance these children further than their peers in the middle class schools, it will sound like a lose-lose proposition. Many dedicated teachers have chosen to work with the needy populations because they care about these kids and enjoy the satisfaction of helping them succeed. These teachers, like others, are interested in higher pay and may well rise to challenges which they believe are achievable and which they have a hand in designing. By contrast, they will hardly look forward to the "challenge" of earning extra awards through an incentive system if they believe the expectations are unrealistic and unfair both to the students and themselves.

It is appropriate to expect districts, schools, and teachers to address school factors that impede student learning for poor and urban children (and for all other children), including teacher quality. Addressing some of these factors may require additional funding, and to that extent state or federal government should also be expected to contribute. Schools may even be able to address some of the other factors identified, though clearly not all. What is not appropriate is to hold schools and teachers responsible for solving problems over which they have no control, or to place the "crisis" of the achievement gap at the schoolhouse door.

Even if policy makers choose to ignore the differences among children, good teachers will not. They will not work in schools where they believe the expectations are unrealistic, and will certainly not risk lower pay or other sanctions for failing to advance some kids to the level of their better prepared peers. If we are to achieve the goals of a revised teacher compensation system, it is critical to understand how standards and expectations for students interact with student and school demographics. Teachers certainly understand this dynamic, and no performance pay scheme will be successful unless it finds a way to address the realities of American society that enter the classroom.

NOTES

1. Iris C. Rotberg, "Quick Fixes, Test Scores and the Global Economy," *Education Week* 27, no. 41 (11 June 2008): 27, 32.

2. James S. Coleman et al., *Equality of Educational Opportunity* (Washington, DC: U.S. Department of Health, Education and Welfare, Office of Education, 1966).

3. Debra Viadero, "Race Report's Influence Felt 40 Years Later," *Education Week* 25, no. 41 (21 June 2006b): 1.

4. Debra Viadero, "Fresh Look at Coleman Data Yields Different Conclusions," *Education Week* 25, no. 41 (21 June 2006a): 21.

5. Robert Rosenthal and Lenore Jacobson, *Pygmalion in the Classroom* (New York: Holt, Rinehart, 1968).

6. Rosenthal and Jacobson, *Pygmalion in the Classroom*, 178.

7. Rosenthal and Jacobson, *Pygmalion in the Classroom*, 181.

8. Rosenthal and Jacobson, *Pygmalion in the Classroom*, 179.

9. Rosenthal and Jacobson, *Pygmalion in the Classroom*, 182; Donald B. Gratz, "Leaving No Child Behind," *Education Week* 22, no. 40 (11 June 2003): 27, 36.

10. Jonathan Kozol, *Death at an Early Age* (Boston: Houghton Mifflin, 1967).

11. William Ryan, *Blaming the Victim* (New York: Vintage, 1971), 33.

12. Ryan, *Blaming the Victim*, 38.

13. Ryan, *Blaming the Victim*, 42.

14. Ryan, *Blaming the Victim*, 47–53.

15. Heather G. Peske and Kati Haycock, *Teaching Inequality: How Poor and Minority Students Are Shortchanged on Teacher Quality* (Washington, DC: Education Trust, June 2006), 9.

16. Peske and Haycock, *Teaching Inequality*, 11.

17. Peske and Haycock, *Teaching Inequality*, 15.

18. "Teacher Quality Important, But Cannot Overcome Poverty," *FairTest Examiner* August 2006, FairTest. Accessed 16 July 2007 at www.fairtest.org/examarts/August%202006/Teacher%Quality.html.

19. Jennifer B. Presley and Bradford R. White, *Public Policy Research Report*, 2005, Illinois Education Research Council (IERC). Accessed 16 July 2007 at http://ierc.edu/documents/Teacher%Quality%20IERC%202005-2.pdf.

20. Peske and Haycock, *Teaching Inequality*, 11.

21. Presley and White, *Public Policy Research Report*.

22. Paul Barton, "Why Does the Gap Persist?" *Educational Leadership* 62, no. 3 (November 2004): 8.

23. Barton, "Why Does the Gap Persist?"

24. Richard Rothstein, *Class and Schools: Using Social, Economic and Educational Reform to Close the Black-White Achievement Gap* (Washington, DC: Economic Policy Institute, 2004), 4.

25. Richard Rothstein, "Class and the Classroom," *American School Board Journal* 191, no. 10 (October 2004b): 4.

26. Mary Otto, "For Want of a Dentist," *Washington Post,* 28 February 2007: B01. Accessed 15 February 2008 atwww.washingtonpost.com.

27. Barton, "Why Does the Gap Persist?" 9.

28. Paul Tough, "What It Takes to Make a Student," *New York Times,* 26 November 2006. Accessed 26 November 2006 atwww.nytimes.com; Betty Hart and Todd R. Risley, *Meaningful Differences in the Everyday Experience of Young Children* (Baltimore, MD: Paul R. Brookes Publishing Co., 1995).

29. Rothstein, *Class and Schools*; Hart and Risley, *Meaningful Differences in the Everyday Experience of Young Children*.

30. Betty Hart and Todd R. Risley, "The Early Catastrophe," *Education Review* 17, no. 1 (Autumn 2003): 114.

31. Rothstein, *Class and Schools*, 130.

8

Motivation and Work

The biggest problem with financial incentives is that they are tremendously over-used. Incentives has emerged as the first answer to almost every problem. Are your schools failing? Bribe teachers with incentive pay. Is the medical system ineffi-cient, with vast differences in treatment protocols for the same disease in different regions? Set up a managed care system that provides financial incentives to doc-tors, insurers, patients, and hospitals. Bad customer service? Provide financial in-centives for better customer service. Airplanes not flying on time? Pay employees if the plans fly on time. Too much overtime in garbage collection? Give truck driv-ers a financial incentive to finish early. Stock price not high enough? Give senior management financial incentives to get the stock price up. And on and on it goes, often with disastrous results.[1]

> *Even people who ain't too clever*
> *can learn to tighten a nut forever,*
> *attach one pedal or pull one lever . . .*
> *and that's the vision of Henry Ford . . .[2]*

The assumptions of test-based performance pay for individual teachers as a means to increase student achievement have already been described. They include a set of attitudes towards work and behavior: that work is not rewarding in its own right so people work mostly for money, that people will work harder if the rewards are greater, and that people work hard mainly for extrinsic rewards rather than intrinsic.

This is an extension of the "rational actor" economic theory, which as-sumes that people will act rationally in their own interests, and which de-fines those interests primarily as pay and prestige. With regard to teaching, pay is the reward most often proposed, and this proposition reduces to a few points: First, schools are in crisis—something needs to be done. Second,

155

because teachers are not paid according to the results they produce, they have no incentive to try hard. Without this incentive, and given unsatisfactory results, it is clear that many teachers are not trying hard. To achieve better results, teachers clearly need to try harder. Third, teachers will try harder when the financial rewards are greater for those who succeed. Trying harder may simply mean that teachers work harder, or it may mean that they think more creatively, but the concept is fundamentally tied to a belief in spurring greater effort through financial incentives.

Further, the concept of success through motivation (trying harder) assumes that skills, knowledge, support, and resources needed to do better are not at issue, and that schools and teachers have sufficient control over circumstances to effect significant change. Thus, teachers already know how to get kids to learn more or perform better on tests, they are simply not applying themselves because they don't have an incentive to do so—they get paid the same regardless of how well their students perform. To get teachers to apply themselves more strenuously—to try harder—we need only increase the reward for those who achieve (or the punishment for those who do not).

A parallel set of assumptions addresses the need to recruit the "best" college graduates into teaching. Many believe that the best college graduates choose not to enter teaching because the pay is low and that these graduates—motivated to compete for high wages because they are the best—don't see the potential for getting ahead financially in education. If they saw that potential—if they believed they could do a better job and rise to the top by being excellent teachers—they would be more motivated to teach.

It is likely that most policy makers have a less jaundiced view of teachers (and of humankind) than these propositions suggest. Still, these beliefs regarding human motivation provide the foundation for performance pay, and they need to be explored. Anyone who does not believe in these assumptions should reconsider his or her support for performance pay, or should modify that support—as many have done—and perhaps consider an alternate form of differentiated compensation.

Proponents believe that schools should function as businesses do. Driven by competition, a capitalist approach to work, and a financially motivated workforce (in this view), business provides a model that will lead to harder-working teachers, better schools, and more accomplished students (as demonstrated on standardized tests). In business, they say, workers are primarily judged on how much they produce, and rewarded if they produce more.

Unfortunately, this belief is based on several myths that undercut its conclusions. Business use of incentive pay, which Rothstein called uncommon in 2000, has been increasing according to Pfeffer and Sutton (2006). But it tends to suppress rather than to enhance performance.[3] Furthermore, most of the research into human motivation indicates that money is not the primary motivator for most workers—whether in business or in other fields. It is also true that worker productivity and financial rewards are not closely linked in business, as described previously.

Not surprisingly, most teachers don't subscribe to this belief system, though many do support aspects of performance pay and accountability. This chapter explores the research on human motivation and the practices of business with regard to motivating employees. It ends with a review of teachers' attitudes towards performance pay in Denver and elsewhere.

EARLY MANAGEMENT AND MOTIVATION

The problems of management and human motivation are nearly as old as history, stretching back to early civilizations. Until relatively recently, however, most individuals or families worked simply to feed and clothe their own families—they worked to assure their own survival. There were systems of barter and villagers often supported each other, but people who were not serfs or servants decided when and how much to work. Their earnings were directly related to the quantity and quality of their work.

The work structure changed little until the late 1700s, when factories began to replace small farms and subsistence villages, and the number of people working for someone else (the factory owners) increased. The growth of factories led to larger workforces, increasing the divide between labor and management. Factory productivity became an issue, but unlike the farm or a barter system, factory productivity did not directly affect the individual worker, who was paid a wage. Early attitudes towards motivation were largely intuitive, as Peach and Wren observe, "symbolized by the myths and tales such as the donkey driver who used both carrot and stick."[4]

Incentives are an ancient psychological tool, nonetheless. Hammurabi's code (eighteenth-century B.C.) includes reference to incentives for merchants. In the reign of Nebuchadnezzar, King of Babylonia around 600 B.C., weavers were paid with food, the greatest amount going to the most productive weavers. In the height of the Greek civilization, Aristotle and Plato both advocated a form of sharing and respect for the common good, but Aristotle criticized Plato's advocacy of common ownership of property and a common living for all because it did not provide incentive.[5]

Beginning in the latter stages of the Roman Empire and stretching through the Middle Ages, the concept of a "just price" for services developed. The Church adopted this policy, setting prices for goods and services. Though sometimes ignored, the policy tended to keep incentives low.[6] From the Middle Ages until the industrial revolution, however, incentives existed in the form of piecework, through the individually based economic system that kept most villages afloat.

Artisans and craftsmen were paid based both on the amount of work they performed and the quality of that work. A farmer brought raw wool to one person for carding and spinning and another for weaving. Incentives were self-imposed in such a system: the faster and better one could do the job, the more business one was likely to have (assuming there was competition).[7] Educators were also individual operatives, more often than not, from the early Greek and Roman civilizations through the scholars of medieval Europe to the individual teachers hired at the one-room village school in rural America.

Beginning in the 1700s, industrialization caused new systems of labor to emerge and new theories of labor management and organization to develop. Some of these appear to have been class based: the middle and upper classes viewed the lower classes as substantially different in terms of motivation and industry. For example, the "mercantilist" economists of the 1700s believed in the "hungry man" theory: workers labored to feed themselves, but if they accumulated more money than was necessary they would stop work and spend it until it ran out.

This convenient theory affirmed that the most effective practice for both owners and workers was to keep workers at subsistence wages. "It is a fact well known," one mercantilist confirmed, ". . . that scarcity, to a certain degree, promotes industry . . . a reduction of wages in the woolen manufacture would be a national blessing and advantage, and no real injury to the poor. By this means we might keep our trade, uphold our rents, and reform the people in the bargain." Adam Smith, whose approach was based on an assumption often known as the "economic man," disagreed: "The wages of labor are the encouragement of industry . . . [and] where wages are high, accordingly we shall always find the workmen more active, diligent, and expeditious than where they are low."[8]

During this same period, Malthus predicted that wages in excess of subsistence would lead to geometric population growth that would outpace the food supply. His view of impending disaster if the population was not kept in check gained notoriety at the time, and contributed to decreased support for the poor, including wages. Arguments proceeded about whether people would work harder if paid more, whether higher pay would attract better workers to begin with, and whether, for that reason, the highest paid labor might be the cheapest because of its greater productivity.

ORGANIZATIONAL THOUGHT IN THE INDUSTRIAL AGE

Scientific Management

Frederick Taylor is popularly considered the creator of incentive plans and many other factory-related innovations. He is also known as the father of organizational studies, which he conducted from 1880 into the second decade of the 1900s. His theories of "scientific management," which initially addressed the issue of productivity, soon became entwined with the closely aligned question of human motivation. Taylor's management process began with an overall plan for production, then broke the plan down into simple streamlined elements. Managers were to choose workers appropriate for the various tasks, and to establish a differentiated system whereby faster, more productive, or more skilled workers were paid more. The system was then managed by production supervisors.[9]

Although Taylor believed in "intimate and friendly relations between workers and management," not particularly common at that time, he got his start attempting to combat "soldiering," a labor practice that kept production down. He did not believe in exploiting workers or even in the assembly line model, though he did visit Henry Ford's production plant and found it consistent with his theory. Nonetheless, his strict belief in differentiating tasks and labor sometimes led to exploitative bonus plans driven by unscrupulous or overpressured managers.[10]

Foreshadowing some of today's attitudes regarding group incentives for teachers, Taylor didn't believe in profit sharing among employees because all shared the profits equally, regardless of their contribution. In his view, this provided no incentive for each worker to contribute his maximum daily output.[11] Nonetheless, by studying work and considering how workers performed, Taylor was among the first to formally consider worker motivation.

Scientific management also included defining a standard unit of work and a standard unit of pay for that work. Taylor experimented with various incentives, such as establishing a base which all workers would be paid and creating incentives above it for the faster workers. He conducted experiments over many years, and was followed by many others—such as Henry Gantt, creator of the Gantt Chart, and the Gilbreths, who advanced the idea of time and motion studies.[12] Taylor's experiments to improve industrial efficiency primarily focused on the factory floor, including his experiments with worker compensation.

Faith in the ability of science to solve problems was widespread in the early part of the twentieth century, and many innovations also emerged away from the factory. For example, "scientific" tests to measure intelligence were first developed in this period, starting with the Army "Alpha" and leading to the Intelligence Quotient (IQ). Many of Taylor's colleagues and followers also expanded on or supplemented his views. Among these, Williamson identified the "social value" of pay, in which pay was important not just in itself but in relation to what others were getting paid. And Mathewson described some of the practices and beliefs that led to labor resistance, including the "lump of labor" belief—that there is only so much work in the world and if you do it too fast you'll be out of a job. This belief, along with punitive management practices in some settings, served to justify labor's fears about management tactics and job security.[13]

Human Relations and the Hawthorne Experiments

Perhaps the most well known experiments with productivity and motivation came out of the multiyear work at the Hawthorne Works plant in Pennsylvania, operated by Western Electric. Harvard's Elton Mayo developed a new theory that came to be known as the Human Relations School, based on his work at this plant. Through a series of now famous studies, Mayo discovered (1) that changes in the work environment could improve productivity and (2) that factory workers respond not simply to specific physical changes in their environment, but also to the opportunity to have some control over their working conditions and to interaction with other workers.

Mayo concluded that work is a group activity, and that group norms—the need for recognition, security, and belonging—are more important in worker morale and productivity than external rewards. He came to believe that worker attitudes and effectiveness are conditioned by social forces both within and outside of the factory. Mayo and his colleagues believed that his experiments at the Hawthorne factory proved that the "economic man" theory of the rational actor who responds to financial incentives was dead, supplanted by a "social man" reality.[14]

Mayo was followed by many others. Abraham Maslow identified a "hierarchy of needs" that starts with physical needs and safety, and ascends through affection and belonging, esteem (success and self-respect), and self-actualization. According to Maslow's theory, salaries are necessary for food and shelter, and physical working conditions make a difference, but "management reward systems are now, or should be, endeavoring to satisfy the individual's high level needs for esteem and self-fulfillment."[15]

Though various theories are still advanced regarding human motivation and the organization of work, the practice of human resource management has never really looked back. McGregor categorized the two basic theories of management as Theory X and Theory Y, and identified their assumptions.[16] Theory X is coercive, and assumes that:

the average human dislikes work and will avoid it if possible;
because they dislike work, most people must be coerced and threatened; and
most people prefer to be directed, and would rather have security than responsibility.

By contrast, the assumptions behind Theory Y are that:

work is as natural as play or rest;
if a job is satisfying, workers will commit to the organization;
under the proper conditions, most workers want and will seek responsibility; and
many workers use imagination and creativity to solve work problems.

Experiments in compensation continued in many settings. In the 1980s, during a period of economic strength in Japan, Japanese management practices became popular in the United States. Sometimes known as Theory Z, these practices build on a Theory Y approach, emphasizing teamwork and cooperation over individual job ownership and competition. Though evidence suggests that financial structures were as much responsible for Japan's success (and later failure) as its management systems, the concept of teams as a management strategy has continued to grow and remains popular to this day.

CONTEMPORARY MOTIVATIONAL THEORY

Most initial theories of management were less about worker motivation than about production and organization. From the 1960s forward, however, more attention has been given to theories of motivation—drawing from the Hawthorne and subsequent experiments—and the two areas have increasingly become one. Most current discussions of human motivation have been built on the Human Relations theory and its successors.

In the 1960s, Herzberg identified two types of motivation he labeled Hygiene Factors (extrinsic) and Motivators (intrinsic). Hygiene factors include the work environment: the company, policies, supervisory style, working conditions, status, salary, and security. These factors do not motivate, but can lead to dissatisfaction. Motivators include achievement, recognition, growth or advancement, and interest in the job. These are largely internal. To motivate employees, both sets of factors must be in place. Employees must believe that they are well and fairly treated to minimize dissatisfaction, but work must also be arranged to provide achievement, recognition, interest, and responsibility if the workers are to be truly motivated.

Also in the 1960s, Vroom introduced the "expectancy theory": people should be rewarded in ways that they believe to be important, which may vary from individual to individual. One worker may want a salary increase, while another places more value on a promotion, and managers should plan accordingly.[17] The key in this theory, as in many others, is what the worker expects as a result of his work. "At the heart of this relationship," as English describes, "lies the *expectation* that action X will lead to outcome Y."[18] A substantial body of research has developed on this theory, according to Heneman, which relies on three levels of expectation necessary to motivate: the worker needs to believe that he can do the job on his own (that his action will lead to a particular outcome), that a reward will be forthcoming as a result, and that the reward has value. If one of these components is missing, the worker is not motivated.[19]

Other psychological and economic theories have also been developed: *Equity theory* looks at the reward relative to the particular organization and field. An example of equity theory is sports salaries, where the player is motivated not by the amount he is paid—often far in excess of anything he could possibly need—but by the equity he perceives compared to others of a similar talent level in his sport or position. The same principle applies to teachers or workers in any other field.[20]

Other theories address other potential aspects of motivation. *Goal-setting theory* suggests that people work harder to reach goals they have a hand in setting, a concept that may relate to Denver's experience. The *job characteristics model* proposes that motivation and satisfaction are closely related to meaningfulness, which depends on the significance of the job and the relationship of the worker to the process. That is, people who are more aware of the entire job and whose role is larger or more significant are likely to be more motivated. Rosabeth Kanter developed an *empowerment* model after studying "environments that stimulate people to act." Her model incorporates aspects of theories and models already mentioned, including expectancy and the setting of goals, as empowering workers. Many of these theories, while broadly applicable, have not been tested in education.[21]

Efficacy theory, another theory with similar roots, has more extensive application in education settings. It postulates that workers are more effective if they believe they can be effective. Some studies have shown that workers' behavior and motivation are closely related to their effectiveness as they perceive it. Both students' and teachers' behavior can be predicted, according to this research, based on their perceived efficacy.[22] The conditions that create efficacy include self-actualization, empowerment, and respect within the social/professional network. Though much derided by conservative pundits as part of a liberal and substance-less "self-esteem" movement, efficacy in children has also been shown to be important in the learning process. (This echoes Coleman's conclusion that a student's sense of control over his own destiny is a major contributor to his achievement.)

Researchers continue to look at human behaviors and the attributes of particular organizations, but research in the last quarter century has not replaced the understanding that teamwork, group norms, a feeling of accomplishment, control over the environment, and similar workplace conditions are critical to motivators. As a prominent international consulting organization observes, "The traditional Victorian style of strict discipline and punishment has not only failed to deliver the goods, but has also left a mood of discontent amongst the working class."[23] That is, the "stick" does not work. As for the "carrot," a good salary is important but not a key motivating factor for most people in their day-to-day work; other, more important factors are involved. No accepted theory of worker motivation remains in which humans are motivated primarily by extrinsic factors.

PERFORMANCE PAY IN BUSINESS

Businesses use a range of approaches to performance pay, including group incentives, individual merit pay (based on supervisor evaluation and employee goals), and strict performance-based pay. Some organizations, such as the consulting firm Bain & Company described earlier, use a complex evaluative system that considers a range of attributes from several viewpoints. This process is presumably more fair and equitable, and less subject to bias, though that is not guaranteed.

On the other end of the scale is strict performance pay for particular jobs—jobs involving piecework of some sort, including sales. The few studies that have been done on performance pay have been associated with piecework. These did not occur until the 1960s, and initially consisted of individuals performing rote and artificial tasks, such as college students hired to perform meaningless tasks solely for the purpose of the study. The research has matured, and some studies demonstrate that under certain circumstances higher pay can motivate workers to be more productive.[24] These circumstances are specific, however, and must meet the following conditions:

The job must be something within the worker's control.
The goal must be specific and clear to both worker and management.
There must be a clear and direct connection between the work performed and the result obtained; that is, it must be clear to the worker what he must do to obtain the reward, and that it is possible for him to do it.

Murnane and Cohen provide the following example. Two workers are loading boxes into a truck and the conditions are the same (the boxes are the same weight, the distance between the boxes and truck is the same, the trucks are the same size, and so forth). If one worker loads twenty-five boxes and another loads twenty, everyone understands why the first worker gets paid more. A payment system that pays more for twenty-five boxes loaded than twenty is seen as fair by all parties. This situation answers two critical questions for a successful pay for performance system: Why does worker X get merit pay and I don't? What can I do to get merit pay?[25] If these conditions are not met, or if circumstances for the workers are different, such as heavier boxes or a greater distance to carry them, this acceptance breaks down. Given the multitude of circumstances in classrooms of different schools—and often even in the same school—this point is relevant in education.

Though incentive pay of this type continues to be available, business leaders have increasingly moved away from such systems, at least until recently. The Japanese concept of teams, and the quality movement introduced in the 1980s and still much favored in business today, were designed to build greater team spirit and intrinsic motivation rather than simply bestowing rewards.

Pfeffer argues that the economic models upon which incentive theory is based "portray work as hard and aversive—implying that the only way people can be induced to work is through some combination of rewards and sanctions." Instead, he asserts that the opposite is true; that work can be empowering if the conditions are right: "Companies that have successfully transcended the myths about pay know that pay cannot substitute for a working environment high on trust, fun, and meaningful work."[26] Therefore, even in traditional business, according to Pfeffer,

> [d]espite the evident popularity of this practice, the problems with individual merit pay are numerous and well documented. It has been shown to undermine teamwork, encourage employees to focus on the short term, and lead people to link compensation to political skills and ingratiating personalities rather than to performance. Indeed, those are among the reasons why W. Edwards Deming and other quality experts have argued strongly against using such schemes.[27]

MOTIVATING TEACHERS AND OTHER KNOWLEDGE WORKERS

Schools are often seen as employing a loose factory system. Each teacher is given twenty-five students to process and hand on to the next teacher a year later. In this model, testing children at the end of a year makes some sense. In fact, however, the conditions are often significantly different from one classroom and school to the next, since different children are involved. Teachers know this, of course, so unlike workers loading boxes, they do not believe they can achieve better results simply by working harder. Certainly Denver's teachers argue strongly that they entered teaching for the intrinsic rewards rather than the pay.

Teachers and professors, along with an increasing number of people in other professions, are sometimes called knowledge workers or "mind workers."[28] They function in a different environment from workers in other professions. The classic comparison comes from Bolman and Deal's *Reframing Organizations* (1991), in which they compare McDonald's restaurants and Harvard University—each an exemplary organization of its type. They note that McDonald's exists to promote efficiency and consistency. A Big Mac in Chicago or New York, or even Moscow, should be the same as a Big Mac elsewhere. Managers and employees at a McDonald's have "limited discretion about how to do their jobs" and "cooks are not encouraged to develop new versions of the Big Mac or the Quarter-Pounder." In fact, the mission of McDonald's is specific and limited, and the company is highly centralized despite its international reach. Front-line workers are among the lowest-paid workers, and are supposed to perform the tasks assigned.

Harvard University, by contrast, is decentralized even though it is geographically compact. Each individual school sets its own curriculum, raises its own funds, and "controls its own destiny." Further, "individual professors have enormous autonomy and discretion." Professors design their individual classes in the context of curricula that are controlled largely by the professors as a group. The value of the program resides not in the decisions made by the central administration, by and large, but in the decisions made by individual faculty members, who are each experts in their own domains.[29] Though school teachers do not have the same level of autonomy (and though that autonomy has diminished in recent decades) their success is also dependent on their own skills, attitudes, and experience, as with Harvard's professors.

The other point to be made about knowledge workers is that they are more likely to be members of professions in which professional norms, standards, and expectations hold great sway. This is true of education, health, mental health, and the "helping professions," as well as law and accounting. These professions are characterized by ethics, standards, and goals developed over time, and members are likely to be motivated, at least in part, by their professional expectations.

Based on their history, described in previous chapters, public schools are arranged more like McDonald's than Harvard, with a factory-like division of labor and a specific curriculum to be taught at every level. Most teachers consider themselves part of a profession, however, and have levels of responsibility (if not autonomy) more like Harvard's. The factory similarity has increased as states have prescribed more and more of the curriculum. Periodically, new curricular methods are introduced that push this similarity even further, from the "teacher-proof" curriculum of several decades ago to programs like *Success for All* today. In search of the perfect curriculum or the *one best system*, to use Tyack's term, some argue for a more McDonald's-like structure, in which activities specified to the smallest detail by a central authority are to be carried out as prescribed by the front-line workers—the teachers.

While some standardization of the curriculum may make sense, this concept of schooling is at sharp odds with classroom reality. Children learn and react differently, and are highly complex beings. Teacher skill and knowledge are essential to effective teaching. Teachers need to know not just the subject at hand, but the learning process, child development, the backgrounds and cultures represented among their students, how to address the special needs of different students in their classes, and effective instructional methods. McDonald's, by contrast, offers people who enter its restaurants a limited range of products, and it strives to present these products without variation. Its front-line workers need little training and exercise little discretion.

This institutional divide continues to create confusion around the teaching profession, and leads to discontent among teachers. The structure of the profession comes from the early part of the twentieth century, and is highly industrial, but both the work and expectations for teachers have changed significantly since that time. Teachers, parents, students, and society are all concerned that students learn many things—from subjects to attitudes to skills—and that teachers adapt their presentation based on their own skills, knowledge, and their ability to understand what students need.

Given this, it should not be surprising that teachers resist a payment plan that draws from attitudes of a century past, and in which their activities are consigned to a small set of goals. And they do resist, consistently indicating support for accountability if it is fair and appropriate, but rejecting the piecework implications of strict performance pay. Part of that resistance may be due to fear of losing income or their jobs, but even when the pay is in the form of a bonus, teachers reject the motivational aspect of it.

Not enough research has been done on teacher attitudes to demonstrate the efficacy of different performance pay plans or to fully understand teachers' attitudes towards them. Hodge notes, for example, that teachers tend to have a favorable view of performance pay programs in which they have participated, but it is not clear whether this approval covers the plans as a whole or the motivational aspect of financial incentives.[30] As CTAC found in Denver, there is a difference (see below). A poll commissioned by the Teaching Commission, which favors performance pay, nonetheless found that neither teachers nor the public support it. In fact, while 86 percent of teachers surveyed favored raising teacher pay, only 13 percent believed it should be tied to test scores. When the survey asked the same question of a broader sample of the adult population, the result was a similar split in opinion: 70 percent supported raising salaries, while 41 percent favored linking them to test scores.[31]

DENVER TEACHERS' ATTITUDES

Surveys and interviews of Denver teachers during its pilot showed that even the pilot's strongest supporters did not believe they were working harder. Teachers dismissed this idea for two reasons. First, they were already working as hard as they could, they said, putting long hours into preparation. Second, even if this had not been the case, the small amount of money involved would not have been sufficient incentive to work harder. At the same time, teachers in the pilot came to believe that both they and their schools were more focused on student learning, that this focus led to better results for students whether these results showed up on standardized tests or not, and that the pilot's emphasis on content-based learning objectives, data, and individual growth had improved their success.[32]

Respondents at all levels agreed that the emphasis on learning and achievement (and the increasingly sophisticated support provided by the Design Team) spurred schools to focus more directly on issues of achievement, provided a tool that principals could use to discuss achievement with teachers, and often created a more organized schoolwide effort in support of reading, writing, and math. This result appears to have had less to do with rewarding performance and more with providing support, data, and specific techniques for applying what is known about learning at the school and classroom level. The district's partial realignment around increased support for the schools—particularly the new attention paid to setting learning objectives in the context of school goals—yielded a more concentrated effort at many of the pilot schools.

Thus, improvement in Denver came about primarily for three reasons: individual teachers learned new skills (particularly objective setting), schools focused more clearly on teaching and learning, and the pilot led to substantial improvement in the district's curricular alignment, school support, and assessment. Most of these changes did not have a direct relationship to teacher motivation. Even though PFP was the vehicle for these changes, the steps that appear to have brought about improvement did not require incentive pay. CTAC's study does not conclude that teacher motivation based on increased compensation was a vital factor; instead, it was the new skills gained plus the organizational focus and support that brought about improvement.[33]

In fact, what worked best for teachers were other motivational factors identified in the theories above as most salient to all workers. They were given tools to help them do a better job, were brought together around a common goal, and were asked to use their expertise and knowledge of their students to set objectives. This was not done without oversight, but it was done with the active involvement of teachers.

RECRUITMENT AND RETENTION

So far, this discussion has addressed the motivation of teachers to do a better job by working or trying harder. We focus on motivation because many state plans are founded on the notion of teacher motivation through monetary rewards. A related goal of performance pay is to attract the best teachers into the field and retain them once they have become teachers. These are both laudable goals and are challenges in many districts.

Many of the studies and reports referenced in earlier chapters recommended higher pay for all teachers along with some form of accountability. Stated in that vague form, such a proposal could win the (guarded) support of many teachers, as well as administrators and policy makers. Higher pay might lure more young college graduates into teaching (though people who enter the helping professions are not motivated primarily by money). Most teachers also claim an interest in accountability.

In the abstract, therefore, this idea has traction. The three primary problems in developing a specific proposal are: the nature of the accountability, the respect and support new teachers believe is accorded to the profession, and the conditions of the teaching profession as it exists today.

Suppose a young college graduate with a strong academic record is looking at the range of possibilities open to her. What does she see and what should she see?

- Does she see high pay, or reasonable pay? Would higher pay make her more likely to try teaching?
- Does she see opportunity for growth?
- Does she see a field that is respected in the community, and a position in which she will receive the support and scope she might find in other professions?
- Does she see an opportunity to use her subject area knowledge and skill?
- Does she see the opportunity for fulfillment and self-actualization?
- Does she see a supportive professional environment?
- Does she think she can succeed with her students, and make a difference?

The list of questions could continue, but the answer to too many is probably no. Though this prospective new teacher does not see high pay or the opportunity to make a fortune, she may see pay that is adequate (especially for a student who has majored in the liberal arts). But she may also see a profession that is bashed constantly by those who claim to support it—a profession in which she is not expected to use her own intelligence and knowledge of her subject, but rather to teach to pre-set standards, using a pre-set curriculum and materials. She may also see expectations that are unreasonable, with too little support. Why would a math major want to enter teaching if she is being told what to think about math? Why would this talented college graduate take a position in which her professionalism would not be valued?

It is possible that a significantly higher salary and room for advancement would increase the number of these high-value recruits, just as the potential for earnings in law may attract some to the law profession who would not otherwise be interested in it. But given the respect and conditions of the profession, this is not at all clear. Similarly, this young graduate might easily look at the teaching profession as it now stands, and say to herself, "I want to make a difference, and I'm not sure I can do it here." In fact, I recently heard exactly that message from one very promising young prospective teacher. She saw a public education too bogged down in bureaucracy and tests and too controlled by external constraints to allow her to teach, so she went to work for less money at a private school that shared her philosophy.

Similarly, the reasons teachers give for leaving the profession have less to do with pay and more with lack of support, feeling overwhelmed, and working conditions. Higher pay could help, but in a performance-based system, most beginning teachers would not expect to earn additional pay in the first few years, as they are still learning the job. What is more likely to help, as has been widely discussed in research but for which the funding is often insufficient, is the support and mentoring any young professional needs to translate theory and training into practice. The new teacher must see that she will be helped to improve, so that she can make a difference and gain the sense of professional self-respect and efficacy that is important to all who consider themselves professionals.

CONCLUSION: WHAT MOTIVATES TEACHERS?

Research about people in organizations provides a wide range of both data and speculation regarding what motivates people. It seems clear, however, that while pay and other extrinsic motivators are necessary, they are not sufficient. That is, people need to be paid and to believe that their pay is appropriate relative to their profession. They also need to believe that pay levels for the profession are sufficient and may leave if they are not. But pay, in itself, is not enough to motivate teachers or most other workers. Lack of pay may undermine motivation, therefore, but additional pay does not provide it.

A range of human factors account for motivation, most of which are generated intrinsically. However, managers can create the conditions in which these intrinsic motivations flourish. Beyond physical conditions, these include the belief that the work is worthwhile (sharing company goals), some ability to control the environment (empowerment), participation in and respect from peers as well as management, a sense of belonging to a group, and the belief that the person is making a difference (leading to fulfillment) and is competent (efficacy).

From the management point of view, this suggests a style that is collegial rather than authoritarian. The international management consulting firm Accel-Team provides the following "tools" in its "management toolkit" of motivators, in order of importance:

- approval;
- trust, respect, and high expectations;
- loyalty, given that it may be received;
- job enrichment;
- good communications; and
- cash incentives.[34]

This approach acknowledges that much motivation is intrinsic, as Kohn, Pfeffer, and many others have pointed out, both from education and business perspectives.[35] It also highlights that managers have some ability to create working conditions that foster intrinsic motivation, as well as to provide extrinsic motivators. Indeed, this is not a new concept. Elton Mayo predicted much the same thing in 1948, saying that factory managers would "someday realize that workers are not governed primarily by economic motives."[36]

The question to be asked is not whether performance pay will motivate teachers, but what conditions of teaching—including pay—satisfy the motivational requirements that good teachers seek in employment. Is teaching a respected profession? What do teachers need to be effective and satisfied? How can we offer the list of motivators above?

Teachers do not enter the profession expecting to get rich. People who pursue that goal do not consider teaching as a career, nor do they enter the other helping or arts and culture professions. Salaries are important to teachers, as they are to others, but in the context of the group and with regard to professional respect. That is, teachers are group oriented. Despite concerns about needing to professionalize the profession (both legitimate and not), a strong norm persists within the teaching profession of concern for the student. It may be extinguished or diminished by poor working conditions, as in the stories of burnt-out teachers in distressed schools, but this interest in the student is why most teachers joined the profession to begin with. Motivational plans should start with this understanding in mind.

This chapter has examined what motivates workers, recognizing that while most workers are interested in financial remuneration, getting ahead in their organization or profession, the conditions of the job, and contributing in some way, most workers are not primarily motivated by money. Rather, they are people who consider the social and physical conditions of the job at least as important as pay (once pay reaches a satisfactory level).

Teachers fit this description well, perhaps even more than the average person. Because teaching has never been a profession in which anyone expects to become rich, it has not attracted people motivated by that kind of success. This is a good thing, as pressure on the teacher easily translates to pressure for efficiency, and (unlike on the factory floor) efficiency is as likely to undercut as to improve effectiveness in teaching children. Efficiency is a concept mostly of the factory model, of production, and the primary purpose of education should be development rather than production.

Studies of teacher attitudes have found that teachers find salary important, but less important than other conditions. The Public Agenda and the National Comprehensive Center for Teacher Quality report in a 2007 study that while 78 percent of the more than six hundred first-year teachers interviewed found salary either a major or minor drawback of the job, only a third saw it as a major drawback, and that "this concern ranks well below issues such as unmotivated students, testing and classroom discipline problems." However, the combination of low pay and a "difficult and daunting job" can push new teachers out of the profession.[37]

Teachers consistently say that money is not a motivator for them, even though they would like to be paid more. That is, they are working hard and trying hard. They'd like higher salaries, but they also want support in doing their job better and improved working conditions. With regard to retention, today's younger teachers are less bound to stay in a situation where they can't succeed, which is often a direct consequence of school conditions. As Susan Moore Johnson notes, "Often, they've chosen teaching because it means more [to them] and they want to work with young people. If conditions preclude their success in these classrooms, they're much more likely to leave than their predecessors."[38] Teachers' definitions of success and the impact of No Child Left Behind should be considered in this context.

Based on all of the foregoing, it is not surprising that performance pay, as a standalone reform, has not worked well in education. It is more encouraging that conditions including pay may be improved both to attract good teachers and help students learn, if that is the road we choose to follow. Denver's new plan, plus discussions and experiments around many of the alternative forms of performance pay, provide hope that improvements in the profession and conditions of schooling can be combined to enhance the effectiveness of teachers and the broad array of outcomes for students.

Society is (or should be) less interested in the consistent presentation of a curriculum than it is in whether children are growing and learning. But each individual's view on this point relates to his or her view of the purpose of schools. The factory model of schools and performance pay are closely aligned with the concept of a school producing products rather than developing individuals. If schools are producing products (with the implications of similarity of each product and of quality control), one approach is required. If they are developing individuals, another approach is implied. Teachers understand this, and few are motivated by higher test scores for their students, since they don't see the overemphasis on test scores as in the students' best interests. If our goals are complex enough to embrace a range of desired outcomes, our structures, assessments, and compensation systems must be similarly complex.

NOTES

1. Jeffrey Pfeffer and Robert Sutton, *Hard Facts, Dangerous Half Truths and Total Nonsense: Profiting from Evidence-Based Management* (Harvard Business School Press, 2006), 129.

2. Stephen Flaherty and Lynn Ahrens, "Henry Ford," in *Ragtime: The Musical* (New York: RCA Victor, 1998).

3. Pfeffer and Sutton, *Hard Facts, Dangerous Half Truths and Total Nonsense*, 110.

4. E. Brian Peach and Daniel A. Wren, "Pay for Performance from Antiquity to the 1950s," in *Pay for Performance: History, Controversy and Evidence*, ed. Bill L. Hopkins and Thomas C. Mawhinney (Binghamton, NY: Haworth Press, 1992), 5.

5. Peach and Wren, "Pay for Performance from Antiquity to the 1950s."

6. Peach and Wren, "Pay for Performance from Antiquity to the 1950s," 7.

7. Peach and Wren, "Pay for Performance from Antiquity to the 1950s," 9.

8. Peach and Wren, "Pay for Performance from Antiquity to the 1950s," 10.

9. Peach and Wren, "Pay for Performance from Antiquity to the 1950s"; Cliff F. Grimes, "Historical Perspectives," in *Employee Motivation, the Organizational Environment and Productivity* (London: Accel-Team, 2006); David A. Whitsett and Lyle Yorks, *From Management Theory to Business Sense* (New York: Amacom, 1983); Daniel A. Wren, *The Evolution of Management Thought* (New York: John Wiley & Sons, 1979).

10. Whitsett and Yorks, *From Management Theory to Business Sense*, 81; Grimes, "Historical Perspectives," 38.

11. Peach and Wren, "Pay for Performance from Antiquity to the 1950s."

12. Whitsett and Yorks, *From Management Theory to Business Sense.*

13. Peach and Wren, "Pay for Performance from Antiquity to the 1950s," 18; Wren, *The Evolution of Management Thought*, 123.

14. Peach and Wren, "Pay for Performance from Antiquity to the 1950s," 19–23.

15. Grimes, "Historical Perspectives," 44.

16. Grimes, "Historical Perspectives," 46; Wren, *The Evolution of Management Thought*, 482–486.

17. Grimes, "Historical Perspectives," 55.

18. Fenwick English, "History and Critical Issues of Education Compensation Systems," in *Teacher Compensation and Motivation*, ed. Larry E. Frase (Lancaster, PA: Technomic Publishing, 1992), 16.

19. Robert L. Heneman, *Merit Pay: Linking Pay Increases to Performance Ratings* (Reading, MA: Addison-Wesley, 1992), 25–26.

20. English, "History and Critical Issues of Education Compensation Systems," 16.

21. Mary Rhodes and Rodney T. Ogawa, "Teacher Motivation, Work Structures and Organizational Change: Perspectives on Educational Reform and Compensation," in *Teacher Compensation and Motivation*, ed. Larry E. Frase (Lancaster, PA: Technomic Publishing, 1992), 62–67.

22. Rhodes and Ogawa, "Teacher Motivation, Work Structures and Organizational Change," 62–67.

23. Grimes, "Historical Perspectives," 56.

24. Peter Dolton, Steven McIntosh, and Arnaud Chevalier, *Teacher Pay and Performance* (London: Institute of Education, University of London, 2003); Heneman, *Merit Pay.*

25. Richard J. Murnane and David K. Cohen, "Merit Pay and the Evaluation Problem: Why Most Merit Pay Plans Fail and a Few Survive," *Harvard Education Review* 56, no. 1 (February 1986): 7.

26. Jeffrey Pfeffer, "Six Dangerous Myths About Pay," *Harvard Business Review* 76, no. 3 (1998): 3, 8.

27. Pfeffer, "Six Dangerous Myths About Pay," 5.

28. Charles Taylor Kerchner, Julia E. Koppich, and Joseph G. Weeres, *United Mind Workers: Unions and Teaching in the Knowledge Society* (San Francisco: Jossey-Bass, 1997).

29. Lee G. Bolman and Terrence E. Deal, *Reframining Organizations* (San Francisco: Jossey-Bass, 1991), 43–45.

30. Warren A. Hodge, *The Role of Performance Pay Systems in Comprehensive School Reform* (Lanham, MD: University Press of America, 2003).

31. Aaron Bernstein, "Lou Gerstner's Classroom Quest," *Business Week Online*, 7 April 2005: Daily Briefing. Accessed 6 June 2006 at http://web.ebscohost.com.odin.curry.edu/ehost/detail?vid=4&hid=102&sid=96a0c182-9e45-4839-865401d0f25d7157%40sessionmgr108&bdata=JnNpdGU9ZWhvc3QtbGl2ZQ%3d%3d#db=aph&AN=16756070.

32. Donald B. Gratz, William J. Slotnik, and Barbara J. Helms, *Pathway to Results: Pay for Performance in Denver* (Boston: Community Training & Assistance Center, 2001), 91; William J. Slot-

nik et al., *Catalyst for Change: Pay for Performance in Denver, Final Report* (Community Training & Assistance Center, January 2004), 106.

33. Slotnik et al., *Catalyst for Change*, 11.

34. Grimes, "Historical Perspectives," 56.

35. Alfie Kohn, *Punished by Rewards* (New York: Houghton Mifflin, 1993); Pfeffer and Sutton, *Hard Facts, Dangerous Half Truths and Total Nonsense.*

36. Grimes, "Historical Perspectives," 18.

37. Jonathan Rochkind et al., "Lessons Learned: New Teachers Talk About Their Jobs, Challenges and Long-Range Plans," *Public Agenda.* Accessed 17 October 2007 atwww.publicagenda .org.

38. Debra Viadero, "Working Conditions Trump Pay," *Education Week* 27, no. 18 (10 January 2008): 35–35.

9

Purposes and Goals

Culture is activity of thought and receptiveness to beauty and humane feeling. Scraps of information have nothing to do with it. A merely well informed man is the most useless bore on God's earth. . . . In training a child to activity of thought, above all things we must beware what I call "inert ideas"—that is to say, ideas that are merely received into the mind without being utilized, or twisted, or thrown into fresh combinations.[1]

WHY CONSIDER PURPOSES AND GOALS?

Performance pay is a relative concept. Pay is awarded relative to some standard or definition of performance. Performance itself is also relative, based on institutional or societal goals. If we have different goals, our definitions of excellent performance will also differ.

While academic standards now exist in all states, few people believe that these standards represent the entire range of school goals. Society wants more from its schools than academic performance. In addition, while standards-based instruction is widely accepted as a classroom strategy, people disagree on whether we need broadly applicable standards at all and whether the ones we have are the right ones. There is even greater disagreement about the effect and value of assessing these standards using high-stakes tests.

The public enterprise of education needs broad support to be successful. Community and business leaders need to support their schools, taxpayers need to fund them, and parents need to send their children to them. Though the parties may not agree in all particulars, this support requires a consensus as to basic school goals. When this consensus is not in place, as is now the case, conflict and discord often arise.

ORGANIZATIONAL PURPOSES

In organizing a school or other organization, purposes and goals give focus to the activities of employees and provide a benchmark around which to develop a structure. If an organization is achieving its purposes and meeting its goals, the activities it is engaged in are probably the right ones. If it is not, its leaders should ask whether its actions align with its goals.

A former colleague, the retired CEO of a large business, liked to say that "every organization is perfectly designed to achieve the results it's achieving." I've mentioned this saying to many people over the years, and have found that some resist it. But, in fact, an organization that consistently gets a certain result must be structured to achieve that result, regardless of the result it may be seeking. If the organization is not achieving the results it wants, its leaders need to consider where changes in its structure or practices would better align its actions with its goals.

In providing technical assistance to school districts and other organizations, CTAC calls this *organizational alignment*. The organization that regularly reviews its purposes, that structures itself around goals and objectives flowing from these purposes, that analyzes whether it is meeting its goals and objectives, and that redirects activities and resources based on this analysis, is well aligned. Such an organization—whether large or small, whether public or private—is the most likely to succeed.

The purpose of performance pay is to encourage teachers and administrators to change behaviors to do a better job. But unless that performance and those behaviors are clearly defined, performance pay is unlikely to achieve positive results. The purpose of purpose, in this context, should be clear. Along with our beliefs, discussed below, our purposes and goals shape our actions and provide the benchmarks against which we measure success. If we hope to improve schools, we must agree on what the purpose of school is and what specific goals we are pursuing.

IDENTIFYING PRIORITIES AND DEFINING PERFORMANCE

The public has generally supported raising academic standards, but not at the expense of other goals. This disagreement as to scope and what's important has led to many of today's controversies. As a first step in developing a performance pay plan, with its need for a clear and widely accepted definition of performance, it is critical that communities resolve the question of educational goals and expected performance. General agreement as to goals and measures is possible at the community level, as Denver's experience demonstrates.

To develop a consensus, school districts need to debate their goals and priorities for schools and students, ways to measure those goals, and links between the chosen goals and teacher performance. Though complete agreement is neither likely nor required, a consensus is needed for successful implementation of performance pay or any other major educational initiative. In fact, the need to define performance should demonstrate why changing teacher compensation is only part of a larger reform. It is in identifying goals and realigning organizational strategies, practices, and resources—including teacher compensation systems, if so desired—that organizational improvement comes about.

A compensation system that rewards some goals but not others will inevitably deemphasize the goals that are not rewarded, and will serve the organization poorly. This has already happened with the implementation of standards, but will increase if teacher compensation is added to the equation. If pay is linked closely to a small range of academic goals and a set of tests, any actions schools and teachers now take that serve to limit their focus to those goals and tests may be expected to increase. Similarly, current results and consequences—positive or negative, intended or not—may also be expected to increase. This raises the stakes for children, parents, and teachers, and heightens the need for a broad consensus on appropriate goals for schools to pursue. The divisions that have already been created by high-stakes testing and NCLB will only be further inflamed if the different points of view of stakeholders are not considered. Under such conditions, performance pay will not succeed.

For these reasons, all affected parties—teachers, administrators, parents, and students initially, plus members of the broader community—should be involved in determining the district's goals and purposes. Each of these groups has different needs and expectations for the schools, and all should have a voice in the debate. Given current controversies, reaching this agreement may require time and effort. However, many districts already engage the public when developing district and school plans, as they should. Defining teacher performance means revisiting school goals broadly, and determining what the community wants to achieve and how it might be measured. The remainder of this chapter focuses on school purposes and goals; the next chapter addresses means to assess progress towards these goals.

Performance pay develops from three questions asked in this process. First, what results do we want schools to achieve for students, families, and society? Second, how do we know whether we are achieving them (is it enough to say that test scores have gone up)? Third, how do we determine what impact teacher actions have had on the student results we value?

Without answers to these questions, we will not agree on what students are supposed to accomplish, will not know whether it has been accomplished, and will not be able to associate teacher performance to the results obtained. How can such a plan succeed? Teacher, student, and school performance can only be defined within this context. The history of performance pay outlined previously shows that without consensus around all three of these questions—a consensus which has rarely been developed and which requires a full discussion of organizational purposes—performance pay is unlikely to have a positive or lasting effect.

THE EVOLVING PURPOSE OF AMERICA'S PUBLIC SCHOOLS

The purpose of American schools has always been to educate children, but that has meant different things in different eras. In fact, the intense emphasis on academic standards is relatively new. Early one-room school houses were presided over mostly by young women, many of whom were barely literate themselves. They were supposed to teach students to read and do basic math, but it was often more important that they demonstrate appropriate comportment and behavior than educational skills. Having orderly and well-behaved children in schools was at least as important as having academically proficient ones.

Thomas Jefferson and other early leaders saw education as a means of promoting civilization, of transmitting the values of a new democratic society to new generations of citizens. But Jefferson didn't want a "civics lesson" that consisted only of the mechanics—how bills are passed, how long the president's term is, and so forth. Rather, he wanted to prepare citizens who could think critically and choose wisely. He proposed this vision for a public education system in Virginia:

> To give every citizen the information he needs for the transaction of his own business; to enable him to calculate for himself, and to express and preserve his ideas, his contracts and accounts in writing; to improve, by reading, his morals and faculties; to understand his duties to his neighbors and country, and to discharge with competence the functions confided to him by either; to know his rights; to exercise with order and justice those he retains, to choose with discretion the fiduciary of those he delegates; and to notice their conduct with diligence, with candor and judgment; and in general, to observe with intelligence and faithfulness all social relations under which he shall be placed.[2]

Jefferson believed students should read history ("apprising them of the past, will enable them to judge of the future") and that they should pursue instruction in reading, writing, and arithmetic. But he also saw education as voluntary, relatively short term, and adapted to the needs and interests of the students. After a few years of basic study, some would move into occupations while others would be selected for further academic study, ultimately including "Greek, Latin, geography and the higher branches of numerical arithmetic."[3] Jefferson believed, as was common at the time, that studying Greek and Latin was both a way to discipline or exercise the mind—a form of mental gymnastics—and an opening into the classics. After a period of further study, those with the ability and interest would go to college to pursue a course of their choosing. This was different from but not necessarily better than farming or other professions that required less school.

Jefferson's views were similar to many thinkers over the ages: that the goal of education is not for all children to end up with the same knowledge or skill. Rather, that basic skills and habits of mind should be taught at a young age, as children are encouraged to grow into adults with the ability and skill to think critically, to analyze, and to make sound decisions. "The general objects of this law," he wrote, "are to provide an education adapted to the year, to the capacity, and the conditions of every one, and directed to their freedom and happiness."[4] Clearly Jefferson saw education as having a strong individual purpose. Just as the Declaration of Independence affirmed the right of the people to "life, liberty and the pursuit of happiness," so education should be directed to the "freedom and happiness" of the individual.

John Adams, a principal writer of the Massachusetts Constitution (the oldest in the country), based his theories of education on somewhat similar beliefs, though with more emphasis on society's needs, plus Abigail Adams's observations on the plight of poor children in Boston. The Massachusetts Education Act of 1789, following Adams's outline, set forth that a system of public schools would exist "to impress on the minds of children and youth committed to their care and instruction, the principles of piety, justice and a sacred regard to truth, love to their country, humanity and universal benevolence, sobriety, industry, frugality, chastity, moderation and temperance, and those other virtues which are the ornament of human society and the basis upon which the republican Constitution is structured."[5]

These purposes for education endured into the nineteenth century, influenced in part by European writers such as Rousseau, but with an increasing focus on the path of the individual child. Writing in the late 1800s, Ralph Waldo Emerson urged teachers and schools to help each child develop into the adult he is destined to be.

> I believe that our own experience instructs us that the secret of Education lies in respecting the pupil. It is not for you to choose what he shall know, what he shall do. It is chosen and foreordained, and he only holds the key to his own secret. By your tampering and thwarting and too much governing he may be hindered from his end and kept out of his own. Respect the child.[6]

Each child has his own nature to pursue, according to Emerson; teachers should encourage this pursuit. This does not mean that skills should not be taught; reading, writing, and the precise skills and discipline of mathematics and science are needed. Once the child has these tools, however, "he can learn anything which is important to him now that the power to learn is secured: as mechanics say, when one has learned the use of tools, it is easy to work at a new craft." For Emerson, helping each child explore his own true nature and acquire the tools to pursue his interests and passions is the highest calling of education.[7]

Despite these individually oriented goals, the massive changes of the nineteenth century led the more immediate concerns of society to dominate. As immigration from other countries and migration of workers from the farm to the factory overwhelmed the cities, expectations for schools changed. School goals included teaching children to read, write, and add and to know a little science and history, but also increasingly focused on assuring that children learned their place in society—that children be sufficiently literate and sufficiently obedient to work in the factories. Irish and southern European immigrants arrived in overwhelming numbers as the century progressed—people of a different faith and often a different language from the current citizenry. Schools were enlisted to teach these newcomers American values—the values of current citizens and the existing social order.

The Organizational Structure of School

The structure of American education today dates from the mid-1800s, when it was imported from Prussia to bring order to a system that was overenrolled and chaotic in a society that was changing dramatically. Midnineteenth-century leaders in the United States were reacting to the greatest influx of immigrants the country has seen, as described in chapter 3, in which Boston saw the arrival of 37,000 Irish immigrants to join a population of 114,000 in a single year (1847),[8] and New York's massive immigration would develop into major gang wars between "nativists" and immigrants that terrorized large sections of the city (popularized by the movie *The Gangs of New York* and several books).[9]

Many civic leaders and citizens feared that their societal values could be overrun and that the country's relatively young experiment with democracy was in danger. In this context, schools were expected to educate students to the American way of life. Institutions of all types were created, in America as in Europe, including police and fire departments, workhouses for the indigent, hospitals, and mental asylums. Each of these had its specific purposes, but each was also designed to help keep the public order, schools not least among them.

"The first requisite of the school is *Order*," wrote William Harris, superintendent of the St. Louis schools and a major national figure in education, in 1871: "Each pupil must be taught first and foremost to conform his behavior to a general standard." Modern society, according to Harris, required "conformity to the time of the train, to the starting of work in the manufactory," and other activities of the industrialized age. "The pupil must have his lessons ready at the appointed time, must rise at the tap of the bell, move to the line, return; in short, go through all the evolutions with equal precision."

This discipline required standardizing schools into precision instruments which children moved through in an orderly and precise fashion—graded classrooms organized by age, specific regulations, a standard curriculum.[10] Schools were redesigned and eventually became mandatory in part because they were needed to teach discipline and moral values, not just basic skills, to a range of children and youth whom leading citizens feared could be out of control if not so instructed.

In the nineteenth century, many also believed that a child was "a lump of clay to be molded." It was explicitly the purpose of school to shape children to particular values and beliefs, among which were obedience to authority. Horace Mann described children as pliable: "Men are cast-iron; but children are wax. Strength expended on the latter may be effectual, which would make no impression on the former." Children are "as docile as 'the lithe sapling or the tender germ,'" he said, such that they could be caused to grow in the right direction if they were bent in that direction at an early age.[11] Thus, the authoritarian Prussian model was a good fit for American schools, providing a structure to create order and shape children for the future.

Though a champion of order, Mann was also concerned for the future of the country, given the population changes, and sought to shape the child towards citizenship:

> if we do not prepare children to become good citizens;—if we do not develop their capacities, if we do not enrich their minds with knowledge, imbue their hearts with the love of truth and duty, and a reverence for all things sacred and holy, then our republic must go down to destruction as others have gone before it; and mankind must sweep through another vast cycle of sin and suffering.[12]

While few educators today consider children as lumps of clay to be molded or empty vessels to be filled, we remain with a school structure that promotes this approach. Allowing children to develop at their own rate in mixed-age classrooms, as one example, is nearly impossible in today's schools. Even though standards were supposed to create a fixed academic goal but to relax the rigid timetable by which children need to meet the goal, that key provision—allowing children the time they need to reach the standard—does not exist at most levels. The system was not designed with that kind of flexibility in mind.

In the early twentieth century, John Dewey and others sought to focus the attention of schools on the growth of the individual child. The "progressive era" of which he was a leader emphasized the ways children learn and the individual strengths and interests they bring to the table more than previous generations. For Dewey, the purpose of education was child-centered: to foster the natural desire of the student to learn, and to guide that student in appropriate directions. The turn of the century saw national debates over the purposes of education and the various ways in which it might be structured. Dewey was influential in these debates—the language of education became more child-centered and remains so today—but he was ultimately more important in promoting a philosophy than in his impact on the functioning of schools. Schools adopted some of Dewey's language but few of his practices.

Contemporary Educational Purposes

Current goals and trends can be traced to the 1950s, as described in chapter 6. The launching of Sputnik in 1957 led to a concern with international competitiveness, and the National Defense Education Act, which promoted military preparedness through science. Interest in individual and family differences grew from the civil rights and women's movements, the Vietnam war, and other societal trends. These interests led to legislation to advance the cause of low-income children and families, women and girls, special needs students, and other such populations.

The 1960s reforms also resulted in more child-centered elementary classrooms, in which the student was the center of the curriculum. Alternative schools, "free" schools, mixed classrooms, and a range of classroom and curricular innovations were created—some well designed and some not—to address the boredom and one-size-fits-all mentality of previous schooling.

This child-centered focus eroded in the 1980s, replaced by an emphasis on set academic standards. As with Dewey's ideas, few of the changes of the 1960s above the elementary level have survived. Where "alternative schools" and "schools within schools" serving a range of children of different ages, needs, and interests were created during this time, few are left. In the 1960s, alternative high schools often served the brightest students. Today's students and teachers think of alternative schools, if they think of them at all, as places where kids are sent if no other school can handle them.

Schools as Social Class Equalizers

Civic leaders in the nineteenth century saw schools as a way to eliminate poverty and crime because they saw poverty and crime as moral failures on the part of the poor and criminal classes. If pliable children were trained at a young age in the proper values of American society, crime, poverty, and other social ills would dissipate. These leaders also hoped that the common school would create better understanding across the classes, and thereby reduce friction by educating all children together. The common schools would create a common social class through education, but without changing the economic structure. Horace Mann's view was not "the elimination of class consciousness," according to Spring, "but its expansion across social boundaries." Expanding class consciousness, according to Mann, would "disarm the poor of their hostility towards the rich."[13]

Over time, the belief that schools can solve social problems has evolved, to the point where parents and policy makers now view the schools as means to achieve economic equality as well, noting the gap in relative income between high school and college graduates. Lower-income parents see schools as a means for their children to better themselves. Middle- and upper-income parents connect school success with college entrance, and see graduation from high-prestige colleges as the key to a successful life. Policy makers seem to believe that eliminating the achievement gap, which they think is within the power of schools to achieve, will propel graduates into better-paying jobs and lift families out of poverty. Thus, economic success for students has grown as a dominant public purpose for America's schools, despite evidence that they have not traditionally served this function.

TWENTY-FIRST-CENTURY EDUCATIONAL POLICY

The prevailing view of educational purposes at the policy level is rooted in *A Nation at Risk* and the development of academic standards, as discussed previously. No longer are the child's interests or individual development seen as paramount. Schools have skills and knowledge to convey to all children in equal measure, well beyond the basics. The school's primary job is to teach these skills and facts. The student's primary job is to learn them.

In this view, the purpose of school is both to prepare all students to take their place in society and to create a vital national economy. Our policy belief is that all students need the same preparation regardless of their interests and abilities—a far cry from Jefferson and Emerson. Art, music, and the range of other disciplines and goals have become secondary. "Standards do not imply standardization," according to proponents,[14] but standardized testing does— especially if incentives succeed in getting teachers to concentrate even more on the results of those tests. Such a system reinforces the predominant nineteenth-century model of education, in which the goal for schools is to "produce" a finished product of a particular type and quality, rather than "develop" individuals with different skills, abilities, and interests.

And yet today, as in the past, many people also see schools as promoters of civilization, and many schools still list citizenship and individual student development as important goals. The belief that education should foster the growth of society is ancient—education has always been about passing on the values of the sponsoring religion or society—but the current interest in civilization is less in the need for societal order so prominent in the nineteenth century and more about acquainting students with the civilizing influence of the arts and humanities, and about the responsibilities of citizens in a free society. Parents want to be sure that art, music, and theater opportunities are offered, as well as athletics, foreign languages, the environment, technology, and other topics. These are seen as important both to tap into the talents and interests of individual students and to prepare students to be citizens in a cosmopolitan world.

PURPOSE AND EDUCATIONAL PHILOSOPHY

The Philosophical Spectrum

Contemporary educational philosophies represent two ends of a philosophical spectrum. The first, which draws from philosophies known as perennialism and essentialism, traces its roots to such divergent thinkers as Plato and Thomas Aquinas. At this end of the spectrum, people tend to believe that truth is absolute and that knowledge is universally consistent and external to the learner. The purpose of the teacher is to transmit this knowledge; the purpose of the student is to learn it. The subject matter, not the child, is the center of the educational process.

Great books and the works of acknowledged experts flow from this educational approach. The teacher leads the class and tells students what they need to know. This is an oversimplification, but the roots of these beliefs can be seen in supporters of today's standards. E. D. Hirsch, who developed a concept of cultural literacy and who has published a series of books for different grades called The Core Knowledge Series (*What Your Sixth Grader Needs to Know*, and so forth) is firmly in this camp.[15] Education starts with the curriculum, not the child.

The second group draws more from Aristotle, as well as from Rousseau, John Dewey (progressivism), William James (pragmatism), and humanists such as Abraham Maslow and Carl Rogers. On this end of the spectrum, people are more likely to see the learner as the center of the educational process. Learners must be engaged and active to learn successfully, and to realize their own potential as individuals. Jefferson and Emerson each describe a philosophy along these lines, with the purpose of education related to the individual learner. There are still many basic skills, areas of knowledge, and habits of disciplined work that all children should learn, explore, and acquire. But classrooms should be active learning centers, structured around problems that students can discover and solve, not simply around the transmission of facts.

In this view, the community and world are part of the classroom, and the concern is less that children learn a prescribed set of knowledge and more that they have the intellectual tools—and the inclination—to explore and understand that world. This curriculum may be less precise and detailed than that of the essentialists, leaving time and scope for students to explore their interests. Learners construct knowledge based on experience. The teacher organizes and leads the class as the responsible adult and transmits basic skills and knowledge, but is more engaged in structuring ways for students to learn by experimentation than in simply presenting facts or theories. Thus, experimentation and active learning are more effective than lectures and memorization.

Both approaches are intended to produce critical thinkers and problem solvers: essentialism through the disciplined study of core academic subjects and the thinking of acknowledged masters; progressivism/humanism through the opportunity to think critically and solve problems while in school.

These simplified descriptions represent positions on a spectrum rather than distinct and competing philosophies. It is doubtful that many people fall wholly in one camp or the other. But some beliefs are hard to reconcile. The more prescribed standards and tests we require, the less students will be engaged in developing and pursuing their own interests. The more lecture and drill we use, the less discovery and engagement students are likely to encounter in their classrooms. The more specific content we mandate, the less room schools will have for other content. One view is not necessarily better than the other; the point is that our goals flow from our beliefs and shape our actions. These beliefs and goals must be discussed before we can agree upon a definition of performance.

Teachers often attempt to reconcile a more student-centered approach with a standards-driven curriculum, with mixed success. Attempting to reconcile different approaches to teaching can be stressful, however, and the need to do so contributes to teacher discontent, particularly in low-performing schools where the demands of standards are greatest. Even in adapting and differentiating instruction, popular training for today's teachers, the goal is to adapt a set curriculum according to different children's learning styles. The curriculum may still be set in great detail, however, and the method centers on finding ways to present this set curriculum to different children. The approach is child-centered, but the curriculum may not be.

Views of Children and Learners

Just as the actions we take and the structures we use betray a basic educational philosophy, they also demonstrate a view of children, of teachers, and of education. Though teachers may never have considered the question, their teaching methods imply an underlying belief as to whether children are blank slates upon which to write, empty vessels to be filled, lumps of clay to be formed, or active learners to be engaged.

Similarly, the policies we choose demonstrate our purposes, goals, and views of children. Are children innately innocent or endowed with traits and emotions that must be controlled? Should their interests be developed or redirected? Although these divergent views have predominated at various points in history, most teachers and parents today would likely respond that children are active learners whose interests should be encouraged.

School organization and curricula also embody both a purpose and a view of children that may be at odds with stated goals. If this *implied* view of the school or teaching profession is not shared by many of the people who work in the school or by many citizens, it can cause stress and divisiveness. This is often the case today.

Although most schools and most teachers agree that children's interests are to be engaged, their talents nurtured, and their differences respected, the organization of today's schools—which has changed little in the last 125 years and which has been narrowed by today's standards and standardized tests—implies a different view. It implies that children are to be recipients of a set body of knowledge. They may be passive or active as learners, but their primary purpose is to learn material embodied in state standards; there are few opportunities to pursue their own interests. (In some schools, such beliefs even justify practices like eliminating recess for young children so they can engage in further study. Physical and social development cannot be important goals in such schools.)

Teachers, particularly in the younger grades, are more likely to employ methods that Dewey would support if they are allowed to, but they work in the context of an increasingly rigid organizational system reinforced by rigid standards (particularly in urban and poor schools). This mismatch of ends and means works against school effectiveness, and against the recruitment and retention of teachers. The more employees embrace the goals of the organization, the more motivated and productive they are. To the extent they don't support the goals or practices of their schools or profession, they are less engaged and less effective (and harder to recruit and retain). Further, if schools are organized around goals that are not fully shared by their primary constituents—teachers, parents, and students—they are also less likely to be effective.

Freire (1968) makes a critical and now famous distinction drawn from his work in rural Brazil, where he was teaching illiterate adults to read. His point is that the teacher's purpose and beliefs lead to a critical distinction in how reading is taught. If his purpose for teaching reading was to continue the oppression of the impoverished natives—either by the government or as useful factory workers—he might teach in one way. If his purpose for teaching reading was to liberate these peasants, to allow them to connect with a larger world and make decisions for themselves, his teaching would take on a different character. Either way these adults would learn basic reading skills, but the context and impact would be entirely different. Freire chose liberation. "The important thing," he concluded, ". . . is for men to come to feel like masters of their thinking by discussing the thinking and views of the world explicitly or implicitly manifest in their own suggestions and those of their comrades."[16]

This distinction also applies in classrooms for children. Sylvia Ashton-Warner used a similar approach to teach Maori children in New Zealand, detailed in her book *Teacher* in the 1960s, tailoring reading to the words and concepts the children wanted to know.[17] This approach also aligns with Coleman's conclusion that students' sense of control over their own destiny is a critical factor in student success.

It is not sufficient to teach children to read so they can follow instructions. Most people believe we should be promoting an attitude or disposition towards reading—for children to enjoy and value reading, and to use it to explore their worlds, answer questions, pursue interests, and become responsible citizens and productive adults. This is why most school districts' goals address more than reading and computation skills. It's why they set goals like creating lifelong learners, fostering each child's innate strengths, thinking critically, or promoting good citizenship. We should not forget these goals.

Implied Goals

Some school goals are implied in the external critiques of schools and in their organizational structure. A number of these implied goals and purposes have been mentioned in previous chapters, including results blamed on schools in reports of "schools in crisis." They include:

Exceed all other countries in test scores on international tests.

Close the academic "achievement gap" between poor and middle-class children and between racial minorities and whites, creating greater economic equality.

Solve student health problems (such as obesity).

Produce workers with the skills of the twenty-first century.

Increase worker productivity.

Produce an American economy that leads the world.

Whether these are or should be goals of the schools are questions worth asking. If they are goals we want to achieve, the decision should be explicit and the expectation clear. We may want schools to focus on providing students with the skills of the twenty-first century, as discussed below. If so, we need to consider what these skills are and how to address and measure them.

If something is not a primary goal, however, schools should not be expected to pursue or achieve it. Schools might be expected to contribute to the welfare of children and society in many ways, but that is not the same as being responsible for particular results. School lunches should be healthy and promote good eating practices, for example, and vending machines should not contain soda, candy, or low-quality snacks. But that is not the same as holding schools accountable for childhood health or obesity.

Similarly, schools should acquaint students with an understanding of basic economics, but it is not clear that they should bear the responsibility for the country's future economic health. If schools are unable to fully address a particular goal—if other institutions and resources are needed—it is hypocritical to hold schools solely responsible for it. Further, if some result is not a goal for the schools, it can hardly be a crisis if the schools don't achieve it.

EDUCATIONAL GOALS IN THE STANDARDS ERA

Following *A Nation at Risk,* the standards movement promised a changed model of education. No longer was age supposed to be the mark of progress, but accomplishment in meeting specific standards.[18] Students would be task- and standard-oriented, and would move from one stage to the next when they had accomplished the appropriate tasks. The standards would be the same for all, but the *time* different students would take to reach various standards would be expected to vary. Thus, high standards would be fair and attainable for everyone.

This vision has not come to pass. The academic standards remain, but the main flexibility provided for students is the opportunity to give up their summers (sometimes a requirement), to spend afternoons in tutoring, or to repeat tests at the high school graduation level. They must still move from one grade to the next with each year in age, however, unless they have been held back as defective. By the time they reach high school, weaker students have failed or done poorly for many years (and been so labeled). This is a far cry from the promise of early standards backers.[19]

If the *organization* of school has changed little, the *practice* of education has been enhanced. The standards movement, despite its rigidity at the state level, has given rise to greater interest in adapting and differentiating instruction based on the differences among children. (This is still a content-based approach, as described above, but it recognizes differences among learners.) Standards-based instruction, which does not require external standards but which has enhanced classroom practice, is becoming common in schools across the country. More teachers have learned to define learning goals in advance, and to shape instruction, assessment, and student expectations around them. Formative, learning-centered assessments are much more common than in previous eras.

Still, even as more teachers have learned to be explicit about their instructional goals and to adapt their instruction to help students meet these goals, the mandated curricular goals are as numerous and rigid as they have ever been. The structure of school also remains unchanged. Children still start school at a given age, move annually from one grade to the next (ready or not), and graduate with the same high school diploma, riding the conveyor belt of education until they are dumped off at the end of grade twelve. Teachers still tinker with each child in this model of education, making adjustments as she goes by. The child is relatively passive, not actively engaged in determining the direction of her own learning. Teachers who struggle to engage children are not helped by such a structure.

With higher standards and harder tests—but without the extra time for children to reach these new goals—the result has been pressure on teachers and students to bridge the gap. Growing globalization and a softening economy, plus a somewhat belligerent political mood, have created a call for greater accountability just as standards and test expectations are raised. The burden is placed on teachers and children, with the mantra that all children can learn (and if they don't it must be somebody's fault). Re-enter performance pay.

And yet, the country is far from agreed on what it wants, what it believes in, or what it thinks teachers should do. The most recent Gallup/PDK poll shows that parents and citizens generally support standards but are leery of tests. The percentage of citizens who view NCLB unfavorably has doubled from 20 to 40 percent in the last three years, while the number viewing it favorably has gone up only 7 points, to 31 percent. In addition, the more citizens become familiar with the act, the less they like it. "It seems fair to say," observe the study's authors, "that, as the public knowledge of NCLB grows, the public's view of NCLB is becoming less and less favorable." Survey results also show that a growing percentage of all respondents believe that schools place too much emphasis on standardized tests.[20]

Opposition to testing has been growing across the country, particularly when it comes with high stakes, and there is increasing concern about the loss of art and music, sometimes history and science. Citizenship, lifelong learning, and critical thinking are not tested and are rarely pursued (though some claim that word problems in multiple-choice tests can measure critical thinking). When asked what they really want, however, neither parents nor citizens seek either test scores or subject matter knowledge as their main priority.

SKILLS OF THE TWENTY-FIRST CENTURY

One of the studies cited previously—one that claims that the future workforce is "woefully ill-prepared for the demands of today's (and tomorrow's) workplace"—presents a list of basic and applied skills that workers of the present and future will need. The four participating organizations—The Conference Board, Parnership for 21st Century Skills, Corporate Voices for Working Families, and Society for Human Resource Management—interviewed four hundred employers across the country and came up with a wish list of skills. The list includes skills in every academic subject from reading and math to the humanities, arts, and history—plus a comprehensive set of applied skills—that add up to the perfect employee. It is doubtful that any employee at any of the businesses interviewed, or at the sponsoring organizations, possesses all of these attributes and skills. In developing this list, however, the report's authors note that the most important skills that employers regularly cite are the four listed below, and that applied skills generally "trump basic knowledge and skills" such as reading and math. The four areas are:

- Professionalism/Work Ethic
- Oral and Written Communications
- Teamwork/Collaboration
- Critical Thinking/Problem Solving.[21]

If these are what parents want for their children and businesses want for their employees, why do they receive so little attention in the testing regimen of most states?

My own town engaged in a small study several years ago, when it convened a series of focus groups to discuss the question of what graduates of the local high school should have, know, or be able to do. All groups, including parents, educators, miscellaneous citizens, and realtors among others, ended up with the same basic hierarchy, in which traditional academic skills were at the bottom. In this suburban community, college attendance and some level of academic success are assumed for most students. Still, it is interesting that the goal of standards and state tests—the goal into which we pour millions of dollars every year—appears last in the list of desired results among all respondent groups. These priorities are remarkably similar to those identified in the study above, which came out six years later. They are, in order of importance:

1. Personal competence: problem solving, social interaction, decision making, respect for others and themselves
2. Metacognitive skills: critical thinking, learning how to learn, research and study skills
3. Oral and written communication skills
4. Traditional academic skills[22]

Rothstein and Jacobsen's 2006 study of a cross section of adults produced a similarly broad assessment of goals. Knowledge of basic skills tops the list in this broader survey, but it is followed closely by critical thinking and problem solving, and thereafter by social skills, work ethic, citizenship and community responsibility, physical and emotional health, and so on. Asked to produce a relative ranking of the importance of various skills (adding up to 100 percent), different groups came up with similar rankings. Averaging responses of all groups, basic academic skills receives the highest rating at 22 percent, while the bottom three categories—physical health, emotional health, and arts and literature—each receive 9 percent. Preparation for skilled work outscores the arts and literature by only one percentage point.

If this ranking of importance were transformed into time in school and measures of accountability, student activity would be divided as follows:

- 22 percent of the students' time would be spent on basic skills
- 18 percent on critical thinking and problem solving
- 12 percent on social skills and work ethic
- 11 percent on citizenship and community responsibility
- 10 percent on preparation for skilled work
- 9 percent on physical health
- 9 percent on emotional health
- 9 percent on the arts and literature[23]

Consider the impact on education if accountability measures, including definitions of school and teacher performance, were similarly weighted. How different might our schools look if we organized around our goals?

DETERMINING (AND PAYING FOR) WHAT WE WANT

It's well past time for a national discussion on the aims of education in the twenty-first century, a discussion that can help shape local efforts. Schools and children are frequently judged to be failing on the basis of goals that are outside their ability to achieve in the time provided and that represent only a portion of what citizens want. The nation should consider whether it truly does care about the other goals often ascribed to schools, large and small, such as citizenship, critical thinking, and an understanding of the arts and humanities. Only when we have determined what we want to accomplish can we decide how to measure progress toward our goals. Before we jointly agree to pay more for something, we need to agree on what that something is.

NOTES

1. Alfred North Whitehead, *The Aims of Education and Other Essays* (New York: The Free Press, 1929), 1.

2. Richard Rothstein and Rebecca Jacobsen, "The Goals of Education," *Phi Delta Kappan* 88, no. 4 (December 2006): 267.

3. Tom Shuford, "Jefferson on Education," *Education Week* 23, no. 42 (14 July 2004): 38.

4. Thomas Jefferson, "Jefferson Proposes New Educational Laws for Virginia," in *The Educating of Americans: A Documentary History*, ed. Daniel Calhoun (Boston: Houghton Mifflin, 1969 [1782]), 107.

5. Stanley K Schultz, *The Culture Factory: Boston Public Schools, 1789-1860* (New York: Oxford University Press, 1973), 9, 19.

6. Ralph Waldo Emerson, "Education," in *Selected Prose & Poetry*, ed. Reginald L. Cook (New York: Holt, Rinehart, 1960 [1884]), 218.

7. Emerson, "Education," 221.

8. David B. Tyack, *The One Best System* (Cambridge, MA: Harvard University Press, 1974), 30.

9. Tyler Anbinder, *Five Points* (New York: Plume, 2002); Herbert Asbury, *The Gangs of New York*, 1928 (New York: Thunder's Mouth Press, Reprint, 2001).

10. Tyack, *The One Best System*, 43.

11. David Nasaw, *Schooled to Order: A Social History of Public Schooling in the United States* (New York: Oxford University Press, 1979), 33, 39.

12. Schultz, *The Culture Factory*, 55.

13. Joel Spring, *The American School: From the Puritans to No Child Left Behind* (Boston: McGraw Hill, 2008), 88.

14. S. Paul Reville, "High Standards + High Stakes = High Achievement in Massachusetts," *Phi Delta Kappan* 85, no. 8 (April 2004): 592; Chester E. Finn Jr., Michael J. Petrilli, and Gregg Vanourek, "The State of Standards: Four Reasons Why Most 'Don't Cut the Mustard,'" *Education Week* 18, no. 11 (11 November 1998): 39.

15. E. D. Hirsch Jr., *What Your Sixth Grader Needs to Know: Fundamentals of a Good Sixth-Grade Education* (New York: Doubleday, 2006).

16. Paulo Freire, *Pedagogy of the Oppressed* (New York: Seabury Press, 1968), 118.

17. Sylvia Ashton-Warner, *Teacher* (New York: Simon & Schuster, 1963).

18. AASA & Panasonic Foundation, "When Standards Drive Change," *Strategies* 5, no. 2 (August 1998): 1–3; Reville, "High Standards + High Stakes = High Achievement in Massachusetts."

19. Donald B. Gratz, "High Standards for Whom?" *Phi Delta Kappan* 81, no. 9 (May 2000a): 681–687.

20. Lowell C. Rose and Alec M. Gallup, "The 39th Annual Phi Delta Kappa/Gallup Poll of the Public's Attitudes Toward the Public Schools," *Phi Delta Kappan* 89, no. 1 (September 2007): 34.

21. *Are They Really Ready to Work?* (The Conference Board, Partnership for 21st Century Skills, Corporate Voices for Working Families, Society for Human Resource Management, 2006), 9.

22. Donald B. Gratz, "Student Achievement: What Is the Problem?" *Education Week* 21, no. 1 (5 September 2001): 62, 80.

23. Rothstein and Jacobsen, "The Goals of Education," 271.

10

Assessing Progress

Now, what I want is, Facts. Teach these boys and girls nothing but Facts. Facts alone are wanted in life. Plant nothing else, and root out everything else. You can only form the minds of reasoning animals upon Facts: nothing else will ever be of any service to them. This is the principle on which I bring up my own children, and this is the principle on which I bring up these children. Stick to the Facts, sir!
Schoolmaster Thomas Gradgrind in Charles Dickens's *Hard Times*[1]

Performance pay in any industry presumes a definition of performance, the ability to measure that performance, and the willingness of the affected parties to accept both the definition and the measurement. In a school setting, a performance pay plan should begin with a clear definition of goals and expected teacher performance, as discussed in the previous chapter. If *student* performance is to be a component of *teacher* performance, student performance must also be defined. In each instance, assessment should encompass the range of desired activity and/or results for students and teachers, not just what is easily measurable.

In a motivational program based on action or behavior, managers define desired behaviors and measure the extent to which they occur. In standard industrial performance pay, the behavior and result are tightly coupled. If a product is to be assembled, a tree planted, or a truck loaded, the behavior (planting the tree) is virtually the same as the result (a tree planted).

Determining the performance of teachers and other professionals is more difficult. First, to the extent that actions and results are not the same, it may not be clear to the teacher or anyone else what specific actions need to be taken to increase student achievement (or meet other goals) and earn the reward. This undermines the incentive value of rewards. For incentives to work, workers must see the incentives as appropriate and achievable, and must believe they have the means to achieve them. Ideally, it is clear to the worker exactly what he or she must do to earn the reward. This is the case in the most successful incentive work programs.

Teacher Actions: Some forms of performance pay use the actions of teachers as their base. These actions include demonstrations of teacher skill and knowledge (either completing training or classroom demonstrations), performing extra duties, assuming a new role such as mentor or curriculum specialist, or teaching in an underperforming school or hard-to-fill subject area. These actions are easy for all parties to understand and to measure.

Student and Teacher Results: Increasingly, however, state and federal officials have pushed the use of student results on standardized tests as an appropriate indicator—and sometimes the exclusive indicator—of teacher performance. Unlike specific teacher actions, the behaviors needed to produce the desired student results are not always known, and may differ from one student, school, or classroom to the next. Further, teachers may not have control over some of the critical factors. The means and ends are loosely coupled—the connection between teacher actions and desired results is often neither clear nor direct.

To the extent that teacher performance is based on student performance, therefore, two additional requirements apply: it must be possible to measure student performance clearly and accurately relative to goals, and it must also be possible to determine the extent to which a teacher's actions influence the results of his or her students. In each instance, teachers and the community must accept these determinations as sufficiently accurate and representative of desired teacher performance to have any incentive value.

Parents, educators, and policy makers are debating whether state tests and the requirements of No Child Left Behind are sufficient or appropriate to judge student achievement or the quality of schools. In addition, to be of value in assessing teacher performance, these tests need to measure student *progress,* not just their final scores, as this is the only way to assess a teacher's or school's influence in a given year.

This chapter considers assessment in the following areas: academic achievement, nonacademic goals, direct measures and agreed-upon surrogates, determining a teacher's contribution, and alternative assessment techniques such as demonstrations and portfolios. These issues are most complex when the performance of individual students is used to judge the effectiveness of individual teachers, and that is a primary focus of the chapter. When groups of students or teachers are assessed, or when indicators of performance change, the complexities of measurement also change. The discussion below presents some of the problems in measuring student and teacher performance for a performance pay system, and some of the ways these problems might be addressed.

ACADEMIC ACHIEVEMENT

The Limitations of Testing

Much has been written on tests and evaluation that will not be repeated here, but the following points are relevant to educational accountability and teacher performance pay.

Academic achievement is a critical goal of schooling, perhaps the most critical goal (though certainly not the only one). If we are to conduct a meaningful evaluation of a school's success, it must include measures of student academic achievement. These measures will most likely include standardized tests in the foreseeable future, but everyone should be aware of the limitations of these tests, and should search for other measurements as well. Nor is it sufficient to select a few areas of academic endeavor and say that these are the only areas of study that count.

It is sometimes forgotten that standardized test results are an approximation of academic success—useful because they are quantifiable and easy to manipulate, but by no means a definitive indicator of student learning. Whereas once these tests were seen as "scientific" and infallible, we know better now. In the 1990s, Congress asked the nonpartisan National Research Council to report on the use of high-stakes testing. Among other findings, this panel of measurement experts issued the following conclusions:

- Tests are not perfect. Test questions are a sample of possible questions that could be asked in a given area. Moreover, a test score is not an exact measure of a student's knowledge or skills. A student's score can be expected to vary across different versions of a test—within a margin of error determined by the reliability of the test—as a function of the particular sample of questions asked and/or transitory factors, such as the student's health on the day of the test. Thus, no single test score can be considered definitive measure of a student's knowledge.
- An educational decision that will have a major impact on a test taker should not be made solely or automatically on the basis of a single test score. Other relevant information about the student's knowledge and skills should also be taken into account.
- Neither a test score nor any other kind of information can justify a bad decision. Research shows that students are typically hurt by simple retention and repetition of a grade in school without remedial and other instructional support services. In the absence of effective services for low-performing students, better tests will not lead to better educational outcomes.[2]

Because statisticians and other assessment experts agree on these points, we have witnessed much talk (but little action) around multiple measures—the use of different kinds of tests that may measure the same areas of achievement in different ways. At the classroom level this is fairly common, but the use of multiple measures in broad state accountability programs is difficult, expensive, and rare.

Growth versus Proficiency

The distinction between measures of student growth or gain and measures of proficiency against a set standard has been a stumbling block in school measurement for many years. This distinction is particularly relevant for performance pay. State standards are generally promulgated with the idea that all children need to attain the same level of achievement (often called proficiency), regardless of where they started—an absolute standard. This resembles a foot race in which the finish line is the same for all but the starting line is different for different runners. In such a race, the runner who crosses the finish line first would not necessarily be the fastest runner, since he might not have run as far as others. We don't set up races this way, for good reason, but if such a race were to be held our concept of "winner" would change dramatically.[3]

Early proponents of academic standards acknowledged that some students and some schools have much further to travel to meet state standards than others. Some educators proposed "opportunity to learn" standards, which would take into account conditions such as resources available to students.[4] These never caught on, possibly because they would highlight resource issues within states and communities—something that would not appeal to governors, legislators, or state boards of education.

To adjust for the reality that different kids start school with different backgrounds, proponents said that the standard would remain set, but that students should not all be expected to reach the standard at the same time: "Instead of time being the constant and achievement among students the variable, standards of achievement would be the constant, and the time required for individual students to meet those standards would vary."[5] This sounds reasonable, but would require that schools not be organized strictly by age. Few schools have altered their structure to accommodate such a system.

If it is true that the standards represent a minimum for advancement—for passing from one grade to the next or for graduation—a fixed goal may make sense. But the use of time as a variable is largely a mirage. Students in most states are allowed to take the high school graduation test multiple times (tenth or eleventh grade), and are often offered extra help in passing. Until that point, however, they move through school from one grade to the next as they always have. They may be passed even though they haven't reached the standard for a particular level (social promotion), or they may be retained (flunked). They may also be given extra help, sometimes pulling them away from other activities, or in after school or summer programs when they have already failed the tests. But fourth graders are not given extra time to prepare for the fourth-grade test. They don't take it when they are ready; they take it when everyone else does. Thus, a principal tenet of standards is not met.

The same problem applies to the assessment of teacher performance. If all students are expected to meet particular standards at the end of an academic year regardless of where they started, and if their teachers are held accountable for their success, teachers in lower-performing schools are expected to achieve more with a needier population of students than their colleagues in higher-performing areas. This is not only unfair and unrealistic, it is a strong disincentive for teachers who have other options to work in the schools that need the most help.

On the other hand, measurement using a growth model may show that some lower-performing students (or teachers or schools) have made substantial progress over a particular period of time, and that some higher-performing students have grown little. Many people believe this approach is more accurate and fair, but some students in a growth model will never catch up to their peers. If all students make similar academic progress on average, the students who start behind will remain behind. Is it realistic or fair to expect that students with fewer advantages will advance *more quickly* than students with greater advantages?

One argument is that intensive support can be arranged for students who need it to help bridge the gap. But this idea needs to be approached with care—especially if the goal is passing a standardized test. If getting extra help in reading and math means missing science, art, or music, is that appropriate? If extra help means drills, do these actually increase learning (as opposed to test-taking)? And if schools were to measure gains in science, art, or music, or health and social growth—if they were to measure the broader range of goals, not just a few—would the disadvantages reappear? All children should be challenged and supported, and some forms of help may allow children to catch up to others developmentally without holding the others back, but when progress is measured comparatively rather than individually, assessment becomes complex, if not unwieldy.

The newest trend in growth measurement is value-added assessment, in which an average of each student's previous growth is used as a baseline predictor for his or her anticipated growth. This method takes into account the student's family background and history, because each child's goal is individually computed. If a student has grown at a certain rate over several previous years, he might be expected to grow at that same rate in his next year. The theory is that since individual variations are accounted for by using each student as his or her own base, more of the growth or lack of growth may be attributed to the teacher (or school).

This approach has merit, but is not a panacea. First, we do not know whether the base years are representative—did the student have a good experience or bad at school, what events took place in his life, and so forth? Second, other circumstances may have changed, either at home or in school, that have nothing to do with the teacher. Third, and most important, this approach still bases significant decisions on test scores: these tests cover a limited range of topics, they are a snapshot of learning but not a comprehensive picture of it, and they can lead to negative behaviors and consequences, such as those mentioned below. A value-added method might help to bridge the gap between those who see the unfairness of a single standard and those who maintain that expectations for all children must be the same, but the methodology has been disputed and the limitations of standardized tests still apply.

INAPPROPRIATE USES AND UNINTENDED CONSEQUENCES

Types of Tests

Growth and proficiency models are generally based on one of two primary kinds of tests: criterion referenced and norm referenced. Criterion-referenced tests (CRTs) are used in a standards-based environment to determine the extent to which students meet the standards set. They are supposed to align with the standards and what is being taught, and to fairly represent the range of standards. As such, they provide the basis for a proficiency model. Criterion-referenced tests create winners and losers depending on where the bar is set. Since students are not compared to each other but rather measured against a standard, these tests theoretically allow all students to meet the standard. However, when students who do not start with the same level of knowledge or skill are expected to reach the same standards in a given year, more is expected from the students who start farther behind, as in the examples above, than of their higher-achieving peers.

Norm-referenced tests are designed to compare students with each other by spreading student responses over a normal curve—so that half the students are above average and the other half are below. While it is possible to determine a student's success against his peers on a normed test in any given year, and to see whether he moves up relative to those peers in subsequent years, the norming process also creates a ranking that is troubling. Since these tests can be used to measure a student's growth relative to the norm from one year to the next, they are also designed to identify winners and losers. Not all children can be above average. Norm-referenced tests account for standards that may be too high (or low), so they have the virtue of representing the reality of student responses rather than an arbitrary standard. But they also assure, by definition, that some students will be identified as successful and others will not.

Problems with Proficiency

With criterion-referenced tests and the standards approach, it is theoretically possible—indeed, it is the stated goal—that all students will do well. The goal of NCLB is for all students to be proficient on their state tests by 2014. Normed tests don't work that way. If all students were to answer 80 percent or more of the questions correctly on a normed test, the test would be "renormed" so that half of them would still be below average. On this basis, a CRT might seem more fair. On a CRT, however, though it is theoretically possible for all children to achieve proficiency, it may not be politically possible. What happens if all students actually reach proficiency? Will officials declare victory, or will they claim that the tests must be too easy and raise the cut score—the score at which a student "makes the cut"?

When Massachusetts decided to raise the passing score on its statewide tests in 2006, for example, board members appeared to believe that too many children were passing. If too many children pass, they reasoned, the test must be too easy.[6] Despite having highly rated standards and favorable notice about its testing program, Massachusetts appeared to demonstrate through this action that it did not believe its own rhetoric. If proficiency represents what students need to succeed in life, and if state leaders actually believe that all students can and should meet proficiency standards, they should not raise the proficiency bar because too many students are reaching it. This is hypocritical—an indication that neither student nor school success are the real goals.

Another problem with the concept of proficiency is that it draws a single, sometimes arbitrary, line for all students to cross. Because of this, teachers are encouraged to put their effort into the children who are just below proficiency on the tests, ignoring both those who have already achieved proficiency and those who are far below. The next time you hear that a school has raised its proficiency rate, ask yourself whether this success might have come about by focusing on test-taking skills with the children who were just below the proficiency line. If so, what has been accomplished?

Finally, the unintended consequences of focusing on test scores are well documented and undermine the credibility and meaningfulness of the tests. Instances of cheating and manipulation by schools, teachers, and students are common, as are the reports of data analysis errors made by testing companies. More important, a range of inappropriate practices has arisen in response to the new standards. These practices are well documented: using classroom time for test-taking drills rather than exploring subject matter; narrowing the curriculum to topics tested; cutting back on art, music, physical education, languages, drama, economics, media, and other subjects; and such steps as eliminating recess, shortening lunch, and curtailing enrichment activities. If these tactics increase test scores without increasing learning—a result which is difficult to measure but widely believed—they also demonstrate the weakness of the connection between the two.

Nichols and Berliner believe that high-stakes tests are corrupting America's schools: "Our research suggests that the incidence of negative events associated with high-stakes testing is so great that, were we the Centers for Disease Control, we would be forced to declare an epidemic."[7] These negative and destructive behaviors are predicted by a social science law known as Campbell's law, which holds that "the more any quantitative social indicator is used for social decision-making, the more subject it will be to corruption pressures and the more apt it will be to distort and corrupt the social processes it was intended to monitor." "[A]s common sense informs us," Nichols and Berliner say, "the pressure to do well on a single indicator of performance from which important consequences are derived can be especially counterproductive and destructive."[8]

This pressure is seen every day in schools, with too many predictable but inappropriate responses. Pfeffer and Sutton point out that the logic of performance pay leads to such negative actions. "After all, if you want to enhance students' performance on a test, one way to accomplish this is by giving students the test or the answers in advance." Further, this kind of cheating is sensitive to the size of the incentive: the higher the incentive, the more likely cheating will occur.[9] In effect, it appears that test-based performance pay works effectively in that it motivates some teachers to produce the specified result—higher test scores. Unfortunately, higher test scores are not really the results that we want, while the unintended consequences are significant and destructive.

TESTING FOR IMPROVEMENT VERSUS TESTING FOR COMPARISON

The purpose of standards-based instruction at the classroom level is for the teacher to align her goals, objectives, assessments, and instruction so they are clear to her and to her students. Assessments against the set standard are frequent and varied, as are student self-assessments. The goal is primarily to aid the student in learning and the teacher in teaching—to specifically show a student how he measures up against the standard that has been set, and give him the opportunity to work on areas of weakness. These assessments are often subjective (measured against a rubric) and formative (they provide immediate feedback). Many are classroom specific. Such rubrics and assessments are designed to help students (and teachers) improve, and successful teachers use them regularly.

On the other hand, tests intended for the purpose of comparison across large groups of students or teachers are designed differently. The need for comparison across many students has led to the development of multiple choice and other short-answer tests with numerical results, and more recently to short essays graded by a quick scan. These can be useful for comparison purposes, and can indicate to a school where it needs to improve, but they are less useful for teaching and learning. As clearly demonstrated in Denver, when teachers set goals based on learning they are more effective than when they focus on raising test scores. Even though increasing learning is the intent of standards, high-stakes tests designed for broad comparability undercut that intent.

A standardized test may easily be used for fact-checking, memorization, or computation as well as for comparison, but most are not developmental or formative. They add little to the learning process. Complex, rubric-driven assessments are good measures of student learning but create practical problems when used widely for comparative purposes. The same attributes that make an assessment useful for comparative purposes—ease of use, universality, relative simplicity—make it less useful as a teaching and learning tool. Conversely, the more individual or specific an assessment, and the more students and teachers become engaged in applying it, the less practical it is for comparison across classrooms.

Essays provide a good example. Some states and now the SAT have incorporated essays into their evaluation schemes. SAT essays are driven by a prompt on a topic about which the student may know little, and are scored by readers looking for general attributes but not for meaning, originality, or accuracy. In fact, however, the mark of a good writer is not his ability to write a five-paragraph essay on a topic he is unfamiliar with, but his ability to take a topic he has studied and turn it into an effective piece of prose—whether to persuade, to inform, or to amuse. This involves marshalling an argument, revising, editing, and honing.

Essay writing can be evaluated through a class rubric or in the development of drafts in ways that help students improve, but mass, impersonal grading is more likely to make student writing formulaic than substantive or imaginative. The need for speed and uniformity works against these outcomes. If teachers are teaching students to succeed in this kind of writing, they may undercut true writing skills. Requiring students to write quick essays on an unknown topic may encourage glib writing rather than good writing.

It is not clear how useful the SAT's writing scores are for colleges seeking to evaluate student writing, but it is doubtful that holistic scores applied by readers who score 220 essays in two eight- to ten-hour days—an essay every two to three minutes—will help students improve their writing, even when those scores arrive. Perhaps as a consequence, only 56 percent of the nation's colleges require the SAT essay.[10] Where essays are used in state tests, however, their results count.

There are alternatives. Some districts have developed rubrics of their own and collect examples of a student's best writing in a year or semester rather than a timed response to a particular prompt on a particular day. This is a much better way to judge the student's writing ability (although if high stakes are attached it could also be open to manipulation). Similarly, systems like Six-Trait Writing may encourage more accurate evaluation of student writing in the classroom. Some schools in Denver used this system in the district's pilot, basing their objectives on improving writing according to this set of rubrics. Once again, however, the Six-Trait scoring system is designed to improve writing, not to allow for broad-scale comparisons. It requires individual reading and assessment of each essay, which is subjective and, if done well, time-consuming.

In the end, it appears that the assessment activities most beneficial to students are those that focus on learning rather than comparison. These learning-centered assessments make comparisons among classrooms more difficult, however, as they are more subjective. This is, in fact, one of the central ironies in testing: those assessments most helpful for guiding instruction are the least useful for measuring results across a large population. Thus, the more we test students for comparability purposes, the less we will use assessment to support student learning. Similarly, the more we focus on comparable measurement—especially if we attempt to add teacher performance to the mix—the more we encourage teachers to abandon the best tools for promoting learning.

This is not to say that both forms of assessment can't be used. They can, and in most districts they are. But we should recognize that the more assessment is used to compare classes and schools, the less useful it will be in helping students learn and improve, and that it may even undercut that learning. Partly for this reason, Denver moved from an initial formulation that included heavy use of the Iowa Test of Basic Skills (ITBS) and later the Colorado Student Assessment Program (CSAP) to a system that employed a broad range of measures. One portion of ProComp includes use of the state-mandated CSAP tests, but Denver continues to focus on teacher-set objectives, an approach that has led to hundreds of different assessments, depending on the teacher's view of student needs. This approach supports teaching and learning and still leaves room for a system of differentiated compensation.

ALTERNATIVE ASSESSMENTS AND NONACADEMIC GOALS

There is no clear national consensus as to the purposes and goals the country expects its schools to fulfill, but individual districts already address a range of goals such as those discussed in chapter 9. In addition to high academic performance, district and school goals frequently embrace lifelong learning or learning how to learn, becoming productive and responsible citizens, communicating effectively, acquiring technological proficiency, being able to work with others, developing critical thinking or problem solving skills, and making good choices (often in reference to drugs and alcohol, but also with regard to diet, exercise, sexual relations, driving habits, and so forth).

In most districts, these goals are largely unmeasured. Even the measures commonly in use (written "word problems" to measure the real-life skill of problem solving, for example) are not widely believed to have much validity. But it is also possible for districts to develop measures that approximate these goals, as some districts have done, or to purchase instruments that are commercially available. For example, they can survey students or graduates on what they are doing or on their opinions. This might indicate whether these graduates are actively engaged in their communities after graduation, the extent to which they have continued their learning, even how often they read a book or how much time they spend watching television. For current students, performances or demonstrations can be used for skill-based goals, such as recitals or performances in music, and gallery presentations in art.

Project-based learning is increasingly recognized as a promising (if sometimes difficult) educational approach. The Met School, an alternative high school in Providence, Rhode Island, has each student complete a project of the student's own devising, with faculty support. In developing the project, students use practical skills of all types, and gain the ability to conceptualize and complete a complex, work-related initiative. With these projects, students demonstrate academic, planning, and thinking skills, and also develop a sense of personal efficacy.[11] This sense of confidence may be as important as specific skills, since this school serves students who have had difficulty in the regular public schools. In fact, such confidence is an important attribute for students who are expected to contribute to society. It may be hard to measure comparatively, but districts can develop surrogate measures to determine whether their students are demonstrating growth in this sense of self.

Problem solving, critical thinking, and the ability to work on a team are important goals, but they are not well-assessed through paper and pencil tests. To the extent that the press or political leaders say that students do or do not have such skills based on these tests, citizens should ignore them. The testing regimen imposed on schools appears to value conformity, not critical thinking, but if we want to encourage critical thinking we should consider how we might measure it.

New measures of such skills are being developed, but it may be that a demonstration or presentation of completed project, as at the school above and as recommended in most assessment models, is the best approach. A problem that a student identifies and researches can provide an excellent learning opportunity, and a demonstration of the solution of that problem can indicate the extent of a student's problem solving and critical thinking skills. Presentations might be difficult to use in any broadly comparative assessment system because they are subjective and time consuming, but can be meaningful at the school or district level.

Similarly, more schools are focusing on developing students' social skills, both to combat bullying and create a more positive classroom environment, and to help students negotiate difficult situations as they get older. Formal measures of these forms of learning have not been widely established, but if we care about these goals for students they must be considered in assessing student progress. Important goals should not be ignored just because quantitative assessments do not exist. A community may certainly adopt such criteria as do exist, or may develop a surrogate assessment that approximates the learning goal to everyone's satisfaction (see below). The key is that the parties agree that the goal is worthy and that the assessment sufficiently measures the goal. With that agreement, much can be done.

If we value particular attributes or outcomes, we should continue to pursue them as goals. If they are goals, we should structure our schools towards meeting them—through providing resources, time, and opportunities appropriate to the goal. We should also attempt to determine whether they are being reached. In a performance pay system, we should consider all goals, both academic and nonacademic, in assessing teachers' and schools' performance.

Direct Measurement and Agreed-Upon Surrogates

Since the implementation of performance pay depends on the ability of schools to measure teacher performance with sufficient validity and rigor to justify awarding or denying compensation, various evaluation techniques must be considered. But, as noted above, measuring complex goals with specificity is a challenging task. One approach is to create surrogates for performance that the affected community accepts as reasonable approximations of the goals. Since these are only approximations rather than precise measurements, agreement on their validity and appropriateness is critical.

Surrogates of this type exist throughout society:

- Opinion polls seek a representative sample of a particular population to gauge public opinion, which is ultimately unknowable. Market research, on which much product development and advertising is based, uses a similar approach.
- Performances are used to demonstrate skills from music and art to debating and physical prowess. Recitals and exhibitions are a normal part of assessment for both college students and professionals in these areas.
- Where comparative judgments are needed (simply watching these demonstrations is not enough) panels of expert evaluators adjudicate everything from speeches to ice-skating competitions.
- Multiple opinions are often used in taste tests or other areas where amorphous concepts like flavor or product appeal are being assessed.

- Multiple opportunities for demonstrating proficiency are sometimes offered. Athletic competitions are often based on multiple trials—the season's results or the best three of five—with the understanding that any particular performance may not be indicative of what a competitor is capable of achieving. Similarly, individual events such as diving, high jump, and gymnastics events allow more than one attempt.
- Practical tests are used to measure practical skills, whether public speaking, carpentry, essay writing, or engineering.
- Imagination and creativity are sometimes tested by a simulation in which people are given items relevant to the situation and asked to create something with these items or perform a task.
- Critics evaluate art, music, books, and movies. Their critical views are informed and important, although they may not match public perception.

Each of these tools is imperfect, whether because it represents a one-time demonstration or because it covers only a small portion of a much broader range of knowledge or skill. Used in the aggregate, however, they can be powerful. For this reason, every leading expert on classroom assessment recommends an array of assessments to address complex goals, such as those above, and still recognizes that they are limited. Each is a sample, attempting to represent a much larger whole.

Despite their scientific veneer, standardized tests have similar limitations. Though many people seem to believe that these tests measure actual achievement, they only measure certain kinds of achievement (related to test-taking) at a given moment on a limited range of potential questions. A test may be well designed or not, but each test is imperfect, a one-time opportunity to demonstrate knowledge or skill. Tests are also surrogates, therefore, just like the surveys and performances above. They are easy to use, however, and easy to compare across students, schools, and communities, lending themselves to mathematical manipulation.

The important point for any of these measures, both with regard to student progress and a teacher's contribution towards that progress, is that teachers, students, and the community must accept that a given assessment is an appropriate indicator of progress towards a particular goal, and that the aggregate of assessments fairly measures student or teacher progress towards the full array of goals. If that agreement exists, many complex goals can be assessed.

Determining a Teacher's Contribution

In measuring any complex field, a balance is needed between the overwhelming whole and a limited representation of that whole. If we try for too much, the measurement becomes impossible to implement. If we try for too little, we trivialize and misrepresent the entire enterprise.

Much of the current debate on assessing performance takes place because the prescribed measures of student, school, and teacher performance fall into the latter trap. In essence, current policy ignores the range of goals stated by schools in favor of the standard academic subjects, then trivializes these by reducing them to a few tests. It adds high stakes to the outcome of these tests, and labels the resulting package *academic achievement*.

If it is true that the best college students are not turning to teaching as a career choice, we may need to look no further than this practice for a reason. The brightest students want challenge and meaningful work; they do not want to engage in a trivial exercise. Many gravitate to nonprofits, where they earn less than teachers but feel they're making a real difference. These students know that test scores are not the equivalent of academic achievement through their own direct experience, and they may suspect that they would not be allowed to use their knowledge of and interest in their subjects because everything is already decided.

How can states entice math or science majors or other promising college graduates? Pay them more, certainly, but give them an opportunity to engage in meaningful teaching. Acknowledge the limitations of testing and stop pretending that learning and testing are the same thing. Invite them to develop meaningful measures of what their students learn. Show that their expertise is valued by involving them in determining what should be happening in the classroom, as Denver has done in the setting of objectives. Above all, don't hold them responsible for something they can't control or don't believe is valuable. Then perhaps more bright young college graduates will be attracted to the profession.

In addition to meaningful goals, teachers want to be assessed fairly for the extent to which they *contribute* to the student's results. Teachers do not control student learning, but they do contribute to it. Since families are complex and student learning styles differ, it is not possible to know all the ways a teacher may contribute to an individual student's learning. Most of the stories adults tell about teachers who changed their lives are not about teachers who taught them specific skills in a particular class or conducted test-taking drills, but about teachers who encouraged them, challenged them, understood them, believed in them, inspired them, helped them overcome adversity, or in some way provided them with the boost they needed to go forward.

How many of these life-changing teacher interventions showed up on end-of-the-year tests, one wonders? We should be smart enough to know that our measures of the impact teachers have on students are limited. This does not mean we can't judge teaching—the attributes of good teaching can be taught and observed—but it does mean that the surrogates we use to approximate the unknowable will only work if they start with the agreement of the parties involved and are applied with a sense of their limitations.

Even in the pursuit of the goal of academic achievement, most people understand that test scores do not tell the whole story. Few dispute, for example, that the easier conditions of suburban schools often attract some of the best teachers. These schools are desirable because they are safer and because teachers can spend more time teaching, so suburban districts tend to have more applicants and more choice. One solution that is becoming more common is a pay increment for teaching in an inner-city school. This incentive is directed at *behavior*, which a teacher can control, rather than *results*, which a teacher may influence but can't control.

Yet results are what we want. Sending experienced or successful teachers to inner-city schools is a surrogate goal—a replacement for or addition to the main goal—which the parties agree is likely to produce better results. These kinds of surrogates are appropriate when the parties agree they are appropriate. Denver and other districts, and some state programs as well, have embraced this particular surrogate as supporting the goal of academic achievement in the inner city. These surrogates, if they are agreed to by the various parties, can measure student results in many areas, engage both students and teachers, and make appropriate forms of accountability possible.

The Portfolio and Multiple Measures

In the classroom, portfolios in which students assemble examples of their work are gaining interest. Students or teachers can put in tests, essays, projects, and demonstrations or performances based on classroom work—items that represent the breadth of the student's ability and learning. Students are often allowed to select their best work, reducing errors related to the one-time administration of tests and increasing student motivation. These examples of work can include indicators of all of the academic and nonacademic goals the school wants to achieve, as well as items reflecting the student's interests. They are appropriate for gifted and talented students as well as those with special needs, limited English proficiency, or other limitations. That is to say, they are appropriate for individual students, because they are individually constructed and assessed.

Portfolios and other compilations of student work can be substantive vehicles for assessing student learning, as long as they are rigorous. Because they are individual, evaluation is more complex, but the positive features of portfolios make them worth considering. Portfolios gain in comprehensiveness what they lose in comparability and ease of use. The question for district and public discussion is which assessments of which goals should be included.

Teacher portfolios are also common. Some districts require teachers to develop portfolios before granting tenure or professional status, and more and more teacher training programs are also requiring them. The National Board of Professional Teaching Standards also requires a portfolio that includes samples of student work, videos of the teacher at work with students, and other evidence of accomplishment.[12]

Denver's ProComp plan also encompasses multiple measures. It is based in part on individually set, classroom-specific goals, reviewed by each school principal. It encompasses academic objectives, district goals such as hard to serve schools and hard to fill subject areas, and a professional evaluation system that identifies the teacher's overall contribution to the students and school. Teachers use hundreds of assessments, making comparability across many teachers or many schools difficult to achieve. However, it's quite possible that personally developed goals within the framework of the district's expectations and with the supervision of the principal will promote the district's overall goals. They might also motivate teachers, if additional motivation is needed, to do their finest work.

CONCLUSION

Americans' goals for children and society are varied and complex. Assessing progress towards these goals is also complex. If we choose to hold schools and teachers accountable, assessment measures must embrace and encompass that complexity—both in terms of student achievement and teacher contribution towards that achievement. We must also remember that the goal of assessing teachers and students should be the same—not just to measure performance but to improve it.

While the arguments for changing teacher compensation are compelling, it is hard to see how a test-based system can succeed in a performance pay plan. Since goals for teachers are extensive, and the links between teacher actions and student test results are often loose and unclear, assessment must be complicated. This is, in part, why resistance to No Child Left Behind and other simplistic and punitive approaches continues to grow, and why attempts to restructure teacher compensation have considered different formulations of teacher success.

Many models for comprehensive assessment of student results already exist. In fact, most assessment experts have proposed comprehensive assessments at the classroom and school level that incorporate most or all of the approaches above. Similarly, principles such as those developed by Fairtest and other organizations provide a basis for understanding the complexity of assessment.[13] These can be developed or modified to apply to the goals determined within particular districts or schools.

Most of the alternative approaches to performance pay recognize the complexities of assessment and move away from overreliance on standardized tests. Some approaches use subjective and individualized assessments of student and teacher performance. Others use surrogates that are research-based but can't be measured on a small scale; still others appear likely to indicate progress without actual proof. These approaches also look at the non-student goals of teacher compensation reform—attracting and retaining teachers—and ask what steps might recruit more top college graduates into the public schools and keep them there. The final chapter of this book considers lessons learned, some of the proposals for teacher compensation, and the principles under which successful changes in teacher compensation—including forms of performance pay—might be possible.

NOTES

1. Charles Dickens, *Hard Times* (New York: Holt, Rinehart, 1854, Reprint 1958), 1.

2. Jay P. Heubert and Robert M. Hauser, eds., *High Stakes: Testing for Tracking, Promotion, and Grading* (Washington, DC: National Academy Press, 1999), 3.

3. Donald B. Gratz, "Fixing the Race: State Tests and Student Progress," *Education Week* 19, no. 39 (7 June 2000b): 32, 34.

4. Nel Noddings, "Thinking About Standards," *Phi Delta Kappan* 79, no. 3 (November 1997): 184–189.

5. AASA & Panasonic Foundation, "When Standards Drive Change," *Strategies* 5, no. 2 (August 1998): 2.

6. Melissa Trujillo, *Board of Ed Votes to Raise Graduation Rates*, AP Wire Service Report, 24 October 2006. Accessed 8 August 2007 at www.boston.com.

7. Sharon L. Nichols and David C. Berliner, *Collateral Damage: How High Stakes Testing Corrupts America's Schools* (Cambridge, MA: Harvard University Press, 2007), 1.

8. Nichols and Berliner, *Collateral Damage*, 25—26.

9. Jeffrey Pfeffer and Robert Sutton, *Hard Facts, Dangerous Half Truths and Total Nonsense: Profiting from Evidence-Based Management* (Harvard Business School Press, 2006), 23–24.

10. Linda K Wertheimer, "Many Colleges Ignore SAT Writing Test," *Boston Globe* (Boston), 20 September 2007, 1.

11. Dennis Littky, *The Big Picture: Education is Everyone's Business* (Alexandria, VA: ASCD, 2004).

12. National Board for Professional Teaching Standards, *National Board for Professional Teaching Standards*. Accessed 25 July 2008 at http://www.nbpts.org/.

13. Monty Neill, Lisa Guisbond, and Bob Schaeffer, *Failing Our Children*, May 2004, Fairtest. Accessed 11 November 2007 at www.fairtest.org/Failing_Our_Children_Report/html.

11

The Road from Here

It is simply not possible to implement a successful performance pay plan without an agreed-upon definition of teacher performance over the long run. Determining that definition should be the starting point of any proposed compensation plan.

Partly in response to No Child Left Behind and the increase in testing, interest is growing both in revisiting the purposes of schooling and in realigning the current system of teacher compensation with those purposes. Some of this interest is misdirected, as in those state plans that continue to regard teachers as the enemy of education or that suggest that standardized test scores are the only legitimate measure of learning. But other civic, business, school, and union leaders now recognize that compensation systems can be changed to the benefit of all. With this growing recognition, the current era is more likely to see such change than any time since the uniform approach to teacher compensation was established in the early 1920s.

Given this potential, we need to assure that any such changes are positive and not punitive, that they are developed inclusively, and that they support a broad range of student learning. Simplistic, state-imposed schemes that focus primarily on test scores will not work and will not last; nor should they. But positive change is possible, if difficult. This final chapter summarizes lessons presented throughout the book, and suggests potential planning and implementation steps based on those lessons.

LESSONS LEARNED I: SETTING GOALS AND DETERMINING ASSESSMENTS

Public Involvement in Public Education

For lasting and substantive change in school practices to occur, stakeholders need to be involved, not just represented. This is possible at the district or school level, but harder for a state. States and the federal government can mandate specific activities, as they have done with standards, accountability measures, and other aspects of education, but these most often lead to compliance rather than long-lasting, substantive change, as past attempts have shown.

States are more successful when they function at the level of enabling policy, not mandating specific programs. They may have success in creating incentives to encourage districts to experiment, as Minnesota has done, but a specific statewide plan—however well constructed—violates the premise of stakeholder involvement. Such initiatives often suffer from lack of support, if not outright opposition. This reaction has been seen in Florida and Texas, to cite two examples, where public discord, cheating, and a range of other problems have arisen. Florida's recent change of direction, in which it now offers more local flexibility, is an attempt to reflect this reality.

The principle of involvement is well understood by those who study the process of change, and it applies in the private sector as well as the public. Speaking of education, Fullan observes, "You can't mandate what matters."[1] Addressing corporate leaders, Kotter warns: "No one individual, even a monarch-like CEO, is ever able to develop the right vision, communicate it to large numbers of people, eliminate all the key obstacles, generate short-term wins, lead and manage dozens of change projects, and anchor new approaches deep in the organization's culture."[2] To succeed, leaders must involve the key stakeholders.

One example of this need is the development of standards and the implementation of associated tests. All the leading proponents of standards from across the political spectrum called for community involvement in setting those standards, but because this work was done at the state level, communities were not involved. Some states convened panels of representatives from cities and towns and had good subject-matter representation in creating standards, but the result was a dramatically uneven and often rigid set of standards with little "buy-in" from the affected communities. States also employed a mechanism for compliance that many oppose—high-stakes standardized tests. No Child Left Behind increased the impact of this approach with no community involvement at all. Districts comply, but the growing resistance is hardly surprising.

Purposes and Goals for Students and Schools

Much of the discussion in this book has been on the purposes of education, the goals for schools and students, and the way these goals are aligned with the structure and activity of the schools—including potential incentives offered to teachers. If compensation plans fail to provide an incentive for teachers or administrators to take steps that will improve results, or if these plans reward teachers for counterproductive actions, results will not improve. If communities have not defined the desired results both clearly and broadly, and if they have not developed means to assess progress towards their goals, how can they restructure in support of their goals?

Perhaps most important, if the results identified do not represent the actual goals citizens have for their children, conflict will inevitably arise and support will erode. This happened in Britain in the late 1800s, in the American south during the Nixon years, and again in the past decade with regard to No Child Left Behind.

Assessment is currently much debated in education, often without the crucial prior discussion of what goals and purposes are to be assessed. But goals and purposes are at the heart of assessment, which in turn provides parameters for evaluating both student and teacher performance. Unfortunately, too many attempts at performance pay fail to specify their goals, assuming definitions of teacher and student performance that are too narrow, and leading to controversy without progress.

The arguments around No Child Left Behind embody this difficulty even without the added complexity of performance pay. By depending too much on test scores (and by setting unrealistic expectations), NCLB has undermined the support for educational accountability that allowed it to be passed in the first place. While it used to be common for people to say that they agreed with the goals of NCLB but not its methods, even those goals have increasingly come under fire.

The definition of performance as higher test scores is, remarkably, still common in public policy circles and the press. Not only do these leaders tend to equate test scores with student learning, they frequently vilify those who disagree. But a growing number of parents and citizens see such tests as overused, harmful to children, destructive of schools, and inadequate for measuring learning or teaching. Tests may have their place, but test results are not synonymous with learning.

Even as this narrowed definition of student performance has occurred, however, the definition of teacher performance has expanded. Though test scores still dominate, teacher performance is now defined to include taking on new duties, working in hard to staff schools and hard to fill positions, meeting teacher-set objectives, and demonstrating increased knowledge and skill.

Concurrently, opposition to changes in teacher compensation has softened. When similar progress is made in broadening the definition and assessment of student learning and growth, much of the logjam around measures of accountability for both students and teachers may also dissipate. It is simply not possible to implement a successful performance pay plan without an agreed-upon definition of teacher performance over the long run. Determining that definition should be the starting point of any proposed change.

It should also be clear by now that when teacher compensation is built around goals for students, teachers, and schools, compensation reform *is* school reform. It is not a simplistic version of school reform, in which offering teachers incentives for higher test scores will magically lead to increased test scores. That method has been tried in the past and has failed each time. Instead, it is reform that engages stakeholders to determine the fundamental purposes of the institution, the goals it is trying to achieve, the methods it will employ, the institutional supports the district will provide, and the measures it will use to gauge success. Discussions of goals and purposes, if undertaken collaboratively and openly, are the first step towards real improvement.

Congruent Goals and Appropriate Assessments

Studies of compensation in business show that workers are more motivated in organizations where they share organizational goals than where the organization pursues a set of goals its workers don't believe in. Given the nature of teaching and the desire of teachers to help children, this dynamic is likely to be particularly strong in schools. Teachers are not like the frontline workers at McDonald's, who are unlikely to participate in developing organizational goals. Rather, teachers are professionals whose success is central to the organization's mission. Teachers will be motivated and enthusiastic if they are treated well and respected, and if the definition of student success and the goals and methods for helping children succeed are agreed among the parties. This need for congruence also helps explain why districts that pursue the goals of control and bureaucratic compliance—of which there are far too many—are not filled with motivated teachers. Incentive pay focused on the wrong goals will not change this dynamic.

Because teacher motivation depends significantly on school practices and goals, teachers need to be engaged in identifying purposes and developing those goals. This explains why test-based incentive programs—where tests harm some children and obstruct teachers' attempts to meet their students' needs—undermine teacher morale. A series of mutually developed goals designed to address the broad range of student and community needs may provide an inducement and focus for teachers to be more effective, while goals that teachers see as destructive or not sensitive to the needs of students or schools are more likely to promote cynicism than to produce positive change.

The need for congruent and aligned goals, actions, and assessments is not simply a compensation issue. It is a fundamental tenet of improvement in most organizations that the most successful enterprises are those that workers believe in and are engaged with. Business offers many examples of such organizations, as Pfeffer and others have described.[3]

Denver's experience provides a good example in education. The pilot succeeded not because teachers were paid a small amount for meeting their objectives, but because they were engaged in developing, seeking, and assessing progress towards those objectives. The pilot was truly, in CTAC's phrase, a catalyst for change. ProComp was approved by teachers and later voters— and stands a good chance of success—because teachers and others participated in identifying the goals, objectives, and assessments to be implemented. If district leaders and teachers continue to work together, continued success is much more likely. Teachers should not control the choice of school goals or purposes, but they should be highly involved in defining goals and objectives which everyone can support. Schools need accountability, but both workers and supervisors—teachers and administrators—should jointly determine who is accountable for what, and what supports will be offered.

Teachers, administrators, students, parents, and citizens across the political and occupational spectrum have something to contribute to and something to gain from well-functioning schools. When the work of an organization is aligned with its goals that its stakeholders share, structures that support teachers, students, and the needs of the organization can be put into place. This kind of synergy motivates all participants.

LESSONS LEARNED II: RECRUITMENT, RETENTION, AND WORKING CONDITIONS

Teacher Recruitment

What motivates people to teach? Some supporters of performance pay believe that potential teachers are motivated by the possibility of getting ahead financially. Give prospective new teachers the opportunity to earn more and they will rise to the occasion, according to this view, propelling their students to the top of the charts and raising the proficiency level on tests—even in the most troubled schools. This economic argument postulates that people will behave rationally and do what's best for themselves; that is, they will pursue a course of action that enriches them. It also assumes higher test scores are a universal value, and that teachers know how to improve those scores but lack the motivation to do so. None of these assumptions bears up under scrutiny.

While college graduates want to earn a good living, the evidence suggests that financially motivated college students are not the ones who enter teaching. Even with excellent incentives, teaching will never become a field in which to get rich. Graduates who are motivated by financial success will seek other avenues, as they should. Instead, most teachers are motivated by their students and their subjects, by making a difference, and by helping society. They want to be paid for their efforts, but as long as they make a decent wage, pay is not their primary motivator.

Human motivation is complex. Individuals may be motivated by several goals simultaneously, and different individuals are motivated in different ways. The purposes, goals, and nature of different professions motivate people to enter those professions and, once there, the conditions under which they work are critically important. For teachers, as for other knowledge workers and for those who enter the helping professions, conditions beyond compensation tend to take precedence.

Teachers and workers in similar professions feel most enriched by the rewards of working with children, by the feeling of having done something of value, and by having a place in a community of similarly motivated people. They want to do a good job for their students. The college graduates attracted to teaching are those who are motivated by these same kinds of goals. They seek to work in a setting with like-minded people where their personal goals are aligned with the goals of the organization. They see the success of their students and their status in this community (and the broader community) as their primary rewards. Knowing that teaching is in many respects a solitary profession—teachers spend most of their day with students rather than colleagues and address many challenges individually—they are concerned about their working conditions and the support that will be available to them.

If college graduates perceive that their goals for helping children are not supported by the schools, however, or that as new teachers they may be held to impossible or inappropriate standards, they may choose other professions. In this way, the relentless criticism of schools and often inappropriate expectations placed on them undermine recruitment efforts. Many of the politicians who promote performance pay make it clear that they do not hold teachers or the profession in high regard. Further, at least some potential new teachers—particularly those who are most engaged in their subject areas—will avoid a profession that seems to downplay their own expertise and goals in favor of standards imposed from on high.

Even the best and most committed college students will wonder if they will make good teachers. They need to believe that they will get the support they need, and that they can succeed in ways they feel will be beneficial to their students. In a recent survey of new teachers, only a third saw salary as a "major" drawback of the profession.[4] School goals that are congruent with their own, appropriate class sizes, a supportive working environment, community respect, and the belief that they can make a difference will attract new teachers into the profession.

Teacher Retention

Many of the factors at play in recruiting teachers also apply in retaining them. It is often noted that education is the only profession in which brand new workers are thrown into the same situation as experienced workers and expected to perform at the same level. Many states and communities have introduced new mentoring systems for younger teachers, but this expectation for new teachers remains much the same. We will retain the new teachers who get the support they need in the first few years to be comfortable and effective in their new roles, and who believe that they are, in fact, making the contribution to children and society that was their original motivation. If they are able to grow in the profession and develop their skills by working with more experienced teachers—the way a new accountant, doctor, lawyer, or architect does—they will be more likely to stay.

The possibility of advancement is also important in most professions. While it is less likely that financially motivated college students will look to schools for employment, ambitious and successful young teachers are more likely to remain in teaching if they see opportunity for advancement. And it is important to remember, in this regard, that advancement for many will have less to do with pay and more with responsibility, scope, professional recognition, the opportunity to have an impact beyond their classroom or school, and the ability to make a difference.

Unfortunately, teachers have little room to advance. A small number may become principals or administrators, and some take on coaching or other responsibilities and create opportunity apart from regular school requirements. For most, there is nothing else available except to leave the profession.

At the same time, experienced teachers also need new challenges and ways to improve their skills and grow professionally. Many teachers are happy facing the challenge of new classes each year, but others need new avenues for personal and professional growth. If the opportunities were available, some of those who leave the profession in search of new challenges might stay. Some of the best might be rejuvenated and kept in the profession by helping younger teachers develop, by providing curricular support or developing new curricula, or by working in other ways to serve the school or district.

Mentoring programs and curricular activities do exist in many districts, but mostly as an add-on. Career ladder approaches to performance pay recognize that young teachers, older teachers, and students can all be served by looking for new ways to organize the profession. Reshaping the profession so that more experienced teachers can help the less experienced—a natural arrangement that exists in most professions—is one example of differentiating duties and compensation that benefits all parties.

Teacher Motivation

Performance pay systems often seek to motivate teachers to try harder by offering bonuses, as discussed in previous chapters. Teaching does not provide the conditions under which motivational pay of this type will work, however, even for people who are motivated by financial rewards. In particular, motivational pay works when incentives are associated with specific actions on the part of workers, and when all concerned can see that one worker has accomplished more than others and deserves to be paid more.

Some states are attempting to tie incentives to test results, but teaching is too complex for that approach—part science, but also part intuition and experience. Even where the desired results are specific, it is often not clear to teachers what they need to do to achieve those results. Professional development or mentoring may help, as may additional resources, but teaching is not like loading a truck. Teaching harder or faster is not an option, and incentives dangled in front of people who don't know how to achieve them (or who don't think they are achievable) will be demoralizing rather than motivating. Not only do bonuses fail to provide an incentive in this situation, but they may undermine teachers by encouraging competition rather than teamwork, or by creating the perception that the system is not fair. This breeds cynicism, already too common in many schools and districts.

Some leaders see competition as the motivating force in performance pay, but competition is not motivating if the ends are not desirable, if the means are not clear, or if the means undercut the ends. Those who support competition should also remember that children are not well served by teachers who are not cooperating, who are withholding good ideas and information or who are fighting—just as they are not well served by families with the same dynamic.

Finally, teachers resent the implication that they are not working hard enough—that student achievement would suddenly rise if they would simply try harder. They are already working hard, teachers in Denver and elsewhere say. Bonuses offered on this basis insult the workforce without providing any actual incentive. In short, attempts to motivate teachers simply through financial incentives for test scores are as likely to undercut teacher motivation as to enhance it. Teachers in Denver and elsewhere reject the motivational power of bonuses or increments based on such goals.

Teachers want to be paid fairly for the work that they do, of course, and nothing above should be construed to suggest that they are indifferent to their compensation. But school goals and teachers' goals need to align—teachers need to believe that the schools are pursuing the best goals for their students. They also need to feel that they are achieving something of value, that their expertise is valued, that support for students is available, that supplies and instructional needs are provided, and that the surroundings encourage learning. These are the factors that mean the most to teachers. Engaging teachers in goal-setting is a good place to start.

LESSONS LEARNED III: EVALUATION AND COMPENSATION

Employees of all organizations are paid to accomplish certain purposes or goals, and most employees are evaluated in some way. Evaluation is usually important to the parties concerned, but its importance naturally grows if pay increases or other rewards are tied to it. The evaluation spectrum has two basic scales. One scale runs from informal to formal, the other from subjective to objective.

On one end of the method scale are supervisory evaluations, common in business (particularly small business), where the supervisor evaluates his employees based on his view of their accomplishments and contributions. This may lead to merit pay, where the supervisor's determination of merit is personal, either purely subjective ("I think she's doing a good job.") or on the basis of a definition. Such evaluations are often informal, though they may be formalized with steps and indicators, but in each instance it falls to the supervisor to use his best judgment, a largely subjective approach.

Depending on the nature of the business and of the supervisor, and perhaps on how the supervisor is evaluated by his own superiors, this kind of evaluation may be done well or poorly. Conducted with integrity by a competent and knowledgeable supervisor, it is probably the most comprehensive and effective form of evaluation. A knowledgeable supervisor is able to see and account for all of the things an employee might do to help the organization, many of which might not be apparent through more objective measures.

Conducted without this level of integrity and competence, however, such evaluations are fraught with danger. Supervisors may play favorites, demand favors, or otherwise abuse the system (and some or all of the employees). They may choose to reward some groups over others, leading to race, gender, or age discrimination, or to reward sycophants rather than those who do the work of the organization. Stories of "bad bosses" may outnumber actual instances, but there are enough poor supervisors to make employees fearful of such an arrangement. Unions, quite naturally, reject such subjective evaluations as offering no protection for employees against an ineffective or unfair supervisor. Given the highly political, bureaucratic, and sometimes corrupt history of public institutions (including schools) this position seems reasonable.

Peers or teams may also conduct evaluations as, for example, the process employed by Bain & Company, described in chapter 4. This process is formal and less subjective. It is likely to be more protective of the employee, in that it aggregates the findings of several different people. It is also much more intensive and time-consuming.

On the other end of the objectivity scale are objective evaluations related to performance, as in sales commissions and piecework. These are more likely to be formal, and are assumed to include performance pay for teachers where that pay is based on student test scores or similar measures. At first blush, an objective measure seems the fairest way to proceed. Why not pay people for what they accomplish? What could be more fair?

As already discussed, however, objectivity and accuracy are hard to achieve. A process that may work for piecework or on the assembly line does not work well in education. The apparent objectivity of the tests masks an array of different conditions, and such measures are often too narrow to address the breadth of educational goals. Even here, teachers may accept some form of "objective" measurement as part of a package—as Denver teachers have by including state tests in their plan. Most often, however, teachers' unions have been wary of forays into performance pay, most of which were designed without their involvement and which they perceived as unrealistic, unfair, or counterproductive.

This resistance has left school districts with the "steps and lanes" system since the early part of the twentieth century, when it was implemented to end the practice of discrimination against women and minorities that was then in effect. Steps and lanes provide a mostly objective approach to compensation primarily based on a teacher's longevity and level of education. Critics complain that this approach rewards competent and incompetent teachers equally and creates a disincentive to work hard. Teachers share some of these complaints, but believe that it protects them from the revolving door of principals, superintendents, school boards, and the program du jour approach of politicians. It also allows teachers to work with poor children and in poor schools without penalty (at least until recently).

The mania regarding testing suggests that teachers have a good point. Much of the press and many public officials still fail to see any distinction between test scores and the entire spectrum of learning, or between the preparation and out-of-school readiness of children from the suburbs and those from high-poverty urban areas. Any teaching deficits that now exist in city schools would have been dramatically magnified if a test-based performance pay regimen had been part of No Child Left Behind. Teachers working in the most difficult circumstances would have earned less than their colleagues in wealthier areas, and would have abandoned city schools in droves.

In fairness, the steps and lanes approach does reward teachers for factors that other professions also value. Most professions value years of service, and many require continuing education and professional development, so it is not the case that simply showing up is all that is asked of teachers. Nonetheless, people from all sides of the issue are coming to the conclusion that the single salary schedule is not sufficiently differentiated to fully address issues of accountability or to meet the needs of students, schools, and of teachers themselves.

In this context, schools may find a place for all of the forms of compensation loosely identified as performance pay. Some districts may decide, as Denver has, to identify a range of different goals for teachers and a series of different ways to assess these goals, and to link compensation to some or all of them. Or they may decide to ask teachers to develop portfolios that demonstrate achievement appropriate to their positions. Each compensation alternative addresses a different need or goal for teachers, and each may have a place in the overall package, depending on the purposes the district decides to pursue. The specific approach a district may choose is less important than how the program is developed and structured, and the extent to which it addresses the principles addressed in this book.

For example, some proponents prefer group incentives. A group incentive may tend to create a more cohesive school environment, encourage teachers to work together, and avoid the most difficult issues of measurement. This approach has much to recommend it. Still, if there isn't enough funding for all groups who meet the goals to receive their share, or if the allocation of funds appears to be based more on favoritism than achievement, the program will be undermined. It is also true that group incentives can allow some teachers to get a "free ride," while others do the work. It's not clear how often this happens, but possibilities like this should be discussed openly before a district selects any specific approach.

Similarly, there are generally accepted attributes and actions which can demonstrate a teacher's skill and knowledge, and which can be used for evaluative or compensation purposes. The success of a compensation plan based on this approach will still depend on whether teachers believe the evaluation of these attributes is fairly and accurately administered, and whether the administrators and the public believe that the measures are appropriate. A complex, peer-driven review of teacher skill and knowledge based on teaching best practices may be appropriate as part of the mix in some districts, while a portfolio may work in others. The key is that actions or results tied to compensation must support broadly agreed-upon goals, and must be assessed by widely accepted measures.

LESSONS LEARNED IV: IMPLEMENTATION AND PROSPECTS

Stakeholder Involvement

Most past efforts to introduce performance pay into education could serve as textbook cases of how *not* to implement organizational change. Performance pay is typically done *to* schools, teachers, and students, not *with* them, in Slotnik's phrase, often by politicians who state or imply that the system is "broken," schools are "failing," and that teachers are lazy, incompetent, or both. Teachers often see the goals as unattainable, and as neither in their own best interests nor in the best interests of their students. Means and ends are not clearly linked, and important school and student conditions ignored. Organizational change rarely succeeds under such conditions.

In the case of existing schools, the vast majority of the people who are needed to make any change work are already in the job. If these workers don't believe that the change will work, that it addresses the right problems, and that it takes into account the concerns they see, they are unlikely to support it. The common practice of "adopting" a new program from one setting and attempting to impose it in another with little input or discussion has been a major reason why so many "proven programs" fail in new settings. Though Denver's plan has much to recommend it, any district that simply adopts it without the inclusive process that Denver went through will not achieve Denver's results. Process is an integral component of change.

The method of choice for states and the federal government with regard to educational change is to create new programs through law and regulation. This is what governments do, of course, but laws can be shaped to encourage progress towards goals (the concept of Minnesota's Q-Cap), or they can attempt to force people to do what they don't want to do.

Noted education historian Bernard Bailyn, writing about colonial America, observes that when new laws and regulations are created around the same topic year after year, it suggests that each of the previous laws or regulations failed. Such a proliferation of laws indicates a lack of community support. He makes this observation around a series of early laws designed to force masters to provide education and moral training for their apprentices and servants as well as their children (which had been the tradition in Europe). In some states, the penalty for not providing appropriate education and moral training for apprentices and servants was death. Still, apparently, these laws were not effective despite the harsh threats, and new ones were needed.

Bailyn interprets the introduction of repeated new laws on the same topic as an indication that the laws no longer represent the views of a changing society.[5] When laws and societal values are misaligned, the laws tend to be ineffective. The failure of Prohibition to stem alcohol use provides another instance where a law not supported by the people failed to achieve its purpose, as does the eventual repeal of the testing regime in nineteenth-century Britain. Civil rights laws did not work, to cite another kind of example, until enough attitudes had changed so that the country was ready to support them. This change had many causes, not least the work of many activists who engaged the country in a critical debate of those rights. The new laws supported and codified growing public attitudes.

While it is possible to pressure people to do some things and not to do others, and while laws regarding access to education and resources may be enforceable, the law functions better to restrict or encourage activity than to change beliefs or opinions. It is a clumsy instrument for shaping the goals of families and individuals, the nature of the learning process, or the interaction between teacher and students.

Education is an enterprise that involves the skill, will, and intellect of its practitioners. It is not a practice where they merely perform rote tasks at a slower or faster pace depending on the incentive. To achieve substantive and lasting change in education, as in other professions, the most effective method is to work with people—harnessing their energy, intelligence and commitment—rather than against them. Such an approach to implementing change will always achieve more than the force of law or regulation. Laws are better at ensuring compliance than changing attitudes, and compliance-driven approaches work poorly in education because they don't engage the skill, will, and intellect of the practitioners.

The Complexity of Change in a Complex Organization

Even without all of these considerations, the experience in Denver and other cities shows the complexity of attempting to implement a one-size-fits-all approach to accountability, in which children and teachers are measured in only a few areas, and in which those areas apply to less than half of the teaching population. An approach that emphasizes standardized tests to gauge teacher performance shows itself to be nearly impossible to implement and nearly useless in its results—unless it is combined with a range of other measures that are more appropriate for measuring complex educational goals, and unless it includes measures for nurses, counselors, special education teachers, high school subject teachers, and teachers of art, music, health, media, gym, and other such subjects.

On the other hand, the use of multiple objectives and assessments worked in Denver because, although these were compiled into a large database developed by the district, pilot leadership made no attempt to judge them against a single outcome. This willingness to leave control at the local level—the principal's review of each teacher's objectives—dramatically simplified the process. The complex goals of education require a multifaceted approach, but it is the effort to apply a simplistic formula to everyone and maintain central control that creates the greatest complexity of all. These complex goals cannot be, and have never successfully been, reduced to a single form of measurement.

Unintended Consequences

In any major organizational change, unintended consequences abound. In a test-based system, as we have seen, the curriculum may be narrowed, good teachers may stay away from the neediest students and schools, data manipulation or even cheating may be encouraged, and the joy of learning may be extinguished in the quest for facts that can be regurgitated. To the extent that these negative consequences occur, they undercut both student and societal goals, regardless of what may happen to student test scores.

A frequent criticism of individual teacher incentives, for example, is that they inhibit cooperation among teachers rather than promoting it. This problem did not arise in the Denver pilot but could occur elsewhere if the stakes were raised. Children live in an educational world defined by the school, and discord within the school is no more productive to student learning than discord in the home. While some policy makers believe competition would be healthy for teachers, others cite the negative impact of competition in supporting whole school incentives rather than for individual teachers. This problem is worth considering. It has been shown repeatedly that pressure on teachers translates to pressure on students. Additional pressure may work for some students, but is counterproductive and debilitating for others.

Denver's leaders support an individual incentive plan, as ProComp shows, but they were well aware of the potential for problems when they developed their plan. Both individual and group incentive programs have their plusses and minuses. In either case, districts and communities should make their own determination, as they carefully weigh the advantages and disadvantages. Leaders should pay special attention to the disadvantages and potential unintended consequences of any plan they choose, and should prepare to address them. In a jointly developed program, many unintended consequences may be avoided by including the players who best understand different aspects of the enterprise, and who each have a stake in the outcome. After that, careful assessment of results and a willingness to make mid-course corrections are key factors in successful implementation.

Although process is important, a different kind of unintended consequence can arise when process becomes too important. For example, joint development of goals and strategies can solve many of the potential problems that arise when districts create a new teacher compensation plan, but this approach can also lead to a program that is watered down and ineffective due to compromises and lack of innovative thinking. Ultimately, any plan must be sufficiently rigorous to support the standards of the profession, and must focus relentlessly on the needs of students. It must also exist in a climate of support and trust, where teachers can trust that the system is designed and implemented fairly, and where necessary institutional supports are provided.

This is why an honest discussion of beliefs and purposes is important from the start. A discussion of teacher compensation may end up focusing on pay and working conditions. However, a prior agreement on beliefs and purposes will reinforce and strengthen the focus of all parties on aligning their activities to best achieve their goals for students.

Piloting and Long-Range Planning

School districts and other public agencies have a tendency to adopt plans or programs perceived to be effective in other locales and try to implement these programs in their entirety. This approach is one reason for the failure of "proven programs" to work in many new settings, as has been discussed previously, in part because teachers and others are not directly involved in determining what problems need to be solved, what specific conditions apply, and whether the approach selected is the most appropriate. Without this kind of stakeholder involvement, no large-scale change plan is likely to succeed.

A related point is the role of the pilot. Denver's process for developing its current professional compensation program worked as well as it did in large part because the right players were involved in a long-term developmental process. But Denver also conducted a pilot in a small number of schools in which ideas were tested, skills were developed, results were analyzed, and methods changed over a period of years. Had Denver not implemented a multi-stage pilot in which it tested its ideas at schools that volunteered to participate first, its initial problems would almost certainly have caused the entire project to fail. Instead, the pilot started with thirteen of the district's one hundred plus schools, added more as it went along, and eventually developed a model that used some of the pilot's original ideas but which was also substantially different.

The importance of a phased implementation or pilot should not be underestimated. In a large district, unwillingness to implement in stages may lead to unnecessary failure of the proposed change. Even smaller districts would be well advised to start with a smaller number of schools or individuals who volunteer to undertake the experiment and who, as a consequence, are interested in seeing it work. When implementing a new compensation system, districts should negotiate the process. In most cases, they should allow voluntary opt-in for current teachers, using the current salary levels as a floor— a hold-harmless approach that may be slower but is more likely to succeed over time. Districts that don't proceed in this step-by-step fashion, unless they have strong support from the teachers, will probably wish they had.

The Need for Funds

One final problem that bears noting has to do with funding. If teacher incentives are limited by finances—that is, if not all teachers who perform at a certain level receive the added compensation—any benefit of the plan is seriously undercut. It will be perceived as unfair, causing frustration and discord, and additional criteria will be needed to determine who will actually be paid more.

Teachers often fear that even the most well-intended plan will lose its funding at some time—that they may bargain away protections and be left without the promised increases despite their performance. Given the uncertain nature of school funding, this fear is understandable. In Denver, a substantial guarantee of funding was included when ProComp was put to a general vote. Citizens of Denver supported the plan by voting to fund it over an extended period. Such a vote may not be possible in every district, but any district seeking to change the teacher compensation formula must carefully consider the financial implications and make plans to address them—both to gain support for the change and to sustain it over time.

Similarly, it is important that a performance pay plan is not used to save money. It cannot be a scheme to pay some teachers more while reducing the pay of others (or eventually firing them). This is an approach some teachers fear, but to take this route is to ensure cynicism, division, and mediocrity as the best teachers leave for more favorable working conditions.

SCHOOL PURPOSES, PERFORMANCE, AND TEACHER COMPENSATION

The current overemphasis on basic academic skills is a historical aberration. Throughout American history, we have held a more expansive set of goals for our public schools.[6]

Every day that schools operate, they operate on an assumption of purpose, embedded within the structure of law, policy, organization, and resources. This has led to a school system that, despite its many flaws and the constant complaints of critics, is still one of the best in the world. In fact, some of its greatest flaws have been introduced by the attempt to enforce conformity and uniformity. Given the debates over NCLB and the increasing interest of both labor and management in new forms of teacher compensation, now is the time for both national and local dialogues around educational purposes, goals, and definitions of performance.

A set of goals can emerge from this dialogue that may be flawed, but that represents a consensus within which the parties can live and work. This consensus may be looser at the national level than at the local, but that is an effective response to local conditions and concerns and in keeping with the country's history and diversity. The Tenth Amendment makes clear that education remains the province of the states. As with other areas of public life in which the federal government may provide a framework of support, state and local governments fill in the details. Education should represent and reflect the will of local communities—as, indeed, it has throughout American history—within the broader national purposes, laws, and goals. Finding the balance is the key.

We could decide, as a nation, that our purpose for all students and all schools includes a particular range of student performance and behavior. We could then attempt to implement that system nationwide. This is the approach of No Child Left Behind. Some policy makers, educational researchers, and a few urban superintendents advocate developing a national curriculum and testing program, in the apparent belief that all students need to meet the same academic standards to succeed in life, regardless of their backgrounds, interests, and abilities. Others believe this approach places academic interests defined by the government over the individual interests of students, parents, and communities.

Alternatively, we could abandon the attempt to codify a national curriculum, as the British did in the early twentieth century, opting instead for broad standards as the foundation for a child-centered approach. Each teacher might "think for himself and work out for himself such methods of teaching as may use his powers to the best advantage and be best suited to the particular needs and conditions of the school,"[7] as the British government proposed in 1907, but still operate within a curriculum framework outlined by a state or by national organizations and selected by the district.

Some will argue that this action would leave the child at the mercy of a bureaucracy that is responsive less to the needs of students than to the working conditions of employees—as shown in the low expectations and poor results of some urban schools as in the past. But a student-oriented curriculum can still be rigorous; it can demonstrate that rigor more through student initiated projects and less through standardized tests, building on student interests and talents.

In fact, a system with curricular guidelines set by experts in various fields but without mandatory standards could be both more flexible and more market-driven than the current model of standards and high-stakes tests, as it would let communities choose what they want in their schools. Given the extreme pace of change in industry based on rapid scientific and technological development, it is hard to see how any set of standards beyond the basic skill level will allow teachers and students to adapt to student interests and new work requirements. At the same time, standards developed by experts in different fields will be more likely to stay up to date than state-mandated standards, and could provide a framework for districts to use as a guide.

Education will always be ambiguous, as it addresses the goals of many different stakeholders and the needs of many different children and families. This is not a bad thing, unless we believe that we must design the *one best system* that works for all children in all communities. But, as Tyack notes in his book of the same name, the search for the one best system of education has "ill served the pluralistic character of American society."[8] If we are to have one system, it should be one that allows for diversity of goals and interests, reflecting the diversity of our society.

In the latter years of the twentieth century, the United States became increasingly contentious in its views on education and the public schools, a debate reminiscent of the end of the nineteenth century. It is not surprising that the schools are the subject of much controversy, given their expense to the country and the scope of their work. Education is about our children, about our future, and about our personal and societal values—three concerns about which people care passionately. But we should confront our concerns with a national dialogue rather than warring camps, starting with what we intend to achieve through our schools and how we will know whether we have achieved it.

Helping to launch this dialogue is one of the purposes of this book, but it is a widely shared concern. Rothstein and Jacobsen provide an excellent discussion of the purposes of education in their 2006 essay "The Goals of Education," introduced in chapter 9. They note that No Child Left Behind has led to a "reorientation of instruction" and a "shift in curricular coverage" that "disproportionately" affect lower income and minority children and that are also "at odds with the consensus about the goals of public education to which Americans historically have subscribed."[9]

In other examples, Paul Houston asks, with regard to NCLB, "How can we sustain our creativity while paring down our education to a stimulus-response system of learning that reduces knowledge to a series of test bubbles and communicates to children that what is on the test is the only thing worth learning?"[10] Richard Neumann worries about civic engagement, and observes that "preparing young people for democratic citizenship in the context of an authoritarian school is a contradiction that is all too obvious."[11]

Linda Darling-Hammond observed some time ago that many problems with teenagers are not inherent, but are related to the "mismatch" between adolescents' developmental needs and their school experiences: "When students need close affiliation, they experience large depersonalized schools; when they need to develop autonomy, they experience few opportunities for choice and punitive approaches to discipline; when they need expansive cognitive challenges and opportunities to demonstrate their competence, they experience work focused largely on the memorization of facts."[12] And that was before No Child Left Behind.

What are we preparing our students for, the *American School Board Journal* asks? It concludes: "After interviewing some of the top thinkers and leaders in their respective fields, it remains impossible to say what 'ready' truly is."[13] Yet businesses, political leaders, educators, and parents want students to be prepared for the future. What does "ready" mean, and how can schools get students ready for a future that is unknown?

So far, the national dialogue exists primarily as a debate about No Child Left Behind. The real questions are deeper than NCLB, however, in that they don't presume academic achievement is the only goal of the schools, even if more effective ways to measure that achievement are put into place. Nor do they presume that the purpose of education is either to provide the country with a more productive workforce or to get all students into well-paying jobs (supposing that were possible).

Rather, the discussion should start with what we value as a nation, the purposes of school, and the nature of children and the learning process. When these purposes are determined, we can define terms like "readiness" and "performance," and establish priorities, goals, and means of assessing progress. When we have achieved greater agreement on all of these, including ways to measure progress toward our myriad goals, we can consider a new compensation system.

Reflecting past innovation, the dialogue may exist at many levels but the innovation is most likely to arise locally. It is unlikely that anything beyond a broad consensus will emerge at the national level. While such a consensus would be extremely valuable given the current debates over NCLB and national policy, innovation and programmatic changes will most likely emerge from districts, as in Denver. This is where they have been developed in the past and where they belong. Districts engaged in planning should therefore consider the broadest range of goals for students. If they choose, they can then include teacher compensation as one of the practices that might change to support their goals.

Developing a Local Dialogue

Districts interested in developing improvement strategies that include differentiated compensation for teachers and others should also begin with a discussion of district goals, beliefs and values—as in most planning processes—and ways that the district might achievement them. The major players—teachers, administrators, parents, and students—should be at the table in one form or another, able to provide input and comment on proposals and plans on a regular and sustained basis. It should be clear from all of the foregoing that the method of compensating teachers is only one factor of many in the success of schools, and that changing that method should not be the goal of a reform. Instead, changes in teacher compensation should be discussed in the context of school goals, which form the basis for definitions of student, school, and teacher performance.

A framework for districts considering this process is provided in appendix II. This framework is based on a standard planning process, highlighting the particular considerations of teacher compensation within that planning context. It provides a lens for district planners that addresses the parameters and principles set forth in this book: particularly the principles that teacher performance should be defined in relation to school and district goals, and that stakeholders in the school and district should define these goals in an inclusive and unifying manner.

The framework also embraces the reality that different stakeholders see different purposes in the schools, and that what children, parents, business, and society need and expect from the education process may be different. Such differences must be reconciled to produce the greatest effect. These stakeholder purposes may also be more similar than one might expect, though they may diverge from the conventional wisdom, as described in chapter 9. The critical point is that any planning process a district uses should include both the full range of questions and the full range of stakeholders.

THE CONTINUING SAGA—MORE LESSONS FROM DENVER

As this book goes to press, Denver teachers and the district are involved in a contract dispute over ProComp. Administrators want to increase starting salaries for teachers by $9,000, and to double the incentive for teaching in hard-to-serve inner-city schools. Teachers want to wait to make such changes until results from an ongoing study are complete in a year, and to award a 3.5 percent increase across the board in the meantime.[14] It is not particularly noteworthy that there is a contract dispute. ProComp notwithstanding, the labor–management system is designed to make balanced progress through negotiations. Disputes and disagreements are to be expected.

Two broader concerns arise from these discussions, however. The first is that an interim study conducted by a local professor reports that test scores rose only slightly among classes taught by teachers under ProComp compared to classes taught by teachers who had not opted into the system. While the professor plays down the importance of these results, saying it is too early to make judgment, the key point is that test scores remain the basis for judgment. If a system not designed to raise test scores is judged on the basis of test scores, what will anyone know about its success?

The second concern is drawn from comments by a nonprofit citizens group called A-Plus Denver. This group's leader says that ProComp is "not affecting behavior as we had expected it to," and that "letting ProComp drift into a base-pay-type system doesn't have that surgically precise ability to affect and motivate teachers in an important and direct manner." It is not clear how the group knows how much teachers have been motivated or what it expects from the "surgically precise ability to affect and motivate," but this remark is also troubling.[15]

While the parameters of the upcoming and "more comprehensive" study of Denver's ProComp are not clear, this controversy adds one final lesson to be learned from Denver—a lesson that is at the heart of the discussions in this book. Just as the definitions of student and teacher performance must be clear and agreed to, so must the definition of programmatic success. A program not designed to raise test scores cannot be judged fairly on whether test scores rise. A program designed to "surgically affect and motivate teachers"—though I don't believe that was ProComp's intent—must define what that means and how it will be assessed.

The heart of Denver's program is teacher-set objectives using hundreds of different assessments. It is possible that successful teacher objective-setting will also lead to higher test scores, as both teachers and students become more motivated and engaged. It is also possible that this new approach will be judged by an old and flawed metric. If so, its successes may not even be recognized and its efforts at change may well fail.

THE ROAD FROM HERE

Our research informs us that high-stakes testing is hurting students, teachers, and schools. It is putting the nation at risk. By restricting the education of our young people and substituting for it training for performing well on high-stakes examinations, we are turning America into a nation of test-takers, abandoning our heritage as a nation of thinkers, dreamers and doers.[16]

Successful change in schools cannot simply be implemented by executive order. Of the many education reform plans and models currently being tried in various districts, most have succeeded in some locations and have failed in others. Though some of these models are better designed than others, the difference often lies not in the program itself but in the means of selection and form of implementation. Is it built around goals and values that everyone shares? Were the people who would need to implement the system involved in developing or selecting it? Do they think that it addresses problems that need to be addressed? Do they believe it can work? Have their concerns and issues been discussed and addressed? If these steps have been taken (and if the program has been developed thoughtfully and with similar care), it stands a chance of success. If not, it is likely to fail.

Denver's model is different primarily because it was implemented differently. It was supported by teachers, administrators, and the public—all groups that worked to help it succeed. It's also the result of a multiyear pilot, followed by several years of discussion across the district, led by a labor–management committee. It was affirmed by votes of the board, teachers, and public. If the exact same model were simply "adopted" by another district or by a state, its failure would be virtually assured.

With this in mind, the first step in substantive school change is a review of goals and purposes. In the case of performance pay, where both teacher and student performance play a role in determining teacher compensation, definitions of performance provide the foundation from which measures of teacher performance can be drawn. If teacher performance is not defined in the context of a district's goals for students, those goals are unlikely to be reached and student learning is unlikely to improve.

The real crisis in education is not in teacher compensation or even the achievement gap, though there are significant issues related to each, but rather in the narrowed definition of school purposes, the regimentation of student thinking, and the trivializing of education by those who would have us reduce it to a set of test scores. This has been a national trend, with the overimplementation of standards and the passage of No Child Left Behind, but it is far from universally accepted. Indeed, though most teachers and citizens see some value in both standards and tests, they reject the relentless focus on testing, the substitution of test scores for actual student learning, and the loss of so much that is valuable—from art to music to student engagement—as a consequence of this focus.

Nor, ironically, do the champions of economic growth based on a test-based approach address the needs identified as the skills of the twenty-first century: creativity, critical thinking and problem solving, the ability to work in groups, oral and written communication skills, professionalism, and a strong work ethic. If these skills were seriously addressed with measures that actually tested the attributes being sought, we could have much greater agreement than now.

This disagreement as to goals, more than any other factor, is also the reason for resistance to NCLB. Until a more balanced view of educational outcomes can be achieved, either at a local or national level, no positive change of any substance will be possible. When we do develop a balanced set of goals and measures, teachers' duties and incentives can be structured to support them.

In the passage at the beginning of this section, Nichols and Berliner claim that we are "abandoning our heritage as a nation of thinkers, dreamers and doers." If this is true, we should not be surprised if our schools don't seem to be serving our best interests or those of our children. Thinkers, dreamers, and doers are engaged learners, after all—seekers of wisdom, ideas, and creative inventions or solutions to problems. Test takers are seekers not of wisdom or ideas but of angles, of committee-approved facts, of "what they are looking for." Which, as a country, do we want to encourage our young people to be? Once we decide, we can structure our schools and support our teachers in helping students not just to take tests, but to set and accomplish their own lofty goals.

NOTES

1. Michael Fullan, *Change Forces: The Sequel* (Philadelphia, PA: Falmer Press, 1999), 18.

2. John P. Kotter, *Leading Change* (Cambridge, MA: Harvard Business School Press, 1996), 51.

3. Jeffrey Pfeffer and Robert Sutton, *Hard Facts, Dangerous Half Truths and Total Nonsense: Profiting from Evidence-Based Management* (Harvard Business School Press, 2006).

4. Jonathan Rochkind et al., "Lessons Learned: New Teachers Talk About Their Jobs, Challenges and Long-Range Plans," Public Agenda, 2007. . Accessed 17 October 2007 www.publicagenda.org.

5. Bernard Bailyn, *Education in the Forming of American Society* (New York: W. W. Norton, 1960), 32.

6. Richard Rothstein and Rebecca Jacobsen, "The Goals of Education," *Phi Delta Kappan* 88, no. 4 (December 2006): 267.

7. W. H. G. Armytage, *Four Hundred Years of English Education* (Cambridge, England: Cambridge University Press, 1964), 188.

8. David B. Tyack, *The One Best System* (Cambridge, MA: Harvard University Press, 1974), 11.

9. Rothstein and Jacobsen, "The Goals of Education," 264.

10. Paul D. Houston, "The Seven Deadly Sins of No Child Left Behind," *Phi Delta Kappan* 88, no. 10 (June 2007): 748.

11. Richard Neumann, "American Democracy at Risk," *Phi Delta Kappan* 89, no. 5 (January 2008): 338.

12. Linda Darling-Hammond, *The Right to Learn: A Blueprint for Creating Schools That Work* (San Francisco: Jossey-Bass, 1997).

13. Glenn Cook, "What Is Ready?" *American School Board Journal* 194, no. 9 (September 2007): 17.

14. Vaishali Honawar, "Union Objects to Proposal to Modify Pact in Denver," *Education Week* 27, no. 44 (30 July 2008): 15.

15. Honawar, "Union Objects to Proposal to Modify Pact in Denver," 15.

16. David C. Berliner and Sharon L. Nichols, "High Stakes Testing is Putting the Nation At Risk," *Education Week* 26, no. 27 (12 March 2007): 48.

Appendix I:
Current Practitioners in
Performance Pay

Many districts regularly conduct planning processes on their own, or bring in a local facilitator or planner to help. Beyond these, a few organizations currently specialize in assistance to large districts in planning and implementing changes in the compensation system. Examples of major current practitioners and supporters include the following.

COMMUNITY TRAINING & ASSISTANCE CENTER (CTAC)

The Community Training & Assistance Center has been involved in systemwide improvement efforts, primarily in large urban school districts, since the early 1990s. These efforts have been wide ranging, but have focused on school improvement, accountability, system alignment, and increasing the involvement of health and human service providers as well as the business and philanthropic communities. CTAC was selected by the Denver Public Schools and Denver Classroom Teachers Association in 1999 to provide technical assistance to the Pay for Performance Pilot and to study its impact and results. That relationship remained in place through the pilot and into the development of the professional compensation system described in chapter 5. The center produced two lengthy reports on the pilot, in 2001 and 2004.[1] Since then, it has worked with Delaware's largest school district (Christina), and is currently engaged in Charlotte-Mecklenberg County in North Carolina and DuVal County in Florida.

CTAC's principles include the following:

- Reform must be done with people, not to them. Improvement efforts and change strategies must involve teachers, principals, and community members if they are to succeed.
- Performance pay may be part of a reform, but it is not *the* reform. Changes in compensation can be an important component of a district's overall improvement strategy and can serve, as in Denver, as a catalyst for change. Compensation reform can only succeed if it is part of a larger strategy for bringing all of the district's resources into focus in support of schools and learning.
- Organizational alignment is critical to the success of compensation reform and, more important, to student achievement, however defined. Denver's success, and the success of other districts in improving schools, has resulted from an increased focus of both efforts and resources on organizational goals. This focus comes about through careful goal setting and planning, analyzing structures and expenditures, collecting data on student achievement and school needs, and deploying district resources based on these needs. It requires a willingness on the part of district, union, and community leaders to refocus on behalf of students and schools.
- Any district embarking on such a change needs to conduct long-range financial planning. Changed compensation systems are likely to cost more over time. A compensation plan that does not address the issue of long-term viability may leave teachers and citizens skeptical about the intent of the plan, and may not last if it is approved. In addition to the alignment of organizational structures, CTAC emphasizes long-term viability and advance planning as critical elements of lasting change.

CTAC focuses on district efforts, and works with individual schools in that context. Unlike many other organizations, it does not have a specific model for what a compensation or improvement program should look like. Rather, it assists a district through an inclusive process that is data- and research-based, that involves all of the critical stakeholders, and that focuses on district and school alignment. The results may be like Denver's professional compensation system, or something substantially different, depending on the needs, interests, and resources of the community.[2] Given my long association with the center, it should not be surprising that these principles are similar in many respects to those presented in the foregoing chapters of this book.

TEACHER ADVANCEMENT PROGRAM (TAP)

The Teacher Advancement Program is a program of the National Institute for Effectiveness in Teaching (NIET), an initiative sponsored by the Milken

Family Foundation. The program was developed in 1999 to attract, develop, motivate, and retain high-quality teachers, and now claims a list of five thousand schools that it has worked with. The program's principles include:

- *Multiple career paths:* The concept of multiple career paths is the "career ladder" approach to teacher compensation discussed earlier. Experienced teachers take on additional responsibilities in areas of their interests and skills. In the TAP model, this emphasizes "master" and "mentor" teachers, who are selected through "a competitive, rigorous, performance-based selection process." These teachers become part of the leadership team, work year round, and have specific responsibilities.
- *Ongoing applied professional growth:* This is an effort to provide teachers with school-based professional development during the school day. Led by a master teacher, teachers meet in small groups on a weekly basis. In these meetings, they learn skills like data analysis and research-based instructional strategies.
- *Instructionally focused accountability:* The program comes with an evaluation system, in which teacher evaluations are tied to teaching skills and student achievement. The criteria for evaluation are set forth by the program, and are clearly defined. Evaluations are conducted four to six times yearly by "multiple trained and certified evaluators using the TAP Teaching Skills, Knowledge and Responsibility Standards." Teachers are evaluated both on the learning growth of all students in the school and on the learning growth of students in their individual classrooms. TAP offers training and support.
- *Performance-based compensation:* The TAP program provides bonuses to teachers based on the results of their evaluations and the success of students in their classrooms, as well as additional compensation for teachers who take on additional roles and responsibilities. According to the program's website: "Teachers are compensated differentially based on the increased demands of the positions they hold, how well they perform those positions, the quality of their instructional performance and by their students' achievement growth. Salary is determined by more than simply years of teaching experience and training credits. All teachers are eligible for financial awards based on these factors."[3] Even with initial help from the foundation, these bonuses and other increments must be sustained over time.

The TAP program sounds similar to Denver's Professional Compensation System in some respects, and it addresses many of the issues identified in this book. TAP is being implemented in various ways in a wide range of schools and districts. The success of the programs will likely depend on critical details of how teacher skills are assessed, how student learning growth is defined and measured, and how the elements of each program are identified and developed. One important distinction is that Denver created its own program, whereas TAP comes as a package. While externally developed programs can work as long as the affected parties participate in the selection, that support and participation are critically important.

Also, to the extent that TAP programs or any others are school-based rather than district-based, this may present a problem. One of the lessons from Denver is that improvement results from better focus, both at the school and district levels. Schools exist in the context of districts, and must respond to district leadership priorities. Any significant institutional change at the school level must be accompanied by related district change if it is to last, and changes affecting teachers must be negotiated with unions that represent the entire district. A change developed at a school will not last unless it is actively supported by the district, and such support is not guaranteed. Districts and schools involved in these and other programs should take steps to ensure that the issues identified throughout this book are addressed, and that changes in practice occur at both the district and school levels.

TEACHER INCENTIVE FUND

It has already been noted that government agencies tend to support simplistic notions of accountability and incentives for teachers, and this program is no exception. The Teacher Incentive Fund was developed as a companion to No Child Left Behind. It focuses on rewarding teachers and schools for closing the achievement gap, raising student achievement and producing "real results" for all children (test scores, apparently), and providing incentives for the most effective teachers who choose to teach in low-income schools. Because it invites applications, however, it may still support worthwhile projects. The jury is out. Funds are awarded based on the following four goals:

- Improving student achievement by increasing teacher and principal effectiveness.
- Reforming compensation systems so that teachers and principals are rewarded for increases in student achievement.
- Increasing the number of effective teachers teaching poor, minority, and disadvantaged students in hard-to-staff subjects.
- Creating sustainable performance-based compensation systems.

Two rounds of grants have been awarded, at this writing, and no results of those projects are in. As with most government funding, applications are restricted and political considerations have been known to play a role in the selection of grantees. Nonetheless, for larger districts or those in "high needs" communities, this source of program support should be considered.

The recipients of the first rounds include four awards each in Colorado, Florida, and Texas, with Florida and Texas receiving the largest dollar amounts overall. While the bulk of the awards have been made to school districts, some have also gone to state departments of education, and others to charter schools. At least fourteen of the recipients are working with nonprofit organizations. These include the Teacher Advancement Program and CTAC mentioned above, as well as several others.[4]

Though it is impossible to understand the full scope of the projects from the information made publicly available, a quick review of the summary descriptions of these projects in light of the principles above suggests some areas of concern. The projects that involve working with individual schools in a collection of districts, for example, or that involve only certain schools in a single district, are less likely to produce any lasting impact if the change is only expected at the school and not at the district level, as this approach implies. As discussed above, and as the Denver experience shows, although the school is the focal point for the delivery of education, schools are parts of districts, not free-standing entities. School change is unlikely to last unless it is accompanied by complementary change at the district level.

NOTES

1. Donald B. Gratz, William J. Slotnik, and Barbara J. Helms, *Pathway to Results: Pay for Performance in Denver* (Boston: Community Training & Assistance Center, 2001); William J. Slotnik et al., *Catalyst for Change: Pay for Performance in Denver, Final Report* (Community Training & Assistance Center, January 2004).

2. Community Training & Assistance Center (CTAC). Accessed 1 March 2008 at www.ctacusa .com.

3. *Teacher Advancement Program: The Four Elements of TAP*, National Institute for Excellence in Teaching, 2008. Accessed 1 March 2008 at www.talentedteachers.org/tap.taf?page=main.

4. Teacher Incentive Fund, *Awards—2007 Cohort 1*. List of Funding Recipients, 2007, U.S. Department of Education. Accessed 26 October 2007 at www.ed.gov/print/programs/teacher incentive/awards.html; George W. Bush, *Fact Sheet: America's Teachers: Fulfilling the Promise of No Child Left Behind*, 22 September 2004, The White House: President George W. Bush. Accessed 1 October 2006 at www.whitehouse.gov/news/releases/2004/09/print/20040922-1.html.

Appendix II:
A Framework for Defining School, Teacher, and Student Performance

The framework below raises critical questions posed in this book for those who would like to address issues of performance related to students, teachers, administrators, and school districts. It is not a planning process or a comprehensive manual. Rather, its principles are based on the lessons identified and issues raised in this book, with attention to the elements of successful change. Anyone who has engaged in organizational planning will find the points below familiar.

Any planning process that is inclusive and comprehensive can be used in conjunction with the framework. Some districts may recently have conducted planning in which they developed a mission, listed their values, and developed goals. These districts may not need to repeat the process (though it is worth discussing whether your goals and purposes are broad enough, and whether you have considered the appropriate role of the teacher). A knowledgeable and skillful facilitator can help move a group forward, but outside facilitation is not essential.

The framework consists of twelve points, each of which includes representative questions:

1. Stakeholders: Who should be involved?
   - Who has a stake in the performance of the institution: society, parents, children, business, the community, the state?
   - What is that stake?
   - How are the interests of stakeholders best represented?

2. Values: What's important?
   - What do we value in the process of education?
   - What are our beliefs about the learning process? What do we believe about student outcomes (academic, social/emotional, developmental), teaching and learning conditions, human motivation, etc.?
   - Should education be primarily student-centered or curriculum-centered? How can an appropriate balance be struck?
   - What role should students (and/or their parents) play in determining the nature and content of their own education?
3. Vision: How do we see teaching, learning, and the educational process?
   - What is the nature of the curriculum? Is the curriculum, or the student, the center and driver of the education process?
   - How do we see children as learners (what is their role)?
   - How do we see teachers (what is their role)?
4. Purpose/Mission: What are we trying to accomplish?
   - What is the overarching purpose (mission) of the district in support of its values?
   - What are we trying to accomplish?
5. Defined Goals: How do we define student, teacher, and school performance?
   - Within our mission and in support of our values, what goals do we want to achieve?
     (There should be only a few goals. Specific objectives can be defined once goals are determined. In addition to district-wide objectives, schools should establish their own objectives within district goals. Objectives should be more specific and relatively short term—one to two years or less.)
   - What are our priorities?
   - How do we define student performance, achievement, results, and progress?
   - How do we define the performance, achievement, results, and progress of teachers, administrators, parents, and community members in support of students?
6. Assessment: How do we evaluate student, teacher, and school performance?
   - How will we know if we are making progress towards our goals?
   - What specific measures can be used?
   - What surrogate assessments might approximate our goals and objectives?
7. Roles and Responsibilities: Who shares responsibility for performance?
   - To achieve these goals, what is needed from schools, administrators, teachers, parents, students, and the public? What are their roles?

- What is needed from business, colleges, the community, state and federal governments, the press? What are their roles?
8. Structures: How should we organize to pursue our goals?
    - How should schools be structured to help students and teachers achieve their objectives?
    - How should the district be structured to support schools and hold them accountable?
    - How should classes be arranged?
    - How should teachers and other resources be deployed?
    - How can our teachers and administrator compensation system help us achieve our goals?
    - Do our plans, structures, and compensation systems encourage teachers, administrators, students, and the community to work together in support of our goals?
9. Unintended Consequences: What obstacles, pitfalls, and problems should we anticipate?
    - What obstacles might we encounter in implementing our plan?
    - What are the plan's weaknesses or areas of confusion—what pitfalls might we encounter?
    - What unintended consequences might we anticipate?
    - Might our goals produce negative results for or encourage negative behaviors from some children (or teachers, or other stakeholders)?
    - If so, how can we adjust our plans or prepare for this possibility?
    - Is our plan realistic? Is it overly complex, expensive, confusing, or time-consuming?
10. Research and the Knowledge Base: How do research and the experience of others help us plan?
    - Are we using the best available research and relevant experience?
    - Does our plan address the best available understanding of what children need, how they develop, and how they learn?
    - Does our plan encompass the best available understanding of the motivational needs and interests of teachers?
    - Have we differentiated appropriately among different children, different teachers, and different goals?
    - Have we learned from the implementation successes and failures of others (not just what they proposed, but how they went about it)?
11. Planning and Implementation: How can we successfully initiate change?
    - Is our planning inclusive? Have those who would like to have input had an opportunity to provide that input?
    - What steps are needed to move from our current system to our new plan?
    - Have we developed a staged roll-out of our plan, or an initial pilot, to allow us to learn from our mistakes and make adjustments?

- Do we have a reasonable implementation calendar?
- What are the primary benchmark points?
- Are we prepared to measure progress periodically, and to make midcourse corrections?

12. Communication and Involvement: How can we keep everyone informed and involved?
    - How can we best communicate with and maintain the involvement of stakeholders?
    - Does our plan include regular, ongoing communication from and to the various stakeholder groups?
    - Can we, through this communication and involvement, learn about the flaws and issues in our thinking as we go forward?
    - Can we, through this communication and involvement, continue to develop a constituency that supports the proposed change?

By addressing these points in an inclusive fashion, with periodic sharing of draft documents and serious opportunities for input, a district with the will to create positive change can develop a plan that engages the entire school community in reaching its goals.

The good news with respect to the discussion of teacher compensation, if not accountability and standards, is that the parties are closer than perhaps they have ever been to agreeing on the need for change in teacher compensation and what a new system might accomplish. Many teachers and administrators agree on the need to focus on student growth and success, to provide career ladder options for teachers, to pay more to teachers with special skills or who are willing to take on challenges, and to reward teachers who make the extra effort or do a superior job.

Since there is widespread agreement on these general goals, the next step is for the parties to come together to forge agreements that embrace the needs and purposes identified by different groups, and to develop a series of assessments or indicators that fairly represent student progress and teacher performance. A comprehensive planning process, in which questions such as those above are seriously addressed, will help ensure the success of any new initiative.

Bibliography

AASA & Panasonic Foundation. "When Standards Drive Change." *Strategies* 5, no. 2 (August 1998): 1–3.

America 2000: An Education Strategy Sourcebook. U.S. Department of Education, 1991.

Anbinder, Tyler. *Five Points*. New York: Plume, 2002.

Archer, Jeff. "AFT to Urge Locals to Consider New Pay Strategies." *Education Week* 20, no. 23 (21 February 2001b): 3.

———. "Businesses Seek Teacher 'Renaissance.'" *Education Week* 20, no. 21 (7 February 2001): 1, 11.

———. "NEA Delegates Take Hard Line Against Pay for Performance." *Education Week* 19, no. 42 (12 July 2000): 21, 22.

Are They Really Ready to Work? The Conference Board, Partnership for the 21st Century, Corporate Voices for Working Families, and Society for Human Resource Management, 2006.

Armor, David. J. "Environmental Effects on IQ: From the Family or from Schools?" *Education Week* 23, no. 12 (19 November 2003): 32–33.

Armytage, W. H. G. *Four Hundred Years of English Education*. Cambridge, England: Cambridge University Press, 1964.

Asbury, Herbert. *The Gangs of New York*. New York: Thunder's Mouth Press, (1928) 2001.

Ashton-Warner, Sylvia. *Teacher*. New York: Simon & Schuster, 1963.

Bailyn, Bernard. *Education in the Forming of American Society*. New York: W. W. Norton, 1960.

Baker, Keith. "Are International Tests Worth Anything?" *Phi Delta Kappan* 89, no. 2 (October 2007): 101–4.

Ballou, Dale, and Michael Podgursky. *Teacher Pay and Teacher Quality*. Kalamazoo, MI: W. E. Upjohn Institute, 1997.

Barrett, Laura, and Jerry Spindel. "Tentative Agreement Reached in Springfield." *MTA Today* (Boston), August/September 2006, 9.

Barton, Paul. "Why Does the Gap Persist?" *Educational Leadership* 62, no. 3 (November 2004): 8–13.

Berliner, David C., and Bruce J. Biddle. *The Manufactured Crisis: Myths, Fraud, and the Attack on America's Public Schools*. Reading, MA: Addison-Wesley, 1995.

Berliner, David C., and Sharon L. Nichols. "High Stakes Testing is Putting the Nation At Risk." *Education Week* 26, no. 27 (12 March 2007): 36, 48.

245

Bernstein, Aaron. "Lou Gerstner's Classroom Quest." *Business Week Online*, 7 April 2005: Daily Briefing. http://web.ebscohost.com.odin.curry.edu/ehost/detail?vid=4&hid=102&sid= 96a0c182-9e45-4839-8654-01d0f25d7157%4Csessionmgr108&bdata=JnNpdGU9ZWhvc3 QtbGl2ZQ%3d%3d#db=aph&AN=16756070. Accessed 6 June 2006.

Bharucha, Jamshed. "America Can Teach Asia a Lot About Science, Technology, and Math." *Chronicle of Higher Education* 54, no. 20 (25 January 2007): A33.

Blair, Julie. "Cincinnati Teachers to Be Paid on Performance." *Education Week* 19, no. 1 (27 September 2000): 1, 15.

———. "Teacher Performance-Pay Plan Modified in Cincinnati." *Education Week* 21, no. 3 (19 September 2001): 3.

Blumenthal, Ralph. "Houston Ties Teachers' Pay to Test Scores." *New York Times*, 13 January 2006. http://www.nytimes.com. Accessed 15 January 2006.

Boe, Erling E., and Sujie Shin. "Is the United States Really Losing the International Horse Race in Academic Achievement?" *Phi Delta Kappan* 86, no. 9 (May, 2005): 688–95.

Bolman, Lee G., and Terrence E. Deal. *Reframining Organizations*. San Francisco: Jossey-Bass, 1991.

Bourne, Richard, and Brian MacArthur. *The Struggle for Education, 1870–1970*. New York: Philosophical Library, Inc, 1970.

Bracey, Gerald W. "15th Bracey Report on the Condition of Public Education." *Phi Delta Kappan* 87, no. 28 (October 2005): 138–53.

Bradley, Ann. "A Better Way to Pay." *Education Week* 17, no. 24, 25 February 1998. http://www.edweek.org/ew/articles/1998/02/25/24pay.h17.html?qs=A_Better_Way_to_Pay. Accessed 8 May 2000.

Brown, Marilyn. "Teacher Bonuses Shaping Up." *Tampa Tribune*, 6 April 2006: Metro, p. 2. *Lexis-Nexis*. Curry College. Http://web.lexis-nexis.com. Accessed 1 October 2006.

Bryk, Anthony, and Barbara Schneider. "Trust in Schools: A Core Resource for Reform." *Educational Leadership* 60, no. 6 (March 2003): 40–45.

Bush, George W. *Fact Sheet: America's Teachers: Fulfilling the Promise of No Child Left Behind*. 22 September 2004. The White House: President George W. Bush. www.whitehouse.gov/news/releases/2004/09/print/20040922-1.html. Accessed 1 October 2006.

Business Roundtable. "Pay-For-Performance: An Issue Brief for Business Leaders." In *Publications*. 27 July 27. www.businessroundtable.org/publications. Accessed 28 May 2004.

Campbell, Claire, and Chris Granger. *Ed Trust Statement on NAEP Science Results*. 24 May 2006. www.edtrust.org. Accessed 7 July 2006.

Carnevale, Anthony P. "No Child Gets Ahead." *Education Week* 27, no. 5 (25 September 2007): 40.

Carson, C. C., R. M. Huelskamp, and T. D. Woodall. "Perspectives on Education in America: An Annotated Briefing." *Journal of Educational Research* 86, no. 5 (May/June 1992): 259–310.

Cech, Scott J. "Florida Scoring Glitch Sparks Broad Debate." *Education Week* 26, no. 41 (13 June 2007): 19.

Center for Innovative Thought. *Teachers and the Uncertain American Future*. New York: The College Board, July 2006.

Chamberlin, Rosemary, et al. "Performance-Related Pay and the Teaching Profession: A Review of the Literature." *Research Papers in Education* 17, no. 1 (2002): 31–49.

Cohen, David K., and Richard J. Murnane. "The Merits of Merit Pay." In *Research Report No. 85-A12*. National Institute of Education no. 80, Summer 1985.

Coleman, James S., et al. *Equality of Educational Opportunity*. Washington, DC: U.S. Department of Health, Education and Welfare, Office of Education, 1966.

Conley, Sharon, Donna E. Muncey, and Jewell C Gould. "Negotiating Teacher Compensation: Three Views of Comprehensive Reform." *Educational Policy* 16, no. 5 (November 2002): 675–706.

Cook, Glenn. "What Is Ready?" *American School Board Journal* 194, no. 9 (September 2007): 17.

——. "What's a Teacher Worth? Houston Joins the Push for Merit Pay." *American School Board Journal* 193, no. 3 (March 2006): 4.

Costrell, Robert. "Governor Romney's Differential Pay Proposals." In *Rennie Center E-Forum* 1, no. 1 February 2006, *Rennie Center for Education Research & Policy*. www.renniecenter.org. Accessed 13 February 2006.

Cremin, Lawrence A. *The Transformation of the School: Progressivism in American Education 1876–1957*. New York: Vintage (Random House), 1961.

Danielson, Charlotte. *Enhancing Professional Practice*. Alexandria, VA: ASCD, 1996.

Darling-Hammond, Linda. *The Right to Learn: A Blueprint for Creating Schools That Work*. San Francisco: Jossey-Bass, 1997.

DeGroot, Gerard J. "Sputnik 1957." *American History* 42, no. 5, December 2007: 34–39. www .ebscohost.com. 27077107. Accessed 11 March 2008.

Del Valle, Christina. "Merit Pay for Teachers May not Have Much Merit." *Business Week* No. 3255, 9 March 1992: Top of the News, 38.

Denver Post Editorial. "Right Way for Merit Pay." *Denver Post* (Denver), 27 June 27 1999, Perspective: H-04.

Denver Public Schools. "Denver Considers Bold New Teacher Compensation Plan." *Press Release* (Denver, CO), 18 April 2003.

——. *ProComp: A Collaborative Project of Denver Public Schools and Denver Classroom Teachers Association*. Denver, CO: Denver Public Schools, 2005.

Dickens, Charles. *Hard Times*. New York: Holt, Rinehart, (1854) 1958.

Dillon, Sam. "Long Reviled, Merit Pay Gains Among Teachers." *New York Times,* 18 June 2007. www.nytimes.com. Accessed 18 June 2007.

Dolton, Peter, Steven McIntosh, and Arnaud Chevalier. *Teacher Pay and Performance*. London: Institute of Education, University of London, 2003.

Draper, Norman. "Interest Builds in Minnesota's New Teacher Pay Plan." *Star Tribune* 14 December 2005. http://www.startribune.com. Accessed 14 December 2005.

——. "State Will Test Teacher Merit Pay." *Star Tribune* 14 September 2004. http://www .startribune.com. Accessed 14 September 2004.

DuFour, Richard, Rebecca DuFour, et al. *Learning by Doing*. Bloomington, IN: Solution Tree, 2006.

Edwards, Owen. "Explorer I Satellite." *Smithsonian* 38, no. 10, January 2008: 36. Curry College. http://web.ebscohost.com.odin.curry.edu/ehost/detail?vid=12&hid=102&sid=96a0c 182-9e45-4839-8654-01d0f25d7157%40sessionmgr108&bdata=JnNpdGU9Z Whvc3QtbGl2ZQ%3d%3d#db=aph&AN=28023368. Accessed 11 March 2008.

Eisenkraft, Arthur. "Rating Science and Math." *Education Week* 20, no. 22 (14 February 2001): 68.

El Nassar, Haya. "Soaring Housing Costs Are Culprit in Suburban Poverty." *USA Today* (Arlington, VA), 28 April 1999, 1, 2.

Elliott, Janet. "Gov. Perry Institutes Teacher Merit Pay." *Houston Chronicle*, 3 November 2005: Monday Education. http://www.chron.com. Accessed 3 November 2005.

Emerson, Ralph Waldo. "Education." In *Selected Prose & Poetry*, edited by Reginald L. Cook, 208–28. New York: Holt, Rinehart, (1884) 1960.

English, Fenwick. "History and Critical Issues of Education Compensation Systems." In *Teacher Compensation and Motivation*, edited by Larry E. Frase, 3–25. Lancaster, PA: Technomic Publishing, 1992.

Feldman, Sandra. "Rethinking Teacher Compensation." In *American Teacher* (2004). *American Federation of Teachers*. www.aft.org/pubs. Accessed 2 January 2008.

Figlio, David N., and Lawrence W. Kenny. "Individual Teacher Incentives and Student Performance." In*National Center for Analysis of Longitudinal Data in Education Research* April 2007. *Calder Urban Institute*. Working Paper #8. <http://www.urban.org/publications/1001069 .html>. Accessed 22 February 2008.

Finn, Chester E., Jr., Michael J. Petrilli, and Gregg Vanourek. "The State of Standards: Four Reasons Why Most 'Don't Cut the Mustard.'" *Education Week* 18, no. 11 (11 November 1998): 39, 56.

Fischer, Kent. "Dallas Schools Approve Performance Bonuses for Teachers." *Dallas News*, 29 November 2007. www.dallasnews.com. Accessed 30 November 2007.

Flaherty, Stephen, and Lynn Ahrens. "Henry Ford." In *Ragtime: The Musical*. New York: RCA Victor, 1998.

Flesch, Rudolf. *Why Johnny Can't Read*. New York: Harper & Brothers, 1955.

———. *Why Johnny Still Can't Read*. New York: Harper & Row, 1981.

Frase, Larry E. *Teacher Compensation and Motivation*. Lancaster, PA: Technomic Publishing, 1992.

Freire, Paulo. *Pedagogy of the Oppressed*. New York: Seabury Press, 1968.

Fullan, Michael. *Change Forces: The Sequel*. Philadelphia, PA: Falmer Press, 1999.

———. *The New Meaning of Educational Change*, 2nd ed. New York: Teachers College Press, 1991.

———. "Professional Culture and Educational Change." *School Psychology Review* 25, no. 4 (1996): 496. EBSCOhost: Academic Search Premier. http://web.ebscohost.com.odin.curry.edu/ehost/detail?vid=18&hid=102&sid=96a0c182-9e45-4839-8654-01d0f25d7157%40sessionmgr108&bdata=JnNpdGU9ZWhvc3QtbGl2ZQ%3d%3d#db=aph&AN=9705162412. Accessed 8 January 2005.

Gerstner, Louis, et al. *Teaching at Risk: A Call to Action*. New York: The Teaching Commission, 2004.

———. *Teaching at Risk: Progress & Potholes*. New York: The Teaching Commission, 2006.

Gewertz, Catherine. "N.Y.C. Pressed on Staffing Neediest Schools." *Education Week* 25, no. 3 (14 September 2005): 3.

Gitomer, David H. *Teacher Quality in a Changing Landscape: Improvements in the Teacher Pool*. Policy Evaluation & Research Center. Princeton, NJ: Educational Testing Service, December 2007.

Giunta, Andrea. "Pay for Performance Plan Ignores Kids' Outside Influences." *Denver Post*, 27 June 1999, Perspective: H-01.

Glenn, David. "A Gold Star for Merit Pay?" *Chronicle of Higher Education* 48, no. 35, 10 May 2002. 00095982. Accessed 6 June 2006.

Goals 2000: Educate America Act. Washington, DC: U.S. Department of Education, 1993.

Gonring, Phil, Paul Teske, and Brad Jupp. *Pay-for-Performance Teacher Compensation*. Cambridge, MA: Harvard University Press, 2007.

Goorian, Brad. "Alternative Teacher Compensation." In *ERIC Digest* Number 142 (2000). Eric Clearinghouse on Educational Management. http://search.ebscohost.com.odin.curry.edu/login.aspx?direct=true&db=eric&AN=ED446368&site=ehost-live. Accessed 6 September 2008.

Gratz, Donald B. "Fixing the Race: State Tests and Student Progress." *Education Week* 19, no. 39 (7 June 2000b): 32, 34.

———. "High Standards for Whom?" *Phi Delta Kappan* 81, no. 9 (May 2000a): 681–87.

———. "Leaving No Child Behind." *Education Week* 22, no. 40 (11 June 2003): 27, 36.

———. "Pay for Performance Teacher Compensation: An Inside View of Denver's ProComp Plan." *Teachers College Record* 22 February 2008. Book Review. http://www.tcrecord.org. ID Number 15022. Accessed 22 February 2008.

———. "Student Achievement : What is the Problem?" *Education Week* 21, no. 1 (5 September 2001): 62, 80.

———. "Unique Features—What Sets the Denver Pilot Apart." In *Speech at PFP Press Conference for Governor & Press*. Denver, CO: Denver Public Schools, 22 March 2001.

Gratz, Donald B., William J. Slotnik, and Barbara J. Helms. *Pathway to Results: Pay for Performance in Denver*. Boston: Community Training & Assistance Center, 2001.

Greer, Colin. *The Great School Legend: A Revisionist Interpretation of American Public Education*. New York: Viking, 1972.

Grimes, Cliff F. "Historical Perspectives." In *Employee Motivation, the Organizational Environment and Productivity*. London: Accel-Team, 2006.

Haney, Walt. "Ensuring Failure: How Effective is the Current Test-Driven Accountability Movement." *Education Week* 21, no. 42 (10 July 2002): 56, 58.

Hardy, Lawrence. "Children at Risk." *American School Board Journal* 193, no. 12 (December 2006): 17–21.

Hargreaves, Andy, et al. *Learning to Change: Teaching Beyond Subjects and Standards*. San Francisco: Jossey-Bass, 2001.

Hart, Betty, and Todd R. Risley. "The Early Catastrophe." *Education Review* 17, no. 1 (Autumn 2003): 110–18.

———. *Meaningful Differences in the Everyday Experience of Young Children*. Baltimore, MD: Paul R. Brookes Publishing Co., 1995.

Hatry, Harry P., and John M. Greiner. *Issues and Case Studies in Teacher Incentive Plans*. Washington, DC: Urban Institute Press, 1985.

Hatry, Harry P., John M. Greiner, and Brenda G. Ashford. *Issues and Case Studies in Teacher Incentive Plans*. Washington, DC: Urban Institute Press, 1994.

Hays, Scott. "Pros and Cons of Pay for Performance." *Workforce Online* February 1999.

Heneman, Robert L. *Merit Pay: Linking Pay Increases to Performance Ratings*. Reading, MA: Addison-Wesley, 1992.

Heritage Foundation. *Where We Stand: Our Principles on Improving Education*. Heritage Research, Mandate for Leadership, 2006.

Hershberg, Theodore. "The Case for New Standards in Education." *Education Week,* 10 December 1997. http://www.edweek.org/ew/articles/1997/12/10/16hersh.h17.html?qs=Hershberg. Accessed 27 December 2004.

Hershberg, Theodore, and Barbara Lea-Kruger. "Aligning the System: The Case for Linking Teacher Pay to Student Learning." *Education Week* 25, no. 29 (29 March 2006): 40, 52.

Herszenhorn, David. "City Reaches Tentative Deal with Teachers." *New York Times* 4 October 2005. www.nytimes.com. Accessed 6 October 2005.

Hess, Frederick M., and Martin R. West. "Taking on the Teachers Unions." *Boston Globe,* 29 March 2006: Op Ed. www.boston.com. Accessed 11 April 2006.

Heubert, Jay P., and Robert M. Hauser, eds. *High Stakes: Testing for Tracking, Promotion, and Grading*. Washington, DC: National Academy Press, 1999.

Hiatt, Fred. "Japanese to Buy 51% of Rockefeller Center; Mitsubishi to Pay $646 Million for Stake." *Washington Post,* 31 October 1989. http://www.highbeam.com/doc/1P2-1220284.html. Accessed 24 November 2006.

Higgins, Alexander G. "UN: Korea, Japan at Top of Best Schooling List; U.S., Germany Toward Bottom." UN Report on International Comparisons. 28 November 2002. AP Wire Report. www.sfgate.com. Accessed 26 November 2002.

Hirsch, E. D., Jr. *What Your Sixth Grader Needs to Know: Fundamentals of a Good Sixth-Grade Education*. New York: Doubleday, 2006.

Hodge, Warren A. *The Role of Performance Pay Systems in Comprehensive School Reform*. Lanham, MD: University Press of America, 2003.

Hoerr, Thomas. "A Case for Merit Pay." *Phi Delta Kappan* 80, no. 4 (December 1998): 326–327.

Hoff, David J. "Big Business Going to Bat for NCLB." *Education Week* 26, no. 8 (18 October 2006a): 1, 24.

———. "Governors Seek New Teacher-Pay Methods." *Education Week* 24, no. 21 (2 February 2005): pp, 22, 28.

———. "To Know NCLB Is to Like It, ETS Poll Finds." *Education Week* 26, no. 42 (20 June 2006): 29, 31.

Holt, John. *How Children Fail*. New York: Dell Publishing Co., 1964.

Holton, Gerald. "An Insider's View of 'A Nation at Risk' and Why It Still Matters." *Chronicle of Higher Education,* 25 April 2003: B13–15.

Honawar, Vaishali. "Legislature Votes to Replace Merit-Pay System in Florida." *Education Week* 26, no. 29 (28 March 2007): 16.

———. "N.Y.C. Unveils Merit-Pay Plan for Teacher in High Need Schools." *Education Week* 27, no. 9 (18 October 2007): 6.

———. "Performance System Slow to Catch on in Minnesota." *Education Week* 26, no. 19 (17 January 2007): 5, 13.

———. "Union Objects to Proposal to Modify Pact in Denver." *Education Week* 27, no. 44 (30 July 2008): 1, 15.

Houston, Paul D. "The Seven Deadly Sins of No Child Left Behind." *Phi Delta Kappan* 88, no. 10 (June 2007): 744–48.

Hull, Dana. "Push for Teacher Merit Pay Vote Underway." *Contra Costa Times,* 4 May 2005. www.contracostatimes.com. Accessed 5 May 2005.

Investing in Teaching: A Common Agenda. National Alliance of Business, Business Roundtable, National Association of Manufacturers, Chamber of Commerce, 9 January 2001.

Ip, Greg. "The Gap in Wages is Growing Again for U.S. Workers." *Wall Street Journal,* 23 January 2004, A1.

Janofsky, Michael. "Teacher Merit Pay Tied to Education Gains." *New York Times,* 4 October 2005, A12.

Jefferson, Thomas. "Jefferson Proposes New Educational Laws for Virginia." In *The Educating of Americans: A Documentary History,* edited by Daniel Calhoun, 107–10. Boston: Houghton Mifflin, (1782) 1969.

Johnson, Susan Moore, et al. *Leading the Local: Teachers Union Presidents Speak on Change, Challenges.* Education Sector Reports. Washington, DC, June 2007.

Joint Task Force on Teacher Compensation. "At a Glance . . . Professional Compensation for Teachers, Tentative Agreement." 2004. www.denverteachercompensation.org. Accessed 28 March 2004.

———. *Recognizing and Rewarding Teachers in the 21st Century.* Newsletter of the Joint Task Force on Teacher Compensation. 2003.

Kaczor, Bill. "Florida Lawmakers Trying to Revamp Merit Pay Plan for Teachers." *Orlando Sentinel,* 1 April 2006. www.orlandosentinel.com/news/education/sfl-0401lawmakers,0,6468689 .story. Accessed 11 April 2006.

Katz, Michael B. *The Irony of Early School Reform: Educational Innovation in Mid-Nineteenth Century Massachusetts.* Cambridge, MA: Beacon Press, 1968.

Keller, Bess. "Fla. Ready to Demand Bonuses Based on Test Scores." *Education Week* 25, no. 24 (22 February 2006): 26, 31.

———. "Florida Union Challenges Teacher-Bonus Program." *Education Week* 26, no. 6 (4 October 2006): 16.

———. "New Teachers Outdo Peers of Last Decade on Academic Scales." *Education Week* 27, no. 16 (19 December 2007b): 1, 14–15.

———. "No Easy Project." *Education Week* 27, no. 4 (19 September 2007): 21–23.

———. "Some Florida Districts Opting Not to Pay Out Performance Bonuses." *Education Week* 24, no. 44 (10 August 2005): 1, 19.

Kelley, Carolyn, and Allan Odden. "Reinventing Teacher Compensation." In *CPRE Financial Briefs* (Consortium for Policy Research in Education, 1995). http://www.cpre.org/images/ stories/cpre_pdfs/fb06.pdf. Accessed 8 May 2000.

Kerchner, Charles Taylor, Julia E. Koppich, and Joseph G. Weeres. *United Mind Workers: Unions and Teaching in the Knowledge Society.* San Francisco: Jossey-Bass, 1997.

Kliebard, Herbert M. *The Struggle for the American Curriculum,* 2nd ed. London: Routledge, 1995.

Koerner, James D. *Miseducation of American Teachers.* Cambridge, MA: Riverside Press, 1963.

Kohn, Alfie. *Punished by Rewards.* New York: Houghton Mifflin, 1993.

Kotter, John P. *Leading Change.* Cambridge, MA: Harvard Business School Press, 1996.

Kozol, Jonathan. *Death at an Early Age.* Boston: Houghton Mifflin, 1967.

Kuttner, Robert. "Another Year, Another Wage Loss." *Boston Globe*, Op Ed, 2 September 2006. www.boston.com. Accessed 2 September 2006.

——. "The Boom in Poverty." *Boston Globe* (Boston), 21 March 1999, E7.

Lambert, Lisa. "Half of Teachers Quit in 5 Years." *Washington Post*, 9 May 2006: A07. www .washingtonpost.com. Accessed 9 May 2006.

Latham, Gary P., and Vandra L. Huber. "Schedules of Reinforcement: Lessons from the Past and Issues for the Future." In *Pay for Performance: History, Controversy and Evidence*, edited by Bill L. Hopkins and Thomas C. Mawhinney, 125–50. Binghamton, NY: Haworth Press, 1992.

Lefkowitz, Laura. "Pay for Performance Teachers Should Earn Their Raises." *Denver Post*, June 27 1999, Perspective: H-01.

Linn, Robert L., and Carolyn Haug. "Stability of School-Building Accountability Scores and Gains." *Educational Evaluation and Policy Analysis* 24, no. 1 (Spring 2002): 29–36.

Littky, Dennis. *The Big Picture: Education is Everyone's Business*. Alexandria, VA: ASCD, 2004.

March, James G. *A Primer on Decision-Making*. New York: The Free Press, 1994.

Matus, Ron. "State Force Teacher Bonuses." *St. Petersburg Times*, 6 July 2005. http://www.sptimes .com. Accessed 7 July 2006.

McElroy, Edward J. "Teacher Compensation: What Can Be Done to Maintain (and Improve) Teachers' Wages and Benefits?" In *TeachingK-12* 8, August/September 2005. www.TeachingK-8.com.

McNeil, Linda M. *Contradictions of School Reform: Educational Costs of Standardized Testing*. New York: Routledge, 2000.

Meier, Deborah. "NCLB and Democracy." In *Many Children Left Behind*, edited by Deborah Meier and George Wood, 66–78. Boston: Beacon Press, 2004.

"Merit Pay a Start to Building Better-Performing Schools." *Chicago Sun-Times*, 6 November 2006: Editorials. www.suntimes.com/news/commentary. Accessed 6 November 2006.

Mishel, Lawrence, Jared Bernstein, and Syliva Allegretto. *The State of Working America 2006/2007*. Ithaca, NY: Economic Policy Institute, Cornell University Press, 2007.

Mishel, Lawrence, and Richard Rothstein. "False Alarm." *Phi Delta Kappan* 88, no. 10 (June 2007): 737–40.

Moran, Chris, and Helen Gao. "Proposed Merit Pay for Teachers Poses Some Sticky Issues." *San Diego Union Tribute*, 7 January 2005. www.uniontrib.com. Accessed 7 January 2005.

Murnane, Richard J., and David K. Cohen. "Merit Pay and the Evaluation Problem: Why Most Merit Pay Plans Fail and a Few Survive." *Harvard Education Review* 56, no. 1 (February 1986): 2.

Myerson, Harold. "Devaluing Labor." *Washington Post Weekly*, 4–10 September 2006, 26.

Nasaw, David. *Schooled to Order: A Social History of Public Schooling in the United States*. New York: Oxford University Press, 1979.

National Board for Professional Teaching Standards. *National Board for Professional Teaching Standards 2008*. http://www.nbpts.org/. Accessed 25 July 2008.

National Commission on Excellence in Education. "A Nation at Risk: The Imperative for Educational Reform." April 1983. *A Nation at Risk*. U.S. Department of Education. www.ed.gov. Accessed 12 December 2004.

Neill, Monty, Lisa Guisbond, and Bob Schaeffer. *Failing Our Children*. May 2004. Fairtest. www.fairtest.org/Failing_Our_Children_Report/html. Accessed 11 November 2007.

Nelson, Wade. "Timequake Alert: Why Payment by Results is the Worst 'New' Reform to Shake the Educational World, Again and Again." *Phi Delta Kappan* 82, no. 5 (January 2001): 384–89.

Neufield, Sara. "States Turn to Teacher Bonuses." *The Baltimore Sun*, 5 September 2006, 1A.

Neumann, Richard. "American Democracy at Risk." *Phi Delta Kappan* 89, no. 5 (January 2008): 328–39.

News in Brief. "43 Percent of School Districts Join Texas Merit-Pay Plan." *Education Week* 27, no. 13 (26 November 2007): 4–5.

Nichols, Sharon L., and David C. Berliner. *Collateral Damage: How High Stakes Testing Corrupts America's Schools*. Cambridge, MA: Harvard University Press, 2007.

Noddings, Nel. "Thinking About Standards." *Phi Delta Kappan* 79, no. 3 (November 1997): 184–89.

Odden, Allan. "New and Better Forms of Teacher Compensation Are Possible." *Phi Delta Kappan* 81, no. 5 (January 2000): 361–65.

Odden, Allan, and Carolyn Kelley. *Paying Teachers for What They Know and Do.* Thousand Oaks, CA: Corwin Press, 1997.

Olson, Lynn. "The Down Staircase." *Education Week: Special Report.* 25, no. 41S (Diplomas Count 2006): 5–6, 10–11.

———. "Economic Trends Fuel Push to Retool Schools." *Education Week* 25, no. 28 (3 March 2006): 1, 20, 22, 24.

———. "NAEP Gains Are Elusive in Key Areas." *Education Week* 25, no. 09 (26 October 2005): 1, 22–23.

———. "Pay-Performance Link in Salaries Gains Momentum." *Education Week* 19, no. 7 (13 October 1999): 1, 13.

Otto, Mary. "For Want of a Dentist." *Washington Post,* 28 February 2007: B01. www.washingtonpost.com. Accessed 15 February 2008.

Peach, E. Brian, and Daniel A. Wren. "Pay for Performance from Antiquity to the 1950s." In *Pay for Performance: History, Controversy and Evidence,* edited by Bill L. Hopkins and Thomas C. Mawhinney, 5–26. Binghamton, NY: Haworth Press, 1992.

Peske, Heather G., and Kati Haycock. *Teaching Inequality: How Poor and Minority Students Are Shortchanged on Teacher Quality.* Washington, DC: Education Trust, June 2006.

Pfeffer, Jeffrey. "Six Dangerous Myths About Pay." *Harvard Business Review* 76, no. 3 (1998): 109.

Pfeffer, Jeffrey, and Robert Sutton. *Hard Facts, Dangerous Half Truths and Total Nonsense: Profiting from Evidence-Based Management.* Harvard Business School Press, 2006.

Pinzur, Matthew. "Performance-Based Pay for Teachers OK'd." *Miami Herald,* 22 February 2006. www.miami.com. Accessed 22 February 2006.

———. "Teacher Pay May Hinge on Test Scores." *Miami Herald,* 27 June 2005. www.miami.com. Accessed 4 July, 2005.

Presley, Jennifer B., and Bradford R. White, *Public Policy Research Report.* Illinois Education Research Council (IERC), 2005. http://ierc.edu/documents/Teacher%Quality%20IERC%202005-2.pdf. Accessed 16 July 2007.

Pressman, Jeffrey L., and Aaron Wildavsky. *Implementation,* 3rd ed. Berkeley, CA: University of California Press, 1984.

"Professional Compensation." In *American Federation of Teachers,* Hot Topics Statement, n.d. www.aft.org/topics/teacher-quality/comp.htm. Accessed 2 January 2008.

"Professional Pay: Myths and Facts." In *National Education Association,* n.d. www.nea.org/pay/teachermyths.html. Accessed 2 January 2008.

Protsik, Jean. "History of Teacher Pay and Incentive Reforms." *Journal of School Leadership* 6 (May 1996): 265–89.

Reville, S. Paul. "High Standards + High Stakes = High Achievement in Massachusetts." *Phi Delta Kappan* 85, no. 8 (April 2004): 591–97.

Rhodes, Mary, and Rodney T. Ogawa. "Teacher Motivation, Work Structures and Organizational Change: Perspectives on Educational Reform and Compensation." In *Teacher Compensation and Motivation,* edited by Larry E. Frase, 61–104. Lancaster, PA: Technomic Publishing, 1992.

Richard, Alan. "Researchers Tally Costs of Education Failings." *Education Week* 25, no. 10 (2 November 2005): 6–7.

Rochkind, Jonathan, et al. "Lessons Learned: New Teachers Talk About Their Jobs, Challenges and Long-Range Plans." Public Agenda, 2007. www.publicagenda.org. Accessed 17 October 2007.

Rose, Lowell C., and Alec M. Gallup. "The 37th Annual Phi Delta Kappa/Gallup Poll of the Public's Attitudes Toward the Public Schools." *2005* 87, no. 1 (September 2005): 41–57.

——. "The 38th Annual Phi Delta Kappa/Gallup Poll of the Public's Attitudes Toward the Public Schools." *Phi Delta Kappan* 88, no. 1 (September 2006): 41–57.

——. "The 39th Annual Phi Delta Kappa/Gallup Poll of the Public's Attitudes Toward the Public Schools." *Phi Delta Kappan* 89, no. 1 (September 2007): 33–48.

Rosenthal, Robert, and Lenore Jacobson. *Pygmalion in the Classroom*. New York: Holt, Rinehart, 1968.

Rotberg, Iris C. "Quick Fixes, Test Scores and the Global Economy." *Education Week* 27, no. 41 (11 June 2008): 27, 32.

Rothstein, Richard. *Class and Schools: Using Social, Economic and Educational Reform to Close the Black-White Achievement Gap*. Washington, DC: Economic Policy Institute, 2004.

——. "Class and the Classroom." *American School Board Journal* 191, no. 10 (October 2004b): 17–21.

——. "Lessons: Arguing Against Merit Pay as Incentive for Teachers." *New York Times*, 26 April 2000: Section B, page 11. www.nytimes.com. Accessed 6 June 2006.

Rothstein, Richard, and Rebecca Jacobsen. "The Goals of Education." *Phi Delta Kappan* 88, no. 4 (December 2006): 264–72.

Rudolph, Fred. "Mark Hopkins (1802–1887)." Williamstown, MA: Williams College Archives.

Ryan, William. *Blaming the Victim*. New York: Vintage (Random House), 1971.

Sacchetti, Maria. "Extra Pay Urged at Poorest Schools: Teachers' Unions Propose Incentives." *Boston Globe*, 30 November 2006. www.boston.com. Accessed 30 November 2006.

——. "Springfield Teachers OK Merit Pay Contract." *Boston Globe* (Boston), September 9 2006, B1.

Sacchetti, Maria, and Tracy Jan. "Romney Wants Teacher Merit Pay." *Boston Globe*, 22 September 2005. http://www.boston.com. Accessed 12 December 2005.

Sack, Joetta. "School Groups in 'Dogfight' with California Governor." *Education Week* 24, no. 29 (30 March 2005): 8.

Sauer, Roger T. "Jencks Reassessed, One Career Later." *Education Week* 22, no. 37 (21 May 2003): 32, 34.

Sawhill, Isabel. *Opportunity in America: The Role of Education*. Princeton, NJ: Brookings Institute, Fall 2006.

Schemo, Diana Jean. "When Students' Gains Help Teachers' Bottom Line." *New York Times*, 9 May 2004: Section 1, Page 1. http://query.nytimes.com/gst/fullpage.html?res=9505E2DD153CF93AA35756C0A9629C8B63&scp=1&sq=&st=nyt. Accessed 16 October 2006.

Schultz, Stanley K. *The Culture Factory: Boston Public Schools, 1789–1860*. New York: Oxford University Press, 1973.

Sherry, Allison. "DPS Teachers Approve Performance-Pay Plan." *Denver Post*, 18 March 2004, 1–2.

——. "Pay-Reform Plan for Teachers OK'd." *Denver Post*, 2 November 2005.

Shuford, Tom. "Jefferson on Education." *Education Week* 23, no. 42 (14 July 2004): 38.

Silberman, Charles. *Crisis in the Classroom*. New York: Random House, 1970.

Sirotnik, Kenneth A., and Kathy Kimball. "Standards for Standards-Based Accountability Systems." *Phi Delta Kappan* 81, no. 3 (November 1999): 209–14.

Slotnik, William J. Discussion of Denver Pilot and PFP. Boston, 10 July 2008.

——. "Mission Possible: Tying Earning to Learning." *Education Week* 25, no. 5 (28 September 2005): 32–33, 40.

Slotnik, William J., et al. *Catalyst for Change: Pay for Performance in Denver, Final Report*. Community Training & Assistance Center, January 2004.

Spencer, Jason. "HISD Chief Pitches Bonus Plan." Monday Education. 18 November 2005. http://www.chron.com. Accessed 20 November 2005.

——. "HISD Has Incentives to Change Merit Pay." *Houston Chronicle*, 4 April 2005: Local & State. http://www.chron.com. Accessed 4 June 2005.

Spillane, Robert R. "Pay for Performance in Fairfax County, Virginia." In *Teacher Compensation and Motivation*, edited by Larry E. Frase, 413–24. Lancaster, PA: Technomic Publishing, 1992.

Spring, Joel. *The American School: From the Puritans to No Child Left Behind*. Boston: McGraw Hill, 2008.

Stansbury, Meris. "Voters Urge Teaching of 21st Century Skills." *ESchoolNews*, 15 October 2007. www.eschoolnews.org. Accessed 30 November 2007.

Stevenson, Richard W. "The Wisdom to Let the Good Times Roll; The Clinton Legacy." *New York Times*, 25 December 2000: A.1. Late Edition (East Coast). http://query.nytimes.com/gst/fullpage.html?res=9D0CEEDB1238F936A15751C1A9669C8B63&scp=1&sq=&st=nyt. Accessed 26 November 2007.

Stutz, Terrence. "Some Schools Pass up Bonuses." *Dallas News*, 2 October 2006. www.dallasnews.com. Accessed 10 October 2006.

Teacher Advancement Program: The Four Elements of TAP. National Institute for Excellence in Teaching, 2008. www.talentedteachers.org/tap.taf?page=main. Accessed 1 March 2008.

Teacher Incentive Fund. *Awards—2007 Cohort 1*. List of Funding Recipients, 2007. U.S. Department of Education. www.ed.gov/print/programs/teacherincentive/awards.html. Accessed 26 October 2007.

Teachers Union Reform Network (TURN), 2008. www.gseis.ucla.edu/hosted/turn/turn.html. Accessed 13 July 2008.

"Teacher Quality Important, But Cannot Overcome Poverty." *FairTest Examiner*, August 2006. FairTest. www.fairtest.org/examarts/August%202006/Teacher%Quality.html. Accessed 16 July 2007.

Tomsho, Robert. "More Districts Pay Teachers for Performance." *Wall Street Journal* No. Eastern Edition, 23 May 2006: B.1.

Tonn, Jessica L. "Houston in Uproar Over Teachers' Bonuses." *Education Week* 26, no. 22 (1 February 2007): 5, 13.

Tough Choices or Tough Times: Executive Summary. New Commission on the Skills of the American Workforce. Washington, DC: National Center on Education and the Economy, 2007.

Tough, Paul. "What It Takes to Make a Student." *New York Times*, November 26 2006. www.nytimes.com. Accessed 26 November 2006.

Trujillo, Melissa. *Board of Ed Votes to Raise Graduation Rates*. AP Wire Service Report, 24 October 2006. www.boston.com. Accessed 8 August 2007.

Tucker, Marc S. "Making Tough Choices." *Phi Delta Kappan* 88, no. 10 (June 2007): 728–32.

Tucker, Marc S., and Judy B. Codding. *Standards for Our Schools*. San Francisco: Jossey-Bass, 1998.

Tyack, David B. *The One Best System*. Cambridge, MA: Harvard University Press, 1974.

Tyack, David B., and Larry Cuban. *Tinkering Toward Utopia*. Cambridge, MA: Harvard University Press, 1995.

Urbanski, Adam, and Roger Erskine. "School Reform, TURN, and Teacher Compensation." *Phi Delta Kappan* 81, no. 5 (January 2000): 367–70.

U.S. Department of Education. *No Child Left Behind Executive Summary*, 2001. www.ed.gov/nclb/overview/intro/execsumm.html. Accessed 16 March 2005.

"U.S. Poverty Rate Rises To 12.7 Percent." *New York Times*, 30 August 2005. www.nytimes.com/aponline. Accessed 30 August 2005.

Viadero, Debra. "Fresh Look at Coleman Data Yields Different Conclusions." *Education Week* 25, no. 41 (21 June 2006a): 21.

———. "Race Report's Influence Felt 40 Years Later." *Education Week* 25, no. 41 (21 June 2006b): 1, 21–24.

———. "Study Links Merit Pay to Slightly Higher Student Scores." *Education Week* 26, no. 18 (10 January 2007): 8.

———. "Suprise! Analyses Link Curriculum, TIMSS Tests Scores." *Education Week*, 2 April 1997. http://www.edweek.org/ew/articles/1997/04/02/27timss.h16.html?qs=Surprise. Accessed 5 September 2008.

———. "U.S. Seniors Near Bottom in World Test." *Education Week*, 4 March 1998. http://www.edweek.org/ew/articles/1998/03/04/25timss.h17.html?qs=Near+Bottom. Accessed 26 February 1999.

———. "Working Conditions Trump Pay." *Education Week* 27, no. 18 (10 January 2008): 34–35.

Wade, Richard C. "Foreword." In *The Culture Factory: Boston Public Schools, 1789–1860*, Stanley K. Schultz, v–viii. New York: Oxford University Press, 1973.

Wagner, Tony. *How Schools Change*. New York: RoutledgeFalmer, 1994.

Walsh, Mark. "More Incentives Would Drive Schools to Improve, Business Alliance Argues." *Education Week* 19, no. 23 (16 February 2000): 8.

Weber, Dave. "Critics Give Failing Grade to Merit Pay for Teachers." *Orlando Sentinel*, 3 January 2007. www.orlandosentinel.com. Accessed 4 January 2007.

Weiss, Rick. "Genes' Sway Over IG May Vary with Class." *Washington Post* (Washington, DC), 2 September 2003, A01.

Wertheimer, Linda K. "Many Colleges Ignore SAT Writing Test." *Boston Globe* (Boston), 20 September 2007, 1.

Whitehead, Alfred North. *The Aims of Education and Other Essays*. New York: The Free Press, 1929.

Whitsett, David A., and Lyle Yorks. *From Management Theory to Business Sense*. New York: Amacom, 1983.

Whoriskey, Peter. "Fla. to Link Teacher Pay to Students' Test Scores." *Washington Post,* 22 March 2006. www.washingtonpost.com. Accessed 11 April 2006.

Wilms, Wellford W., and Richard R. Chapleau. "The Illusion of Paying Teachers for Student Achievement." *Education Week* 19, 3 November 1999, 34, 48.

Wolk, Steven. "Why Go to School." *Phi Delta Kappan* 88, no. 9 (May 2007): 648–58.

Wren, Daniel A. *The Evolution of Management Thought*. New York: John Wiley & Sons, 1979.

Zehr, Mary Ann. "Texas Plans New Test-Security Measures as Cheating Allegations Swirl." *Education Week* 26, no. 41 (12 June 2007): 19.

Index

About the Author

Donald B. Gratz (PhD, Boston College) is currently professor of education, director of the Master's program, and chair of the education department at Curry College, outside of Boston.

Prior to this appointment, he served for a decade as Director of School Reform for the Community Training & Assistance Center (CTAC). In that capacity, he coordinated long-term, district-wide improvement efforts in school districts across the country, including Cleveland, Ohio; Newark, New Jersey; Palm Beach County, Florida; Salt Lake City, Utah; and districts in San Jose and Los Angeles Counties in California. The position involved working with superintendents and school boards, principals and central administrators, teachers, parents, and community members to build school improvement and accountability efforts around the needs of children and schools. He also served as an evaluator in the first round of California's Immediate Intervention—Underperforming Schools Program (IIUSP).

Before leaving the CTAC staff, he led the research team for the first half of Denver's Pay for Performance pilot, for which the center provided technical assistance and studied pilot processes and results. He was a founder of CTAC and remains an officer of the board.

In addition to this national involvement in public school leadership and management, he has served for ten years on the board of the Needham, Massachusetts, public schools—twice each as chair and vice chair. He is also vice chair of The Education Cooperative (TEC), a collaboration of districts addressing special education, professional development, and policy issues. Finally, he has bargained with teachers on behalf of his district in three different rounds of negotiations, and is also a member of two unions, for which he has helped develop positions and engaged in bargaining. He is author or coauthor of papers and commentary on issues of teacher compensation, school improvement, assessment, and accountability, plus reports on Denver's Pay for Performance pilot and the effects of the state takeover of the Newark, New Jersey, public schools.